The Flying 400

The Flying 400

Canada's Hydrofoil Project

Thomas G. Lynch

Nimbus Publishing Limited

Canadian Cataloguing in Publication Data

Lynch, Thomas G.
The Flying 400

Includes index.
ISBN 0-920852-22-X

1. Hydrofoil boats — Canada — Design and construction — History. 2. HMCS Bras d'Or (Hydrofoil) — History.
I. Title.

VM362.L96 1983 623.8'204 C83-099276-6

ISBN 0-920852-22-X

Published by **Nimbus Publishing Limited**, Halifax, Nova Scotia.
Typesetting: McCurdy Printing &
Typesetting Limited, Halifax, N.S.
Printing & Binding:
Seaboard Printing,
Bedford, Nova Scotia

Contents

Author's Preface

Bras d'Or was one of the most daring, innovative ideas that Canadians had ever had in naval design, making the evolution of the St. Laurent class destroyers in the early 1950s seem small in vision. This ship and her concept thrust Canada years into the future . . . perhaps too far for most critics within and without the country. With her demise, Canada reverted to being the consumer of military hardware instead of a manufacturer.

I have found the researching of this book one of the most rewarding experiences of my life. I have met some tremendous people, both in the military and civilian side of life and with few exceptions have found an undying pride that they had a part to play in the *FHE-400* Programme. Through them, I gained some small insight into what made them proud to be Canadians. I only wish that I could put into words their pride; it might go a long way in filling that great gap in our national identity that Ottawa has tried to patch with millions of dollars and slogans for the past 15 years.

The last portion of the book and the conclusions reached by the author have recently been vindicated by the new Minister of Defence, Jean-Jacques Blais, when he mentioned *Bras d'Or* in passing, while signing a contract connected with the new Canadian Patrol Frigate on August 23, 1983. In this remark, he stated that he was looking at the possibility of reviving Canada's military hydrofoil programme, but the clincher came in his next direct statement: "Perhaps we abandoned it too soon." (the *FHE-400* Programme.)

From this book I hope the reader can reach their own conclusions about the blunderings of the government and the Navy . . . the same government that is, eleven years and $52.7 million later, reviewing its position. As ill-fated as the Avro Arrow still it seems there may be a belated chance at resurrecting what has been up to now a great loss.

Thomas G. Lynch,
Halifax, N.S.

August 31, 1983

Foreword

Firstly, it is a pleasure and an honour to have been asked to write the foreword to a book about a vessel I loved. As I look back at my thirty-five-year naval career HMCS *Bras d'Or* stands out as the biggest highlight overall. It was truly an adventure, and for Canada at least it was similar to something like the space programme. Everything was new and untried, and thus the day-to-day challenges were immense. In my opinion *Bras d'Or* rose up and met every challenge admirably.

When I was posted there I went with mixed feelings, particularly, I suppose, because I had never even considered it. I was expecting to be sent to some staff college or other, and was fully prepared for that. There was even the possibility, based only on rumour, that I might have gone as the new "Sea Trainer". It came as a shock but when I got used to the idea of *Bras d'Or*, I was indeed delighted.

If one is at all keen in the navy, the first thing one does is to contact the incumbent, to find out all about the new job. When I contacted my predecessor, 'Tino' Cotaras, I frankly admit I was not given much optimism. When I suggested we should eventually, during trials, live onboard, he stated "never". I expressed my feelings that an extended trip should be part of the trials programme, and he said "forget it", and when I suggested that we stock the wardroom bar, he only gave me a look of incredulity! All this is not intended to be criticism, because these were honest feelings from an officer with a lot of experience in the ship, not all pleasant.

Well, I didn't change my mind, and we did all those things. First, a twenty-four-hour trip, then a forty-eight-hour trip into the Gulf Stream, and finally the two-week saga to Bermuda and Norfolk. We lived onboard, and we did stock the bar, needless to say providing some cheer in what could have been, on occasion, despondency. One last thing that I decided was vital. I declared we would never again be towed back into harbour! That statement almost came back to haunt me several times, but in my year of command, we were never towed back. *Never*!

As always, I now look back at the best things: the rough weather trials, figure eights around every destroyer I could find, circling George's Island at 50 knots, speed trials on the range with HMCS Margaree where our combined closing speed was 75 knots, Armed Forces Day where our foilborne pass actually sprayed everyone in *HMCS Protecteur*, the 300 plus visitors that went foilborne and of course, Bermuda and Norfolk.

The facts behind possibly arriving twenty-four hours "early" in Norfolk because of engine problems are well outlined in this book. This alone created a certain amount of incredulity in Norfolk and many decided they would see it before they really would believe it. The ETA was scheduled for 1300. It was a hazy day with about one mile visibility, and at about 1255 the people on the jetty were getting somewhat skeptical about ever seeing *Bras d'Or*. At exactly 1300 we came out of the mirk and went by the jetty doing 50 knots. The skeptics were impressed. The Canadian officer at Norfolk, Captain "Pop" Fotheringham, who up to that time had been under some duress, said that it was the proudest "Canadian" day of his life!

Naturally being quite proud of *Bras d'Or* we showed her off whenever we could. During a fleet demonstration in Bedford Basin with a large number of ships present, I overdid it a little. After doing a slalom down the formation of ships, then a turn around them all, I gilded the lily by going past the flagship literally "waggling" my wings. Clearly I had stolen enough thunder from the rest of the fleet and I was accordingly told by Commodore "Willy" Hayes, "That will be quite enough." Any naval officer can quickly grasp the significance of the adjective 'quite' and so I quickly left Bedford Basin.

In Norfolk one US Admiral said to me "Well son, that is a great ship, but what are you going to do with it?" My reply was a little less than tactful, but I did think that it was a stupid question from an Admiral: "You're the Admiral — you tell me." (This caused quite a lot of amusement when it was subsequently printed in the Norfolk newspaper).

I suppose all along I had many doubts about *Bras d'Or's* operational role in

ASW because of the high towing speeds required. Yet, in a "sprint and drift" mode, the ship would have been able to conduct high speed searches. If the sonar could maintain contact at high speeds, even at relatively short ranges, then it could have been an effective attack vehicle. Its great attribute would have been its relative immunity from counter-attack; therefore it could have operated safely alone.

However it was in all the other areas of operation that it could have been most effective at relatively low cost. Search and rescue, pollution control, sovereignty patrol, and in wartime, a superb attack craft if equipped with a surface-to-surface missile. Clearly the British could not have taken such a craft all the way to the Falklands, however, it is certain that the Argentines could have used them with great effectiveness.

The real pity is that due to our lack of foresight and perseverance we will never know.

I think that I would be very remiss if I did not mention the key to the successful completion of vehicle trials — the people. Co-operation between everyone was absolutely outstanding, and the team of civilians and military worked as one toward the same goals. There are too many names to mention but my boss, Dudley Allan (now President of Control Data Canada) gave me counsel, leadership and support throughout. The DeHavilland Project Officer, Dick Becker, knew where he was going and ran his team accordingly. While we did not always agree personally, we had a fine working relationship with regard to our objectives. I think that the Defence Research Establishment Atlantic was vital to the project, and credit there must mainly go to Mike Eames. Finally I should thank my loyal executive officer, LCdr Ian Sturgess, who when he wasn't performing his normal duties provided us with much-needed comic relief.

This fine book by Tom Lynch will help all Canadians remember a project they almost pulled off and undoubtedly provide some lessons for the future.

Gordon Edwards

Chapter One

From Bell to 'Bras D'or'

Canadian interest in hydrofoil craft far pre-dated the *FHE-400*; indeed it dates back to the first decade of this century when the team of Alexander Graham Bell and Frederick Walker Baldwin began to experiment with ladder-arranged, surface-piercing hydrocurve surfaces, arranged in airplane configuration. Through extensive model testing they entered into a series of hydrofoil craft that culminated in the highly successful *HD-4* in 1918. With a new set of engines in 1919, the craft finally achieved a world speed record of 70.86 miles per hour on September 9th, 1919. This record stood until 1929 and remained a record for a hydrofoil craft until well into the late 1950s.[1]

However, as a commercial enterprise, the hydrofoil proved to be a disaster. Frozen out of the British market by protectionist attitudes and finally all markets because of warship limitations under the Washington Treaty, the hydrofoil craft remained an oddity, far ahead of its time.

During this period and indeed throughout the years leading up to the Second World War, the Canadian Navy remained an avid observer. When war broke Baldwin was ready with lightweight hydrofoil target designs that proved to be far more robust and could be towed with a fraction of the horsepower required for a conventional displacement target. These were acquired by the Canadian Air Force, Canadian Navy and the United States Navy, with mixed results. However, hydrofoil research and development was ignored throughout the war years by the Allies, only being exploited by the Germans in the latter half of the war. Luckily, Allied bombing and the invasion of Fortress Europa finished off these efforts before they could produce tangible weapons in great numbers.

Canada did develop a high-speed smoke-layer after it was found that aircraft detailed for this job were highly susceptible to ground fire. Baldwin quickly produced a scow-like craft with main foils forward and the stern set also acting as the rudder. Designed for a ten-minute operational lifetime, the craft performed successfully for over two hours with two men aboard during trials. It should be noted that the operational craft was to be radio-controlled and therefore a great deal lighter.

Although a success in every way in late 1943, the so-called Comox Torpedo was supplanted by a cheap, smoke-producing unguided rocket in 1944 and joined the ranks of the nearly-successful hydrofoil craft that had preceeded it. The Comox Torpedo and an aborted self-propelled target were the last dying gasps of hydrofoil efforts in Canada by Baldwin and marked an end to hydrofoil research until after the war in 1945.

At this time Lt.-Cdr. Duncan Hodgson, RCN (R), who had been involved with the Comox Torpedo development laid plans to build a record-breaking hydrofoil craft, now that he had returned to civilian life and approached Mr. Philip Rhodes of New York to design such a craft.[2]

At the same time, the recently-formed Defence Research Board, through the offices of Mr. E. Ll. Davies, Vice-Chairman, asked Commander D. M. Hodgson and Captain W. F. Gray to prepare a statement of development of hydrofoil craft. Since both had been involved extensively in the testing of the Comox Torpedo, they had first-hand knowledge on which to base their assessment.

When the report was tendered in late 1947, Mr. Davies was confirmed in his faith in hydrofoil craft principles and recommended that D.R.B. should actively support research in this field. The recommendation was passed on to the Chief of the Naval Staff, Vice-Admiral H. E. Reid.

First, Gray and Hodgson were recalled to active service and then 'loaned' to D.R.B. to further develop a hydrofoil design. Davies had prevailed upon Hodgson sometime earlier to suspend developing the design of his 'record breaker' and Mr. Rhodes was instructed to redesign a craft to reflect intended Naval demonstration purposes. Length was set at 45 feet overall and structural design limits were stated as being capable of rough-water operation. Rhodes, who had designed some of Casey Baldwin's later hydrofoil craft, willingly submitted a design in 1948.

The contract was awarded to McCrea's Boat Shop at Lake Massawippi, near North Hatley, Quebec in June, 1949. According to a report from the Committee of Massawippi Boat Project, D.R.B. to the Chairman, dated July 11, 1949, several difficulties arose during the first five weeks of construction, the first being necessary modifications to McCrea's roof trusses, brought about because of the increased size of the hull and foils. This cost, some $200.00, was approved at the same meeting. Additionally, the Robert Mitchell Company of Montreal, who were manufacturing the foil components, had closed down for annual vacation and hence there would be manufacturing delays in New York. The hull would be ready for roll-over on August 6th and mechanical installations could then be made.[3]

As an historical aside, the members of this committee should be noted, largely because of their far-reaching decisions in the infant days of *Massawippi*;

Mr. E. Ll. Davies, Vice-Chairman, D.R.B.
Rear-Admiral (E) J. G. Knowlton, RCN
Dr. G. S. Field, Deputy Chairman, D.R.B.
Commander W. F. Gray, RCN (R)
Commander (S.B.) D. M. Hodgson, RCN (R)

As a last item on this agenda, it was decided that Halifax would be the best place for experimentation with *Massawippi* and that all correspondence should be treated as 'Secret' in future.[4]

The construction of *Massawippi*, officially known by her DRB file number *R-100*, was completed in January, 1950. She was moved from the heated shed to a railway flat car, ready for her train ride to Halifax under the anxious eyes of Commander Hodgson. On arrival it was found that the rough handling had sprung the straps, allowing the hull to work in its cradle. This had loosened the forward propeller shaft strut. Worse, the temperature change from the heated shop to the frigid outdoors resulted in a $\frac{1}{8}$″ misalignment vertically and about $\frac{1}{16}$″ athwart.[5]

It was felt that a few days soaking might correct the warping. When the lift was first attempted, the three-way lifting bridle broke at $\frac{3}{4}$ safe loading without damage to the vessel. A new four-way bridle was fabricated, two stainless steel lifting straps fitted aft, replacing the single bronze eye originally fitted. This delay also afforded the time to complete unfinished items and to modify others. A complete set of wooden handrails was fitted, running along both sides and the centre of her length. A copper and plexiglass waterproof shield was fabricated and fitted over the switchboard on the dash and a $\frac{1}{8}$ inch thick aluminium deflector screen fabricated for rough water trials.

Most importantly, the copper bilge traps and electric bilge pumps were removed and a large single tank installed. These tanks, made necessary because of the Merlin engine's ability to cough back up to two quarts of high-test gasoline on a false start, were to contain this fuel and then void it safely over the side.

After plugging all the water outlets and openings to prevent freeze-up, the hull was lifted into the water by a boom defence craft and allowed to soak two weeks. When re-examined in the first week of February, it was found the warping had corrected itself in great measure and only minor shimming at the engine end of the drive-train would be necessary. *Massawippi* was then moved to Shearwater on February 21, 1950 for engine start-up, lubrication and coolant systems checks.[6]

Although the *R-100* is described more fully in Table 1-1, a general description is given here.

The craft had a hard-chine hull, 45 feet long overall, 8 feet 6 inches in beam and 4 feet 5 inches midship depth. The original all-up weight of the craft was 8,000 lb. and it was powered by a Packard-Merlin 31 marinized aero-engine, developing 1,250 BHP at 3,000 rpm. The stern was pointed and a special bow design in which the chine swept up to meet the gunwale about three and a half feet abaft the stem head was fabricated. The corresponding forward sections were very fine underwater compared with an orthodox hard chine form, with the lines developed conically. The skin of the hull consisted of two layers of half-inch plywood sheeting.[7]

The engine was mounted well forward at the deepest point of the hull between frames fourteen and seventeen and a half, immediately over the original hydrofoil unit mounting points. It drove the craft via a $1\frac{1}{2}$ inch driveshaft inclined 9.5°, supported by struts and a tail bearing in the base of the rudder assembly. The original propeller was driven through a 2:1 step-up planetary gearing from the engine, thus giving a shaft speed of 6,000 rpm at full power and being below and just forward of the lower rudder foil. Original pitch was 15″ x 23″, but various others were fitted later.

Abaft the engine compartment, two watertight cockpits were fitted, the most forward accommodating the driver and mechanic, plus all the controls. The after compartment was initially used by observers and later for trials instrumentation in the 1952 tests. In the stern, a fuel tank holding fifty gallons of high-test aviation gas provided about twenty minutes endurance at full power.

TABLE 1-1 Specifications, *R-100 Massawippi* Hydrofoil Boat.

General:				
Dimensions:	Length	Over hull:	45′	
		Overall:	45′ 8 1/8″	
	Beam	Over hull:	8′ 10 1/4″	
		Over original foils:	13′ 7″	
		Over intermed. foils:	14′ 5″	
	Freeboard deck above run line:	4′ 9″ at stern		
		6′ 10 1/2″ at stem.		
	Static draft of keel:		6″ at no. 1 frame	
			1′ 9″ at no. 18 frame	
	of running line:		2′ 2 3/8″ at no. 1 frame	
			3′ 2 3/4″ at no. 18 frame	
	Minimum height of keel above run line: 1′ 4 1/4″ at no. 12 frame.			
Weights:	(Dec. 1952) Hull:	6614 lb.	Vert cent grav.	LCG
	Fuel & Machinery:	2892 lb.	5.11′	27.83′ from A.P.
	Outfit, etc.:	923 lb.		
	Instrumentation:	1,061 lb.		
	Crew (approx):	720 lb.		
	Ballast (approx):	290 lb.		
	All-up weight	12,500 lb.	4.50′	24′ from A.P.
Hydrofoil System:	Three point suspension Bell-Baldwin Ladder System. Two main hydrofoil sets, five foils per side. 25% M.A.C. point of no. 1 foil — 31′ 8 1/2″ forward of A.P. One rudder hydrofoil set, two foils- 25% M.A.C. point of no. 1 foil, 2 1/8″ abaft A.P. Foil base (between 25% M.A.C. points), 31′ 10 5/8″ Further hydrofoil specifications in Table 2-3 Further specifications on engines in Engine Specifications Appendix B			
	Post-Intermediate	Foil Refit: Three point suspension "V" foil Ladder system Two main hydrofoil sets — four foils per side Foilbase: 36′ 3″		
	One ladder "V" foil rudder set — five "V" foils in set. 6% Walchner "C"/NACA 16-1009 sections. See Hydrofoil particulars Table 2-3.			
	Intermediate Revised Dimensions:			
	Length	Over Hull:	45′	
		Overall:	46′ 7/8″	

The foil layout was classic Bell-Baldwin, with the two main support foil units forward and the third aft, acting as a rudder as well. The foil sections were classical as well, having a flat bottom or face, sharp leading and trailing edges and a parabolic curved back with a maximum thickness (4-5% of chord) at about 40% of chord. The 14° dihedral on the main sets provided geometrical 'reefing' of the foils and the angle of incidence with the design running line of 5° for the lowest or number one foil, increasing to 11° for number five foil. The unit was raked 5° to the vertical.

The rudder foil unit consisted of two hydrofoil surfaces 8 inches wide by 41.5 inches long overall. These were not designed to 'reef' and were mounted to the rudder blade tips. These braces in turn mounted to a collar just below the lower rudder post bearing.

Tests began in February, 1950 and extended into July. Particulars of these tests are contained in Table 1-2 and only important points will be followed here. With the main foils shifted aft some two feet after the stern had refused to lift in the first runs, the engine was unable to swing the craft into foilborne mode. A small bow preventer foil was fitted to help maintain bows-up attitude for take-off, but it wasn't until the stern foil assembly was rebuilt that this 'squatting' was cured. (see Table 1-3). Thereafter, the craft rose smartly, but the engine was clearly overloaded. The main foils were returned to their original position and on July 13, 1950 *R-100* achieved the speed of 64.28 knots at 2800 RPM with 14 pounds of boost on the supercharger. However, the overloading persisted and the overstressed 2:1 gearbox gave up the ghost in August, 1950. Repairs took until October 15 with a compromise made in the gearbox. The manufacturer in error had shipped a 2.2:1 gearbox instead of the 1.8:1 as ordered and rather than stall the

R-100 Qualitative Trials Results Table 1-2

DATE	PROPELLER (dia × Pitch)	Gear Ratio (up)	Engine RPM	Max. Speed (knots)	Remarks
STAGE ONE — Preliminary Trials					
February	15 × 23″	2:1	2650	30	Hydrofoils as Modification A (Table 2-2). Stern not
to	16 × 21″	2:1	2650	32	lifting. Runs made with main hydrofoils moved
July, 1950	16 × 21″	2:1	2250	38*	two feet aft. Engine overloaded. Stern not lifting.
	16 × 18″	2:1	2200	34*	
STAGE TWO — Step-Up Gear Trials					
5 July, 1950	16 × 18″	2:1	2750	55.38*	Large span stern foils fitted — Modification B
8 July, 1950	16 × 18″	2:1	2800	64.28	(Table 2-3). Stern lifting. Main foils returned to original
13 July, 1950	16 × 18″	2:1	2500	Approx. 50	position. Stern still lifting. First sea trials 2-3 ft chop on 6′ × 50′ swells.
August, 1950	—	—	—	—	2:1 gearbox failed due to overloading.
15 Oct., 1950	16 × 18″	2.2:1	2250	48	Wrong gearbox shipped. Engine badly overloaded.
28 Oct., 1950	16 × 18″	2.2:1	2300	48	First episode of porpoising with this craft.
18 Nov., 1950	15 × 14″	2.2:1	3000	35-40	Propeller clearly too small.
22 Nov., 1950	15 × 14″	2.2:1	1400	20-25	Behaved well as displacement craft in heavy seas.
December, 1950	—	—	—	—	2.2:1 gearbox failed to overloading.
STAGE THREE — Direct Drive Trials					
9 Jan., 1951	18 × 24″	1:1	3200	40	Propeller too small but very rapid acceleration noted.
23 April, 1951	18 × 28″	1:1	3000	46	
24 April, 1951	19 × 26″	1:1	3000	51.5	Stern lifting dangerously high: fear diving.
4 May, 1951	19 × 26″	1:1	3000	53	Stern hydrofoil area reduced — Modification C (Table 2-3)
May-Oct., 1951	19 × 26″	1:1	—	—	Instrumented stability tests-Mods. D and E made (Table 2-3)
Oct., 1951-Jan. '52	—	—	—	—	1½″ diameter shaft replaced with 1 ¾″ shaft.
9 Jan., 1952	20 × 28″	1:1	3000	55	Very rapid acceleration.
STAGE FOUR — Load Carrying Trials					
9 Jan., 1952	20 × 28″	1:1	3000	55.4	All-up weight: 9,880 lb
9 Jan., 1952	20 × 28″	1:1	3000	55	All-up weight: 10,880 lb
10 Jan., 1952	20 × 28″	1:1	3000	50	All-up weight: 11,880 lb
10 Jan., 1952	20 × 28″	1:1	3000	45	All-up weight: 12,880 lb
10 Jan., 1952	20 × 28″	1:1	3000	50	All-up weight: 13,880 lb
15 Jan., 1952	20 × 28″	1:1	3000	55	All-up weight: 11,060 lb (1000 lb on extreme stern reduced porpoising.)
January/52-Sept./52	—	—	—	—	Overhaul, installation of instrumentation. Mod. F made to foils.

HYDROFOIL PARTICULARS — *R-100 Massawippi* Table 1-3

Modification Letters	Foil no.	Span (in.)	Chord (in.)	Act. Area (sq. ft.)	Aspect ratio	Angle of incidence		Foil space	Foil reef	Chamber/c ratio (%)
MAIN FOIL SET (one only)		DIHEDRAL: 14°			RAKE: -5°					
A to I	5	40¾	8	2.26	5.10	11°		—	—	4.2
A to I	4	39⅞	8	2.21	4.98	9°		8″	8″	4.2
A to I	3	38¾	8	2.15	4.84	7°		8¾″	4″	2.4
A to F	2	37⅝	8	2.09	4.70	5°		8¾″	8⅜″	2.4
D, E tips added								8¾″	2¾″	2.1
A to F	1	36½	7½	1.90	4.86	5°				
G to I	2	47⅝	8	2.65	5.95	5°		8¾″	8⅜″	2.4
G to I	1	46½	8	2.58	5.81	5°		8¾″	12¾″	2.4
RUDDER HYDROFOILS (ONE SIDE OF RUDDER ONLY)				DIHEDRAL: 18°	NO RAKE					
A	Upper	12	8	0.67	1.50	7°				2.4
A, C to F (E, F tips)								8½″	—	
	Lower	18	8	1.00	2.25	3½°				2.4
B	Upper	28	10	1.94	2.80	7°				1.9
								8½″	—	
	Lower	24¾	10	1.72	2.48	3½°				1.9
C to I	Upper	19½	10	1.35	1.95	7°				1.9
								8½″		
								8½″		
G to I	Lower	26	8	1.44	3.25	3½°				2.4
Intermediate Set										
MAIN FOIL SET (one of)			DIHEDRAL: 30°	STRUT RAKE: 15°						
	1	48 in.	9⅝	3.20	5.0	2.0°	2.3°	9.32 in	¼ span	6% t/Walchner 'C'
	2	48	9⅝	3.20	5.0	5.5°	6.4°	9.32 in	¼ span	6% t/Walchner 'C'
	3	48	9⅝	3.20	5.0	9°	10.4°	9.32 in	¼ span	NACA 16-1009
	4	48	9⅝	—	5.0	12°	13.9°	9.32 in	¼ span	NACA 16-1009
Stern Foil:										
	1	48	9⅝	3.20	5.0	4°	4.6°	9.32 in	¼ span	6% t/Walchner 'C'
	2	48	9⅝	3.20	5.0	7°	8.1°	9.32 in	¼ span	6% t/Walchner 'C'
	3	48	9⅝	3.20	5.0	10°	11.6°	9.32 in	¼ span	NACA 16-1009
	4	48	9⅝	3.20	5.0	10°	13.9°	9.32	¼ span	NACA 16-1009

Massawippi with *KC-B* designator, on Naval Day, 1950, Halifax harbour. The engine space covers are open and the induction cowl is not fitted. This view shows the bow 'preventer' foil. *Credit: Nat. Def. Photo.*

testing further, this was installed. This proved unfortunate, since it was only possible to become foilborne by hand priming and solid injection with boost at 10 pounds of the engine. Best speeds were reached on October 15 and 28, being 48 knots, but longitudinal instability or 'panting' and porpoising made their first appearance with this craft in this configuration. It was found this condition was most apparent during calm water trials, minor choppy water greatly reduced the porpoising. However, the overloaded 2.2:1 gearbox brought the testing to a halt on November 29 when it failed. The decision was made then to couple the engine directly with the shaft. This would serve to eliminate the gearboxes and secondly, would reduce the shaft speed to 1:1. This was seen as a definite advantage, since cavitation problems were being experienced with the current line of propellers. Thirdly, the reduced propeller 'blast' would effect the rear foil surfaces less, something that was identified just prior to the rough water trials some five days before the gearbox had expired. However, the direct coupling now overstressed the driveshaft and this had to be replaced with a 1¾-inch unit that was on-hand on January 9, 1951.

Testing continued through January, with another change in rudder hydrofoils necessary when the new 19″ x 26″ pitch propeller showed these surfaces were generating too much lift. This caused the craft to trim bows down, leaving it in serious danger of sliding forward off her main foils and crashing into the water bows-first. The rudder foils were finally sorted out by May 4, 1951.

The longitudinal instability persisted and photographic measurements showed cyclic oscillations in heave, pitch and roll above speeds of 30 knots through the later half of 1951. These decreased in amplitude but increased in violence up to 55 knots, where growing hydrodynamic forces reduced this to only sharp roll oscillations. This was reduced progressively by adding extension plates to the second foil in the main sets and to the bottom stern foils until they showed only slow rates of oscillation and pitch was a gentle movement. However, this was brought to a head when the load testing commenced in late January, 1952. Increased weight set up violent porpoising if placed forward of the centre of gravity. Loading aft of this point stopped this, but prevented the stern from clearing the surface. Loading of 1000 lb. over the extreme stern was the best in preventing porpoising, but buried the stern hopelessly. Cavitation remained a limiting factor in preventing the engine from developing maximum thrust and horsepower. A general overhaul was undertaken in February, when the full instrumentation package was finally installed.

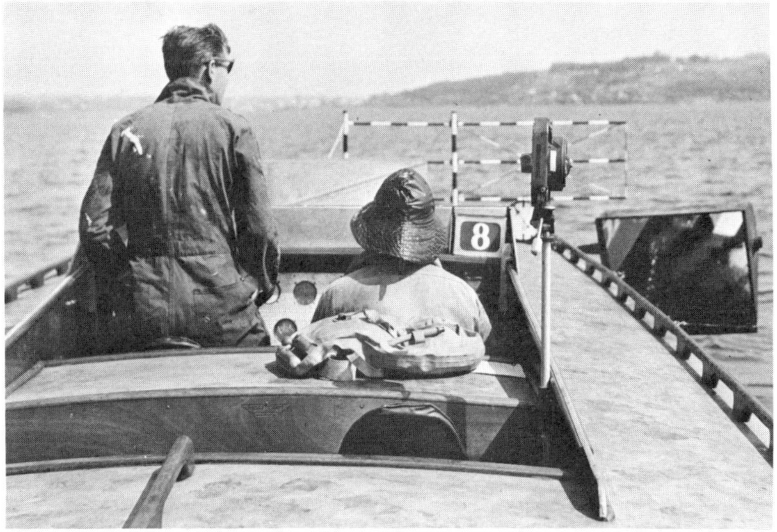

Aboard *Massawippi.* The observation equipment was fairly primitive. Note the cine camera, the mirror and the grid bars for measuring roll and pitch. *Credit: N.R.E.*

Looking back over the preceeding period, it must be realized that all results and remedial actions were based on the best traditions of Bell-Baldwin — direct observation by eye and camera. A system of trial and error were the only guidelines; it was slow progress over the first year.[8]

It should be noted that capital expenditures up to 1952 for the *R-100* programme totalled $2,498,946.16 covered under Vote 400 of the DRB Budget and approved April 4, 1952.[9]

Mechanical unreliability haunted the project throughout 1952, with the weakness of an aero engine adapted to a marine environment becoming more and more apparent. Repairs were costly and time-consuming. Trials under Stage IV were exhaustive with the full instrumentation package aboard, beginning in August. Finally, with the recorded results, N.R.E. scientists had concrete information to work with. Cavitation problems with the 20″ x 28″ and 22″ x 26″ pitch propellers and the modified foils were identified, with porpoising reaching dangerous levels at 37-38 knots. The foil system was found to be overloaded by a factor of three times the original loadings. Foil tips were in complete breakdown, cavitating into uselessness thereby increasing the load on the main blade sections between the struts. The rear foils were reluctant to trim up, thereby throwing the main foils off their angle of attack, further eroding their performance. This lack of stern foil lift was traced to the down-wash of the propeller, coupled with the unexpected disturbance of the main foils. Measurements showed that this disturbance and cavitation of the propeller were restricting delivered horsepower of the engine to 800, when the engine was capable of 1200 even after allowances for shaft loss.[10]

It was determined the entire foil system would have to be replaced. New blades were fitted and the craft returned to service in November, 1952. Although the foil system now worked reasonably well, the greater lift height left the propeller in an increased state of cavitation, since it was closer to the surface, inviting surface ventilation. Clearly a propeller that could operate in a supercavitating state would be necessary! However, this was a virtually unknown field in 1952.

Fences were fitted to control the limited amount of surface ventilation to the lower foils and the craft was rushed into service with these improperly finished on November 29 for demonstrations for Saunders-Roe representatives. Results were not judged representative until the V-2 and V-3 trials in January, 1953, when pitch was recorded as reduced by 40% and heave practically eliminated. Ride was noticeably smoother too. Clearly the ventilation of the foil surfaces had been delayed until after the 40-knot range by the fences. Trials continued until February 6 when a general maintenance period was started.

Conclusions reached from these tests were that the foil system as it existed was incapable of stable lifts nearing 12,500 lb. at speeds greater than 30 knots. A new set of foils would be necessary to further explore lifting ranges in the future. Also, a supercavitating propeller would be necessary to fully utilize the engine's thrust and horsepower and the rudder foils would have to be moved clear of the propeller's blast to operate anywhere near efficiently.

It should be noted that D.R.B. had taken over the *Massawippi* Project as of 1950, tasking the Naval Research Establishment, Dartmouth with trials, testing and development. Being a project of the Engineering Group, N.R.E., the head man was Mr. R. P. Blake. The research team built up for the 1952-53 period consisted of Mr. R. P. Blake, Mr. M. C. Eames, Mr. E. A. Jones, Mr. G. K. Naas and Mr. K. R. Bezanson with Mr. K. R. Enkenhus working the instrumentation from mid-1951 to mid-1952. On the Naval side, the Superintendant, HMC Dockyard, Halifax, Commodore (E) W. W. Porteous, RCN took a keen interest in the project and contributed to its progress by providing many Dockyard services and facilities. Cdr. (E) F. Harley, RCN, Lt. P. Baldwin, RCN and Captain A. F. Peers, RCN, assisted with the project as well.

During September a series of tests to further refine the deficiencies in the *R-100* foil system were undertaken. However, a failure of the bearing pillow block under high-speed conditions finished these. A report of October 9, 1953 stated that the frame inboard stringers from frame 9 to 12 were shattered, the inner keel from frame 11.5 to 16 was fractured, the floor from frame 12 to 14 was damaged and started away from the hull planking. This damage would have to be repaired and the decision was taken to build a new set of foils along the lines proposed by Saunders-Roe for the *R-101* design study.[11]

Redesignated under Project D12-05-70-02, the "Canadian Hydrofoil Project", the new foil design by M. C. Eames would allow the *R-100* to operate at weights realistic for a larger operational craft. Dominion Engineering Works of Montreal was contracted to build the new foil sets in 1955. However, a series of complications arose in the design and manufacture of these foil units delaying delivery by some eighteen months. These foils, which were intended to explore the design to be later utilized by the *R-103* which was then under construction at Saunders-Roe in Britain, were completed and fitted too late to have any impact upon this design because of this delay. Hence the 'Intermediate' designator for the foils was misleading: these would in fact be the last configuration for *R-100*. Details are given in the Table 1-3.

The new foil units, when delivered in 1955 used NACA 16 series and Walchner 'C' sections. There were four foils per unit and marked a significant departure from earlier straight dihedral ladder types employed on *R-100* and in the *R-102* study. (See section on *R-103*.) The new all-up weight was 16,800 lb. or 7.5 tons, representing an increase of 4,300 lb. or 34.4% of the maximum all up weight of the original *R-100* in 1952 and a 100% increase over the estimated 8,000 lb. of the original design. Fifty knots was set as a reasonable top speed for the craft, requiring a horizontal thrust of 3,360 lb. and thrust horsepower of 516. This was deemed possible, employing the Merlin's supercharger in low gear and utilizing an N.R.E.-designed 25″ x 30″ pitch propeller with an efficiency factor of 0.43.

The main foil locations were moved forward and the rudder foil shifted further aft, but on the same rudder post. Foil base was increased some 4 feet 7.5 inches with the centre of gravity 24 feet forward of the stern post. Final trimming would be accomplished by shifting of ballast weights, carried as payload.

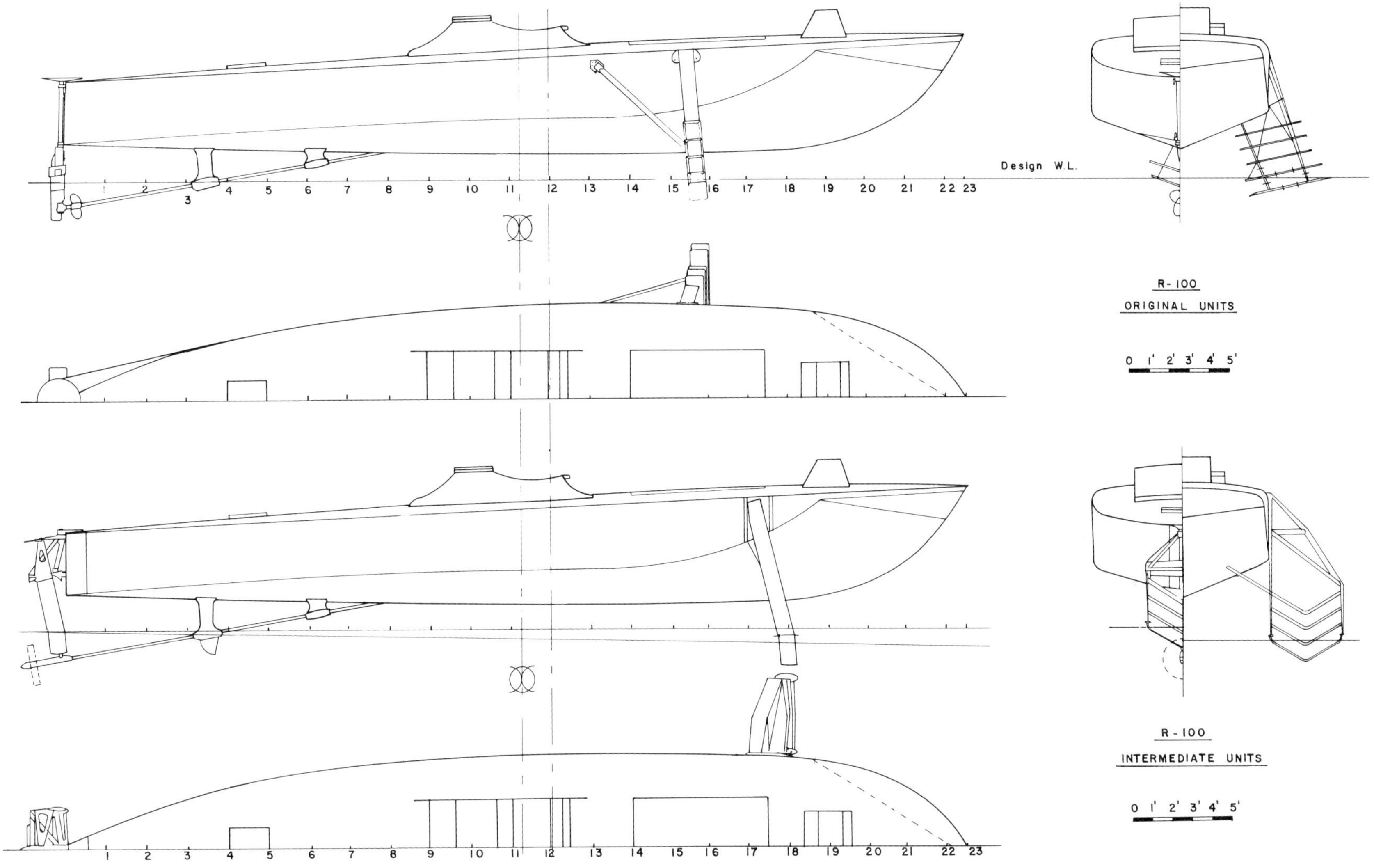

R-100 Original Units
Intermediate Units

In manufacturing, the new foils proved to be more complicated and exacting than expected. These units were of all-welded construction and the material of chrome-molybdenum alloy steel meeting SAE 4130 specification in normalized condition. Yield strength of 70,000 lb/in^2 were typical of this material, with 100,000 lb/in^2 maximum. The blades were planed in continuous lengths for construction simplicity and bent around a cylindrical surface having its axis parallel to the base line of the foil section to form the 'V'. Specialized jigs which were manufactured for the building of these foils by Dominion Engineering were partially responsible for the delay in building. Firstly the wrong dimensions were used in the building of the jigs, necessitating another unit being built and a breakdown of the only planer capable of the task. Secondly an underestimation of time allocated for engineering and a strike at the plant caused serious delay.

Initial tolerances set down as $\frac{1}{10}$ inch were found to be unrealistic, without inducing unacceptable stress in the material, so this was relaxed to 0.25 of a degree. During welding, it was found that weld-induced stress cracked certain welds before the units could be normalized. It was necessary to grind out these welds and reweld, with disastrous loss of time. More delay was caused in the final polishing of these units, largely because of the complex shape and the hardness of the material.

To allow the question of down-wash and propeller blast to be investigated more thoroughly, the rudder foil was made adjustable in rake. Complicating the unit further, the stern foil was used as the mount point for the propeller and shaft. This made it necessary to thicken the apex of number one foil's 'V' to accommodate this bearing.

When *R-100* re-appeared in 1955, she presented a fairly radical change in looks and performance, more closely resembling a possible scale model of a 50-ton naval hydrofoil craft, with increased hull clearance of 1 foot 7 inches for rough water trials. Trials showed that the porpoising problem had nearly disappeared and the craft operated at 45 knots in seas of 6 feet, a truly remarkable performance for a 45-foot craft. Additionally, the foils proved to be an efficient damper of hull movements at hullborne speeds, something of great importance for later hydrofoil craft designs.[12]

Another achievement for *Massawippi* was the use of super-cavitating propellers. David Taylor Model Basin, (Washington, D.C.) had developed the theory and a practical method of designing such propellers. However, there wasn't a suitable test craft in the USA. N.R.E. was approached by DTMB to allow these propellers to be tested on *R-100*. The need for actual testing became apparent immediately, since the first propeller crumpled on initial take-off. This design had not allowed for increased stresses before super-

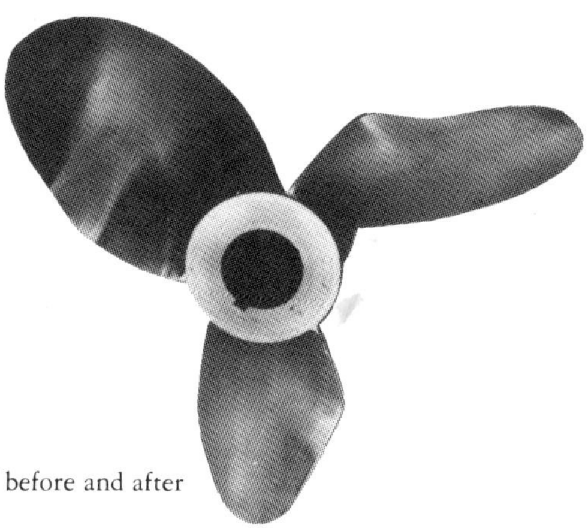

The DTMB supercavitating propeller from *Massawippi* before and after testing.
Credit: N.R.E.

cavitation was established. A second, strengthened propeller was rushed to Halifax and tested, found successful and thus allowed DTMB to further their research.[13]

At the completion of the 1956 test season it was agreed that the Bell-Baldwin foil system represented the best compromise between reasonably high-speed, seaworthiness, stability and load-carrying capacity. The results of this research proved that a hydrofoil vessel suitable for operational naval use in open waters was feasible. However, it would remain up to *R-103* to either prove or disprove that a suitable craft was within technology's means.

R-103 Bras d'Or — Anticipating a satisfactory outcome of both *R-100* and scale model tests, it was felt it was necessary to initiate a design study of a similar type of hydrofoil craft which would be large enough and suitably designed to meet a naval operational need. This was initiated in late 1951 and the craft project number was R-102. Design work was undertaken by Mr. Philip L. Rhodes but, due to continued ill health, he was forced to transfer the design study contract to Messrs. Saunders-Roe Ltd., and Mr. Rhodes was retained in a consulting capacity. After transfer of the contract it was engineered by this company that a considerable relaxation of specification limits came about to allow coverage of a wider range of possible designs of craft ranging from 80 to 100-foot lengths, using various available engines. When the *R-102* study was tendered in 1953, it was found to be marginal. The RCN was interested in a 100-ton plus ASW vessel, but available propulsion plants, even those on the drawing boards, would be incapable of powering it. Saunders-Roe proposed an alternative craft, weighing 50 tons and capable of construction immediately, labelled *R-101*.

As far as DRB were concerned the project nearly died at this time, but Admiralty encouraged them to ask Saunders-Roe to embark on a second design study into the *R-101* concept. Admiralty was extremely interested in a 50-ton hydrofoil craft capable of operation in English coastal waters by Coastal Forces, the W.W.II MTB crowd. Canada considered the design too limited for ASW operations and balked at such an ambitious endeavour without obvious applications for Canada. However, the impasse was resolved when DRB offered to build a smaller craft, while Admiralty funded the scale-model testing and announced that they would build the full scale, 50-ton *R-101* prototype, assuming that tests on the manned model substantiated the promise. Admiralty agreed and since so much new technology was involved, it was felt that the manned scale model would be the best route to follow.

The proposed package would be the smallest craft, capable of incorporating the mechanical features necessary in the full-scale design, such as hollow built-up foils and Z-drive transmissions.[14]

Defence Research Board authorized a contract in September 1953 and awarded this to Saunders-Roe Ltd, Cowes, Isle of Wight.[15] Contract DRB/218 authorized the building of a ⅓-scale manned model, to be identified as serial #2UK2-2201, with an authorized expenditure ceiling limit of $644,000 1954. However, technical problems and design changes by Saunders-Roe caused this amount to be inadequate and because the contract was on a cost-plus basis, necessitated because the final design could not be specified by N.R.E., completion date was set for April, 1956.

Drawings of the craft were completed and construction of the hull started in late 1953, but, the finalized hydrofoil design was not known and would have to be investigated, following the *R-101* proposal. True, the ladder-type Bell-Baldwin design, with two units forward and the third doing double-duty as rudder and support, was confirmed, but foil shape, angles of attack, rake, materials, manufacture were still only proposed specifications on paper in the *R-101* proposal. It was hoped that the intermediate foils of *R-100* would assist in this configuration for the ⅓-scale manned model, but delays in producing the *R-100* foils precluded any input in the *R-103* foil design, with disastrous results. Only model testing would have any bearing.[16]

Saunders-Roe began construction of 1/14-scale models for tank testing at their Osborne, Isle of Wight site. Design criteria were based upon input accumulated from scale tests and actual data on *R-100* over the past years. Three test tanks were utilized, including a huge towing tank. Resistance, spray behaviour, stability and response in head, quartering and following seas were investigated, with several differently-configured models of 1/14-scale. Impact accelerations were measured, 'take-off' speeds and attitudes calculated and tested, high-speed turns were investigated and foil behaviour observed. From these and hundreds of other tests, the design of the hull, sponsons and foil units was developed to give the best performance in all anticipated sea conditions. In all, some 20,000 test runs were made in the test tanks alone, while construction of the actual vessel slowly kept pace with the resultant research findings.

Additionally 1/4.4 scale tests were carried out with a radio-controlled model in sheltered waters near the plant. Accuracy of scale was exact in structural and instrumentation design to achieve a correctly-scaled craft and weight.

Speeds of over 20 knots were possible in open water, allowing for studies in random 'seas'. Test results thus gathered were compared with tank model tests and adjustments to design criteria then made.[17]

Meanwhile, in Canada a funding formula had been arrived at, in which D.R.B. would share funding with the RCN. Roughly half the projected $1,000,000 expenditure would be covered in Naval Appropriations in the years 1953-1957. However, it should be kept in mind that this was to fund the *entire* program, not just the construction costs.

By 1954 the design criteria were firmly locked in and the following craft took shape. The construction of the hull was entirely aluminium sheet, riveted over extruded aluminium ribs, frames and stringers. The shape of the hull was roughly that of a tadpole when viewed from overhead, being widest at the wheelhouse, where the main foil sponsons were attached. Widths were 126.75 inches at #1 engine room hatch, 60.5 inches at the rear cleats and bollard and 36.5 inches at two feet from the stern extremity. Nominal displacement would be 17.5 tons, with a maximum of 19.24 tons. Overall length was 59 feet, with a length between perpendiculars of 55 feet 6 inches. The centre point for all datum measurements was 22.24 inches from station 10 (furthest forward) and 9.445 feet below the centre of gravity.

The foils of 'V' shaped 6% Walchner 'C' sections were the same in all locations, with four blades in the main foils and three in the rudder unit. Width of the foil units was 5.186 feet, distance between blades, measured at the strut were 1.387 feet for all blades. The overall draft of the foils from CG was 9 feet to the CG of the foil. Each blade was approximately 2 inches thick at the centre.

The foil units were unique for this time, since these were of built-up construction, rather than a machined solid as in earlier craft.[18]

Two massive Rolls-Royce Griffon III 12-cylinder, 60° upright-V, supercharged engines of 1500 bhp at 3,000 rpm were fitted in the hull, one either side of the propulsion pod and facing one another.[19] Each had an input shaft into the bevel-gear housing, which in turn directed this thrust through 90°, straight down via two shafts to bevel gears at the bottom. These gears then turned the thrust 90°, back to the horizontal and to the front and rear propellers. The aftmost engine drove the variable-pitch propeller, which had blades of 11⅞ inches and was used in all instances when the craft moved. The foremost engine and the propeller of high-speed, subcavitation type was only used when maximum speed to become foilborne

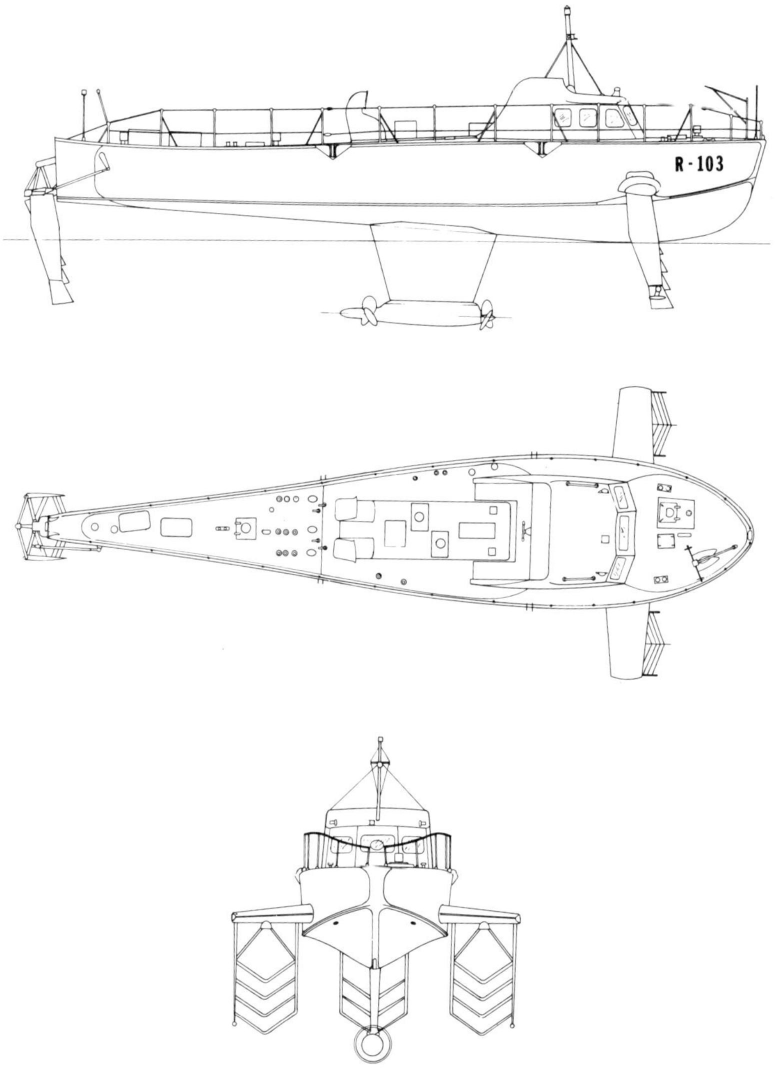

R-103 original foil configuration

was needed. Distance from horizontal centre of gravity to centre of propeller hub boss was 9.445 feet.

The cabin, just forward of the centre of gravity point, was largely given over to test instrumentation and observation space. The helm position was like an MTB, from an open position just abaft the cabin, affording only chest-high protection from the wind and elements . . . truly an adventurous position in foul weather! Forward and below the deck was a typical bos'n store . . . at first glance. Two observation positions through the hull for cameras interrupted the floor area, affording an inside view of the foils when foilborne.

Steering was hydraulic ram, acting on an eccentric arm linkage on the starboard side of the hull, to an anchor point on the rear foil unit.

Air for the engines was provided via baffled ducts on the main deck. Exhausts were at hullborne waterline level on both sides with stop-valves to prevent water entering the exhausts when the engines were stopped or the ports were underwater.

Many engineering problems were encountered during construction and delivery dates were constantly revised. April, 1956 became October, 1956 and then April, 1957. Finally *R-103*, now officially referred to as *Bras d'Or*, honouring the lakes on which the original Bell-Baldwin experiments had taken place, was ready.

Bras d'Or was launched and named on April 29, 1957 at Saunders-Roe Ltd. on the Isle of Anglesey. Officiating at the launching ceremonies was Mrs. A. H. Zimmerman, wife of the D.R.B. chairman, with Dr. Zimmerman, Mr. E. Ll. Davies now Defence Research member of the Canadian Joint Staff in London, plus interested Admiralty, RCN, DRB and N.R.E. personnel present.[20]

Bras d'Or immediately began fitting out and the first trials to demonstrate foilborne ability were undertaken in the summer of 1957. After initial machinery trials, foilborne demonstrations were undertaken with N.R.E. personnel aboard. Speed mounted and the craft lifted onto its foils . . . but briefly. The craft, after attaining its trim at 25 knots, suddenly lurched and fell off her foils, landing on the hull none too gently.

N.R.E. scientists were clearly shocked. The similar foils on *R-100 Massawippi*, designed by N.R.E., but based on the *R-101* principles, had performed so well during the rigorous testing over the past two years. But here were the *Bras d'Or* foils, designed by Saunders-Roe, showing a marked instability.

Saunders-Roe contended that since the craft was capable of foilborne service, albeit with some stringent procedures, they had fulfilled the contract. N.R.E. through DRB, contended that faulty design on the part of Saunders-Roe was responsible. With the dissolution of Coastal Forces in the first months of 1957 and the ending of any requirement for a fast 50-ton coastal craft, Admiralty was non-commital. The whole sorry affair descended into a squabble for politicians and lawyers to sort out.[21]

Since the craft was now DRB property, it was seen that full-scale testing in Canada would be necessary to solve the mystery of *R-103's* instability. This would necessitate moving the craft to Canada, since it was part of DRB's responsibility to instrument and exhaustively test the craft. It was proposed that *Bras d'Or* would be transported to Halifax as part of the deck cargo of the new RCN carrier, *Bonaventure,* then fitting out at Harland and Wolfe Shipyards in England. However, delivery of *Bonaventure* was delayed from that fall until January, 1957 while last-minute improvements were added and the ship put through acceptance trials. She was finally commissioned on January 17, 1957. It was May before *Bras d'Or* left for Halifax, a canvas-shrouded mass stowed next to the 'island'.[22]

Bonaventure arrived in Halifax on June 26, 1957 where she hastily off-loaded *R-103*, snug in her wheeled cradle.

During those last months awaiting the delivery of *Bras d'Or*, N.R.E. had acquired one of Naval Armament Depot's concrete flat barges. A mechanical boom system was fabricated to allow *Bras d'Or* to be secured alongside the barge without damaging the submerged foil units. Additionally, a shed was constructed on the barge and a boom fitted to allow a small, experimental craft designated *Rx* to be retrieved or launched from the shed. Upon delivery, this was where *Bras d'Or* retired at the end of June for instrumentation fitting-out.

First instrumentation calibration tests were run on October 15, 1957, followed by five more before the end of the month. However, it wasn't until April, 1958 that full-scale investigative tests began on the measured mile course on Bedford Basin (see Table 1-4). Priority was given to finding out what had gone wrong with the *R-103* hydrofoil design. Testing was exhaustive, especially in conjunction with *Rx*, which was fitted with similar foils, throughout the rest of 1958, finally winding down in November.[23] The masses of raw data were providing broad clues on the problems in the Saunders-Roe designed hydrofoils. *Rx*, with her to-scale set of *R-103* foils, provided the data to enable N.R.E. to devise a solution to these problems

R-103 on Bedford Basin, 1958
Credit: N.R.E.

and allow rough water trials in 1959, but N.R.E., in its progressive research in 1957-58, had come to the conclusion that perhaps Bell and Baldwin had been mistaken in their orthodox foil unit lay-out! Perhaps they had had it backwards! In the spring session of the Institution of Naval Architects, March 26, 1958, following the reading of Peter Crewe's "The Hydrofoil boat: Its History and Future Prospects", N.R.E. scientist M. C. Eames, dropped this bombshell in the discussion period:

> ". . . Taking the author's comparison of various configurations and extending his ideas a little, one arrives at the conclusion that for craft in the transcavitation speed range, the most logical configuration is one which has not yet been tested . . .
>
> . . . the envisioned system would combine the advantage of the current ladder and Grunberg types by *carrying about 90% of the load on a monoplane foil aft and 10% on a single surface-following ladder unit forward* . . ."[24]

Thus N.R.E. had forestalled any move by Saunders-Roe to apply for exclusive patents on this foil configuration!

The results of the 1958 tests had shown that *Bras d'Or*'s foil system was capable of maintaining stability over only a narrow range of angles of attack — a range too narrow for satisfactory rough-water operation. This, coupled with a tendancy of 'V' foils to be roll-sensitive to slip, had proven to be too much for safe foilborne operation except in conditions found on occasional summer days. Part of the problem was eventually traced to errors in foil nose shape, leading to premature cavitation and encouraging ventilation too extensive to be controlled by fences. Additionally, too low a rate of change of lift with draft prevented her recovery from sudden local losses of lift. This was an expensive lesson in the importance of scale effects, since her model tests and *R-100* had promised exemplary behaviour.[25]

Bras d'Or surrendered her name to the proposed *FHE400* in 1962, becoming *Baddeck*.[26] However, N.R.E. had laid her up in 1959 in favour of work with the *Rx* craft and it wasn't until 1961 that a temporary 'fix' was applied. This primarily called for a reshaping of the foil section, plus an increase in setting angle (see Table 1-5).

R-103 1958 Trials Results Table 1-4

Trial no.	Date	Number of Runs	Indicated rpm	Sea Conditions	Wind	Main Foil Load	Stern Foil Load	Comments
#58/4-2	11/6/58	three	1400	calm	SW 5-7 mph	12,622 lb	13,960 lb	cavitation of #1 foil, involving 0.2 chord.
			1500	calm	SW 5-7 mph	12,622 lb	13,960 lb	cavitation of #1 foil, ½ chord, ventilation of #2
		foil settings: stern: 0° bow: ½°	1600	calm	SW 5-7 mph	12,622 lb	13,960 lb	port foil dipping occasionally, #1 cavitating wholly, ventilation of #2 to inner fence
			1700	calm	SW 5-7 mph	12,622 lb	13,960 lb	aborted; craft dived violently, impacting with surface hard enough to throw crew about. 1300 RPM runs produced runs with minor porpoising.
#58/5-2	16/6/58	nine	1200-1300	8-10″	SW 15-20	12,644 lb	14,719 lb	severe spray, no cavitation
		foil settings:	1400	8-10″	SW 15-20	12,644 lb	14,719 lb	beginnings of cavitation, leading edge
		stern: 0°	1500	8-10″	SW 15-20	12,644 lb	14,719 lb	full cavitation #1, vibration
		main: 0°	1600	8-10″	SW 15-20	12,644 lb	14,719 lb	severe vibration, two rolls, with lower strut fairing completely out of water. Lack of control.
#58/6-2	18/6/58	fourteen stern: 0°, m-1°	1200-1800	4″	W/SW12	14,343 lb	11,772 lb	rolling beginning at 1300-1500. Porpoising at 1600; yawing, loss of directional control at 1800.
#58/7 A&B	1/7/58	eight main; 1.4° stern: 0° 1.9°	(A) 1200-1800 (B) 1200-1800	calm	NNE 2-4	(A) 12,521 lb (B) 12,523 lb	14,373 lb 14,360 lb	difficulty in obtaining 1600-1800; barely f'borne. not foilborne at wide-open throttle; 1800.
#58/8-2	4/7/58	five stern: -.9° main: 1.9° (minus)	1200-2000	calm	NNW 4-6	12,491 lb	14,318 lb	foilborne at 1200, roll perceived, getting harsher as speed increased. Pitching begun at 1800; 1900 was top speed; fixed roll angle to starboard.
#58/9-2	8/7/58	eight stern: -1° main: -1½°	1200-2000	calm	NE 2-4	12,600 lb	17,357 lb	constant list to port at 1200, gentle roll at 1400, roll and pitch at 1600, more violent at 1800, violent pitching, hitting the water at 2000. Engine lube oil overheating to 150°C at last.
#58/10-2	10/7/58	six stern: -1° main: -1°	1200-1800	calm	NE 0-2	13,642 lb	16,959 lb	gentle roll at 1200, port beam under at 1400, heavy roll, slight pitch at 1600, steady at 1800, poor directional control, roll, pitch, yaw at 2000.
#58/11-2	14/7/58	five stern: -1° main: -½°	1200-1800	calm	NNW 5	12,588 lb	14,974 lb	gentle roll at 1200, shorter period/greater amp. of roll, random at 1600, slight dips to stbd at 1700, sudden roll and yaw, loss of directional control at 1800, cavitation span-wise/chordwise on #1.

R-103 1958 Trials Results Table 1-4 (cont'd)

Trial no.	Date	Number of Runs	Indicated rpm	Sea Conditions	Wind	Main Foil Load	Stern Foil Load	Comments
#58/12-2	16/7/58	five stern: -1.9° main: -2.4°	1200-1800	slight chop	SSW 10	12,459 lb	14,365 lb	constant port roll at 1200, slow roll at 1400; more rolling, difficulties with speed at 1600; barely foilborne, loss of directional control, engines overloaded, poor performance.
#58/13-2	17/7/58	six stern: -2° main: -2°	1200-1800	chop	W 15	12,546 lb	14,286 lb	Roll to port at 1200; more at 1400; rolling, poor control at 1600; porpoising, would not stay on foils, engines overloaded, poor speed control.
#58/14-2	22/7/58	two stern: not known bow: not known	1200-1400	calm	none	not given	not given	Constant heel to stbd; stbd foils fouled, deterioratior of marginal performance; discontinued; #58/15 repeat of trial after cleaning.
#58/15-2	23/7/58	five	1200-2000	chop	SW 10-15	not given	not given	slow roll at 1200; more violent at 1400; cork-screw at 1600; more steady at 1800; sharp yaw, pitch, roll, very little directional control at 2000.
#58/16-2	24/7/58	five	1200-2000	not given	N/A	same as #13-2	same as #13-2	slight roll at 1200; roll to beam tips at 1400; alternating steady, rolling, porpoising at 1600; increased violence of motion at 1800; stbd foil dip, diving to surface, yawing, directional control loss at 2000.
#58/17-2	25/7/58	five	1200-1800	6 inch, calm	S 6	same as #16-2	same as #16-2	Heavy roll to beam tips at 1200; heavier, shorter rolls at 1400; partly foilborne with occasional rolls, pitching at 1600; violent motions, complete loss of lift, uncontrollable yaw, dangerous at 1800.
#58/18-2	29/7/58	eight	1200-1800	12"-18"	SSE 20	same	same	small, shifting list at 1200; moderate roll at 1400; rolling and pitching at 1600; unsteady increased rolling/porpoising in following sea at 1800; attempted, but stopped by loss of directional control at 1800+.
#58/19-2	30/7/58	five	1200-2000	calm	S 5	same	same	gentle rolling at 1200; greater rolling at 1400; high on foils, mixed roll and porpoising at 1600; high and steady at 1800; violent loss of lift, port foil, diving at 2000.
#58/20-2	1/8/58	six	1200-1800	flat	SW 0-5	same	same	15-20 sec period roll at 1200; heavy roll at 1400; corkscrew, just foilborne at 1600; steady, level at 1700; port foil lift loss at 1800.

Trial no.	Date	Number of Runs	Indicated rpm	Sea Conditions	Wind	Main Foil Load	Stern Foil Load	Comments
#58/21-2	21/8/58	five	1200-1800	calm	not known	same	same	same as #20-2, however altered foil settings degraded performance in all but the 1800 range, which was as 1800 in #20-2.
#58/22/	11/9/58	seven	1200-1900	calm	not known	same	same	gentle roll at 1200; worse at 1400; foilborne, random roll/dive, landing each time at 1600; high, foilborne, random rolls at 1700; random loss of lift at 1800; violent porpoising and rolling at 1900. Steady, but falling off at 1750 in turns.
#58/23-2	21/10/58	not known	1200-1900	calm	not known	same	same	same settings and performance, other than there being no speed that the craft was stable! Photo session, plus Capt. Kinney, USN.
#58/24-2	30/10/58	ten	various	choppy	not known	same	same	Displacement comparison with YMT-1 by cine camera, take-off attempted through wave wake; craft rolled to beams ends, throttles chopped. Another resulted in foil lift loss, violent landing result in foil damage. (Portugese Cove area).
#58/25-2	21/11/58	three	various	slow swell	not known	same	same	Rough water, slow speed trials (repeat of #24-2) Compared with YMT-1 by direct observation, camera. 6-8 knot comparisons made. *R-103* adjudged better in sea response resistance.

Note: It should be noted that the angles of the foils as a unit were altered between each test, as well as weight shifts in the earlier tests.

These changes were tested in 1962 and resulted in the best performance possible without a major redesign. However, progressive research with *Rx* had left *R-103* technologically in the past. This $1,159,000.00 (1956) investment seemed doomed to be retired, until the investigation of high-speed towed bodies for the *Helen* hydrofoil V.D.S. was undertaken in 1962. This investigation is detailed later in this book, but the conversion of *R-103* in 1963 to a high-speed towing vehicle is chronicled here.

To bridge the gap between laboratory tests and expensive full-scale trials at sea, Defence Research Establishment, Atlantic (DREA), (the former N.R.E.) developed an up-to one-half-scale model test facility for high-speed towed bodies, based upon the 17.5 ton *Baddeck*. In 1962 DREA set out to redesign the foil system for stability in the 25-35 knot range and to install a towed body boom assembly.[28]

The shift aft of the centre of gravity, caused by the addition of the winch and handling equipment was counter-balanced by the increase in main foil weight. Additionally, by altering the vertical placement of the existing stern foil unit on the hull and adjusting the rake an adequate range of loads could be accommodated to cover both the movement of the centre of gravity and the estimated stern down-force due to towing. The modification of mounting positions were made, but the stern unit was not modified.[29]

Thus *Baddeck* then sported two straight dihedral ladder units forward and a steerable 'V'-foil ladder unit aft, with ship weight nearly evenly spread over the three foil units.

Particulars of *R-103 Bras d'Or*- All Configurations Table 1-5

Construction: Aluminium sheet riveted over extruded aluminium ribs and stringers.

Foil Systems: (1957) Conventional 3-point hydrofoil system of Bell-Baldwin ladder, with four 'V' foils per unit forward and three in the rudder set. These foils were of 6% Walchner 'C' section.

Angle of dihedral was 35° and angle of incidence was as follows:

Main-	Rear-
#1 -2°	#1 -3°
#2 -4°	#2 -5°
#3 -6°	#3 -6°
#4 -6°	

Blade thickness, all units; 2″ at $\frac{1}{4}$ chord

Distance between blades at strut; 1.387 feet for all blades 0/a draft of foils from centre of gravity to c/g of foil; 9 feet

(1961) Remedial fix made possible by tests conducted with *Rx* in 1959. This called for reshaping the foil section, plus increased setting angles.

Main-

#1 $6\frac{1}{3}$% modified Walchner 'C' section no setting change.

#2 $6\frac{1}{3}$% modified Walchner 'C' section -4.5 setting change

#3 NACA 16-509 section -5.5° setting

#4 NACA 16-509 section -10.33° setting

Rear-

#1 $6\frac{1}{3}$% modified Walchner 'C' section -3.33° setting

#2 $6\frac{1}{3}$% modified Walchner 'C' section -5.5° setting

#3 NACA 16-509 section -9° setting

(1963) Conversion to high-speed towed body tug saw simple dihedral Bell-Baldwin foils fitted within the original Monel struts. These provided a stable tow platform capable of 40 knots.

Main Chord:	Blade Width:
#1 $19\frac{7}{8}$ inches	$67\frac{1}{2}$ inches for all.
#2 $19\frac{7}{8}$ inches	
#3 $24\frac{7}{8}$ inches	
#4 $24\frac{1}{2}$ inches (adjustable angle of attack.)	

Spacings, main foil; (from bottom)

#1-2 14 inches

#2-3 15 inches

#3-4 $15\frac{1}{4}$ inches

Main foil width, 0/a, per unit; 41 inches

Main foil stance, centre/centre, sponsons; 17 feet 10 inches

Overall foil width; 28 feet 8 inches.

Depth of propulsion pod from hull to bottom; 8 feet $9\frac{7}{8}$ inches o/a.

For the towed body handling gear, the following specifications were suggested for four operational conditions;

Cruising; 8½ kt. recovery at 400 ft/min at 500 lb tension at 45°
Design; 28 kt./stream at 400 ft/min at 3000 lb tension at 30°
Overspeed; to 35 kt. hold 6000 lb tension at 20°
Trailing; 35 kt. hold 3000 lb tension at 5°

Both electric and hydraulic drives were examined, but the latter was chosen, driven by an auxiliary engine. The system promised good variable speed control in both recovery and pay-out, dynamic braking and full-torque from a stand-still. A Volkswagen industrial gasoline engine of 25 continuous h.p. at 3,000 rpm was sufficient and deck mounted, aft of the bridge to maximize air-cooling and minimize fire hazard.

The towing winch, further aft, 17 feet from the end of the towing boom would handle and store 0.375 inch diameter faired cable in lengths up to 300 feet. It was coupled to the hydraulic pump by stainless steel lines below decks, the controls (situated to starboard, beside the pump/engine), allowed variable speed control up to 400 feet per minute. 6000 lb tensions could be held and rapid slipping and abrupt stopping was possible to create step input for transient response studies. An automatic release allowed the cable to pay out freely, if tensions exceeded 9,000 lb.

After leaving the winch, the cable fed through a sheave mounted on a 10-foot stern boom, which could be fixed for steady state towing or oscillated vertically by means of a servo system driving a hydraulic cylinder. A signal generator, fed to the servo system, determined the waveform oscillation, with the tow point capable of 33″ peak-to-peak amplitudes, with periods down to 2 seconds. This oscillation permitted measurement of frequency response of towed systems and controlled simulation of rough water conditions.

During the six years *Baddeck* was in use, she accorded DREA a unique high-speed facility, capable of towing various-shaped towed bodies, not only in the Variable Depth Sonar research but in other related hydrodynamic testing. The use of faired cables aboard every destroyer and frigate of the Canadian Navy, plus numerous other worldwide applications, is a direct result of DREA's efforts and the tow facility. In this role she more than made up for her 1956 cost and provided a stable, high-speed test platform. Truly she earned a place in Naval Research history, after her ignoble beginnings, and in a role unforeseen at the time of her conception.[30]

Rx — During the construction of *Baddeck (R-103)* in Britain, N.R.E. was

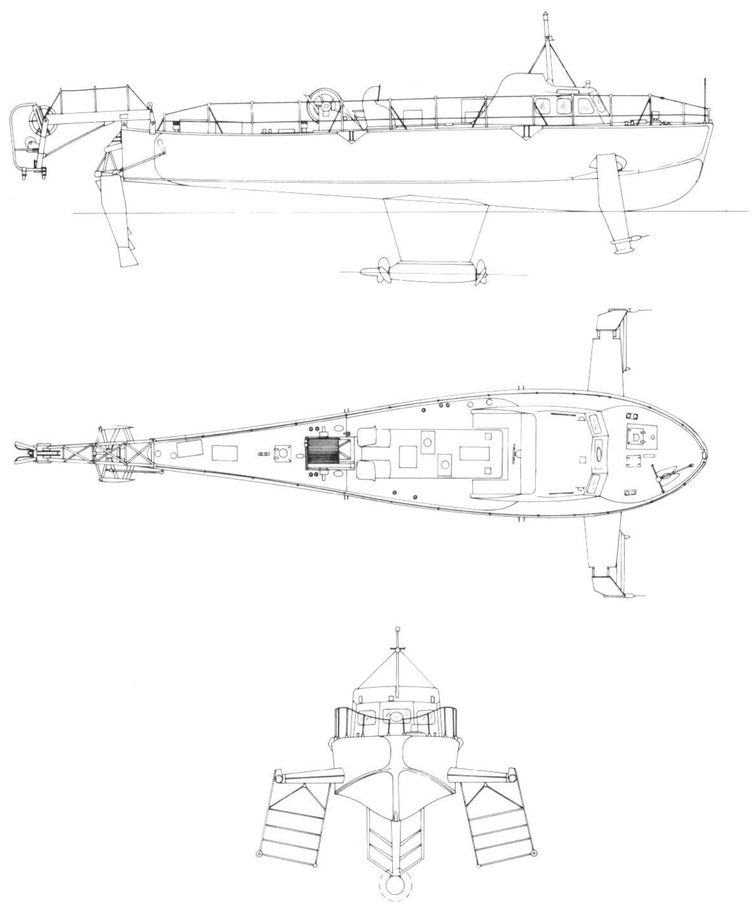

Baddeck foil configuration as high-speed tug

made painfully aware of their lack of a high-speed model-test facility in Canada. Therefore, in 1954 a purely research-oriented hydrofoil work craft was designed and built in 1955. She was built by the N.R.E. workshops in Dartmouth, N.S. Assuming only foil-borne performance tests, the hull was designed to be as simple as reasonable strength, seaworthiness and resistance considerations would allow. A 3-ton, scow-like plywood-hulled craft was the result. The exceptional strength was based on two main longitudinal members, spaced 21 inches apart, laminated from ¾ inch fir plywood to a thickness of 1½ inches, increased to 1⅞ inches midships where they acted as engine bearers. Frames were spaced on 18 inch centres and were 1 × 2 inch fir with ⅜ inch plywood knees and floors. All joints were glued and screwed and a hull 'skin' of ⅜ inch plywood treated similarly. In 1959-60 a thin layer of fibreglass mat was applied to reduce water absorption and maintenance time and costs.

For research purposes a propeller was used. The power-plant was a marinized water-cooled Chrysler Imperial type M45 V-8 gasoline engine, offering greater reliability over an automobile engine. Normally rated at a conservative 235 h.p., N.R.E. modified the engine through the use of a Latham supercharger, special carburetion, racing camshafts and strengthened connecting rods until 365 h.p. at 4500 rpm was realized. (See Engine Spec Appendix B)

The engine was located horizontally amidships and a 'V'-drive gearbox with a 2.05:1 reduction ratio brought the shaft out at an inclination of 20°. A single, cast-aluminium intake was fitted at the lower end to pick up cooling water for the engine. The 22 inch propeller normally used was a conventional subcavitating type, having a pitch of 21 inches. Fuel was carried in two 15-gallon tanks located in the engine bay, handy to the craft's centre of gravity. Two watertight bulkheads, the first ahead of the engine and the second behind the cockpit divided the hull. These spaces served as buoyancy tanks, and were sufficient to float the craft in case of flooding.

The hull gunwales were straight and parallel over the whole hull length and reinforced with aluminium rails on top. These rails simplified the mounting of cross-beam attachments which in turn supported the main foils, allowing the ready stationing of the beam at any point along the hull. The

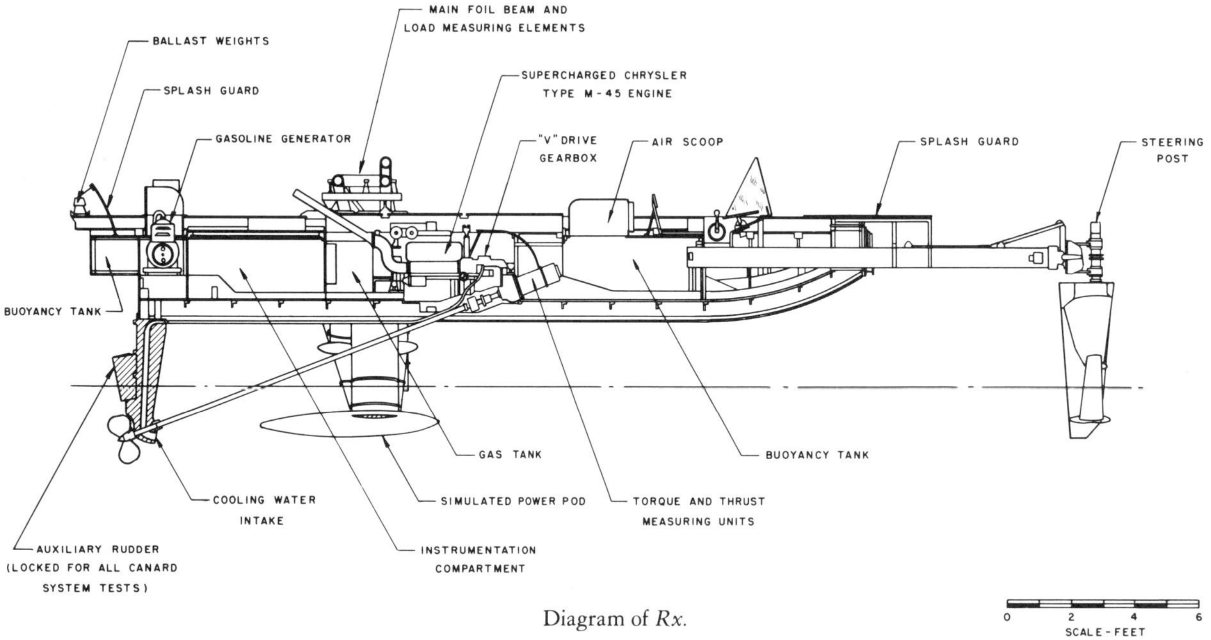

Diagram of *Rx*.

resultant craft was square-sided and looked remarkably like an oversized duck boat; in effect, she was a floating Meccano set.

For three-point configurations, great flexibility in foil base length and load distribution was provided by the use of a telescoping tube to carry the third hydrofoil unit. Stern mounting was first used, the bows streamlined by the use of a false bow. The craft dimensions were:

length; 25′ overall	beam; 6′
deadrise; 25°	hull depth; 3′

The 25-foot length gave exact ¼ to ½-scale modelling of the current hydrofoil craft configurations. A 'V' bottom, plus the 25° deadrise made for low hull pounding when foilborne in waves and the 6-foot width gave reasonable stability. The size, weight, (6640-7300 pounds) gave a craft large enough for full instrumentation, fast enough for scale testing, but small enough to facilitate handling by a small crew and reduced maintenance costs.

Rx with one quarter-scale canard hydrofoil configuration for *FHE-400*, 1963, Halifax harbour.
Credit: DREA, Dartmouth, N.S.

As completed in 1955, *Rx* modelled a 'V' ladder, stern-mounted steering foil unit on the transom-mounted tube, as configured on both *R-100* and the *R-101/R-103* construction taking shape in the U.K. She was used throughout 1958 to investigate the instability problems in *R-103*, it being easier to shift, alter and modify the foils of *Rx* over the larger, vastly more expensive ones of *R-103*.

However, at the same time, theoretical work was suggesting that a canard configuration would be far better in rough water. *R-103* was too advanced in construction and its tadpole shape precluded changing to a canard configuration for experiments. *Rx* was the ideal test bed.

During 1959 *Rx* was utilized to test supercavitating foil sections and to test 'fixes' proposed to cure *R-103*'s instability problems. In 1960, work was undertaken to develop the proper foil sections and configuration for the proposed *R-200* design.

During 1961 and 1962, the basic DREA design for the *R-200*, which was the origin of *FHE-400*, was developed through design studies by DeHavilland Aircraft of Canada. The role assigned to *Rx* in 1962 was to develop and confirm the design of *FHE-400* foil system. Essentially *Rx* provided a ¼-scale manned model (see Table 1-6).

The bow foil, although modified many times, reflected full-scale design work on *FHE-400*. However, structural and instrumentation requirements dictated main foil differences. The main foil struts sloped outward to clear the hull and thus allowed measurement of foil loads by dynamometers in the foil beam structure. Additionally, the main foil structure was complicated by the need for structural stays from the foil beam to the outer main foil intersections. The altered outline of *Rx*'s foils restricted hull clearance to 23″ to allow proper propeller immersion, 11 inches too low to model *FHE-400* clearance of 11 feet 6 inches at 60 knots correctly, adversely affecting *Rx*'s lower foilborne speeds in any seaway. In the final *FHE-400* design the main anhedral extensions were canted down and made incidence-controlled, but these remained fixed extensions on *Rx*. Additionally, the chord/thickness ratios differed greatly between the two craft.

Rx's foils were machined from solid hard-anodized 75ST aluminium, except the upper main anhedral panels which were fabricated from aluminium sheet. Foils and struts were pin-jointed to all intersections. The bow superventilating foils had to be insensitive to angle of attack, but responsive to changes in immersion. The bow foil spoilers that finally solved the problem of foil flow re-attachment and oscillating lift were pioneered on the *Rx* scale unit. The bow foil, in this configuration, acted as a 'feeler', setting the ship in trim required and allowing the stern foil (bearing 90% of A.U.W.) to anticipate the on-coming wave. It was inherently inefficient and could be kept small, with only 10% of A.U.W. or less being carried.

Obversely, the after foil required a high lift-curve slope, but only needed to respond to immersion changes at its ends for lateral stability. It was efficient and its behaviour enhanced by a large span.

The original bow foil designed by DeHavilland was fitted with conventional delayed-cavitation sections, immediately presented ventilation problems. Anti-ventilation fences were fitted, working quite well until the submerged fence broke the surface, allowing ventilation to flow down the foil until encountering the next fence. At high speeds this accounted for significant lift loss and pitch stability was affected. At 23 knots, almost complete immersion of the bow foil unit, with very slow recovery was the result.

Anticipating the superiority of supercavitating sections and superventilation operation for this design, DeHavilland had provided alternative lower dihedral foils. Supercavitating sections are essentially sharp-nosed, well cambered and set at high angles of incidence. Lift is largely generated by the lower surface, with the only restriction on the upper surface being that it must be thin enough in section to lie completely within the ventilating cavity that is generated by the leading edge. The particular section used for *Rx* had a Tulin-Burkart two-term lower surface and was set at 7° incidence.

Continuous ventilation proved difficult to achieve, especially during transition from wetted to ventilated flow and to maintain in rough water. Low speeds, with full flow attachment, the high incidence and camber developed very high lift and caused trim to increase rapidly with speed to a value of 4° at 8 knots. This remained a characteristic of the system throughout development of the *FHE-400* foil system and was one of the astonishing features of both *Rx* and *Bras d'Or* when becoming foilborne. The original foils ventilated at about 14 knots and the sudden decrease in lift allowed the bow foil to plunge deeply into the water, where flow promptly re-attached, high lift resulted, causing a severe cyclic pitching motion. Bow foil rake was increased from 0° to +3°, thus setting the incidence of the foils to a nominal +10° in order to achieve stable running over a limited speed range.

Leading-edge spoilers were then fitted to the upper surfaces of the foils which allowed stable running at 0° rake. Speeds of 20-25 knots over two to two and a half-foot tug wakes proved encouraging. However, leading-edge spoilers created further drag and spray. The next step was to remove the spoiler, plane the first third of its chord to make it finer and placing the section within the envelope generated by the leading edge. Stable ventilation occurred, but cyclic pitching persisted between 12½ to 16 knots, plus severe pitching in waves, which showed that angle of attack had improved, but the foil section remained too prone to flow re-attachment to be useful in a seaway.

DeHavilland again modified the section, this time adding a spoiler at the 60% chord point which, when tested, prohibited large lift increases by preventing flow re-attachment over the heavily-cambered after section. Since the spoiler remained well within the ventilation envelope at high speeds, it contributed little drag or spray. Testing at speeds of 25 knots in waves 5-6 feet produced its liveliest motions in head or bow seas, where the bow foil frequently left the water, although there wasn't a noticeable re-entry shock. Under the same conditions, the main foil, on occasion, left the water too, followed by a noticeable squatting and deceleration, but without any hull-pounding.

The performance in severe following seas or quartering seas which had proven the downfall of most surface-piercing foil systems was tested under the same conditions. Accelerations seemed less to the crew than in head or bow seas, but in fact were as great, although frequencies were reduced. In two-mile test runs at 25 knots there was no sign of broaching or diving, but there was a greater tendency to roll and steering control was reduced.

Sea trials with the modified superventilating bow foil was good, but modification of the design was desirable to reduce drag and improve pitch response in a head sea. DeHavilland re-designed the unit completely, deleting the upper dihedral panels and developing the required lift from the single diamond configuration.[31]

Production of this unit marked the end of major bow foil development changes. *Rx* continued to perform well in both calm and rough water, but unfortunately, before tests could be completed, the new bow foil was torn off and lost in a collision with a semi-submerged timber derelict in the harbour, November 13, 1963.[32] Naval divers, searching in the harbour mud in eighty feet of cold water were unable to find it, thus a new unit was fabricated by DeHavilland, incorporating some minor refinements in planform and section. Rough water trials proved near-identical for both units.

Main foil development was not nearly as active as the bow foils, since the behaviour of sub-cavitating sections was more fully understood and more readily compatible with small-model testing. Most of the changes necessary were to improve roll stability. As speed increased from rest, the craft heeled until at 13 knots there was a 5° loll which switched unexpectedly from port to starboard. At 15 knots, this developed into cyclic rolling with amplitude of 8° and period of 5.5 seconds. Rolling ceased at 19 knots and the craft was very stable until 23 knots, when the short original anhedral tips left the water and the craft heeled sharply, sideslipping off the foils.

DeHavilland modified the main foil configuration by extending the anhedral tips to the 30-knot waterline, increasing the tip incidence angles from 1°40′ to 3°20′ and changing the section to 5% ERA No. 1. High speed stability was excellent with the new arrangement, but low speed heeling persisted.

No serious attempt was made to correct this problem until the redesigned bow foil unit was fitted in 1962, when the chord and camber of the anhedral main foil panels was increased substantially at the inboard end, giving a tapered planform. This modification succeeded in reducing the steady angle of roll for speeds up to about 11 knots, but cyclic rolling continued between 11-19 knots.

DeHavilland stability studies showed insufficient roll stability for the full-scale design at low foilborne speeds and it was decided to make full-scale extended anhedral tips incidence-controlled. This complicated and expensive modification was not incorporated in *Rx*, but the problem continued to be of interest because *Rx* roll stability was lower than predicted by DeHavilland's model tests and analogue computer studies.

Fairings to the inefficient outboard intersections brought little improvement and the trouble was eventually found to be closely associated with the cyclic pitching instability of the bow hydrofoil unit. Trim changes due to cyclic pitching caused heaving at the main foil surfaces and this, aggravated by ventilation of the main anhedrals, produced strong cyclic rolling. There was very strong mutual roll-pitch coupling and cyclic pitching occurred consistently at twice the frequency of cyclic rolling. This behaviour presented an interesting example of the value of *Rx* tests in demonstrating system characteristics unlikely to have been revealed by theoretical studies. Elimination of cyclic pitching had now led to the virtual disappearance of cyclic rolling.

Although originally designed to investigate a wide variety of hydrofoil systems, *Rx*'s greatest use was in proving the particular system developed for *FHE-400*, particularly in the development of the superventilating bow foil unit. The farsightedness in her design allowed ready adaptability as a ¼-scale version of *FHE-400* and practical testing of capabilities of the system in rough water. She not only verified important design techniques and data, but pointed out unexpected deficiencies and assisted greatly in

Table 1-6 Rx Experimental Hydrofoil

Foil Element	*Incidence*	*Chord*	*Foil Section*
Bow anhedrals	1°40′	16″	7½% NACA 16-40 section
Upper bow dihedrals	1°40′	12″	7½% NACA 16-40 section
Lower bow dihedrals	1°24′	8″ to 16″	7% Walchner 'C' section
Main anhedrals	1°40′	30″	7½% Walchner 'C' section
Main dihedrals	1°24′ to 3°54′	18″ to 30″	7% Walchner 'C' section
Main horizontal dihedrals	1°24′	18″	7% Walchner 'C' section
Main anhedral tip extension	1°40′	30″ to 15″	7½% NACA 16-40 section
Retrofit replacements	Bow foil-		
Lower bow dihedral	7°	—	Tulin-Burkart two-term lower surface, super-ventilating
Deleted upper dihedrals	—	—	1963
	Main foil-		
Changed main anhedral tips by lengthening	3°20′	—	from 7½% NACA 16-40; to 5% ERA no. 1.

Proteus research craft suspended from a launching crane. Note the simplified main foil. The short anhedral foil could be replaced by others of various lengths, thereby increasing or decreasing the width of the foils. The stack of ST6 can be seen right aft. *Credits: DREA*

their correction. She emphasized the value of a large-scale, manned model in open-water trials, considered essential and an integral part of the design process.

Proteus — The very successful utilization of *Rx* in the development of the *FHE-400* hydrofoil system and conversion of *R-103* to a high-speed towed body tug during the 1960s encouraged DREA to make a design study for a replacement of both craft, but with greatly increased experimental testing facilities and abilities. DREA had at this time entered the field of hydrodynamics in a far broader scope, actively engaging in research and development in the field of fluid dynamics. By 1966 this establishment had a set of design parameters leading to the completion of full working drawings by spring of 1969.

First, tests of a 3/8 scale model were undertaken at the National Research Council's towing tank in 1967, both with, and without, scale foils. Tests of this model continued through 1969, simulating loads of up to 10,000 GVW. The craft exhibited a tendency to porpoise when propelled only by simulated marine propeller thrust, but this was traced to an incorrectly modelled vertical centre of gravity. Testing of the foils in all attitudes proved the model craft exceptionally stable and the foils to be a superior descendant of the work undertaken for the DeHavilland *FHE-400* project. However, it must be kept in mind that DREA was no longer actively involved in a hydrofoil research programme and the design criteria for the *Proteus* system was vastly different.[33]

The resultant design, named *Proteus* (derived from her design objectives of *P*ropulsion *R*esearch and *O*cean-water *T*esting of *E*xperimental *U*nderwater *S*ystems) was submitted to the Department of Supply and Services, Shipbuilding and Heavy Equipment Branch, Ship Procurement Division that spring who then sent out a letter of inquiry to sixteen firms in Canada, a cross-section of the shipbuilding, aerospace and specialized machine tool industries.[34] Seven confirmed interest in tendering and were invited to tender in June 1969.[35] Four did so and after examination, DSS awarded the contract for the hull to Canadian Aircraft Products Ltd., Richmond, B.C. that Oct. 17 with a contract bid of $175,000 (see Table 1-7).

The hull was loaded aboard a railway flatcar and delivered to DREA, Dartmouth, N.S., in August, 1970. Fitting out was begun over the winter of

1970-71. The 'Z'-drive, supplied by Hydro Drive of Seattle, Washington State to DREA specifications, was delivered in late 1970 and tested on a mock-up of *Proteus*'s stern to test the match-up of components. The lightweight bow foil was delivered at the end of 1970, but the main foil unit was not delivered until early 1973. After fitting out the propulsion system, the deckhouse and instrumentation package, *Proteus* was first run as a planing craft on July 29, 1971 to test the entire system and calibrate the instruments. Several trips were made that summer, but serious full-scale testing did not commence until the main foil was delivered by DeHavilland. The first foilborne test was conducted on May 9, 1973.

An extensive series of investigations into hydrofoil performance, dovetailing with previous research done by N.R.E. and investigations into propulsion and cavitation problems with sub-cavitating propellers was undertaken that same year. However, by 1974, the hydrofoil research had dried up with Canada's lack of interest in naval hydrofoil craft and propulsion/cavitation problems became the overriding research work. This continued throughout 1976, when research was narrowed still further into the realms of propulsion. Investigation centred on the audible noise problems of sub-cavitating propellers at 25-27 knots, searching for a compromise configuration that would work well at this speed without the attendant noise of cavitation.

By 1979, troublesome electrical problems were being found in the ship's wiring, rendering instrumentation unreliable. Additionally, micro-circuitry was making great strides and it would be necessary to completely re-wire and re-instrumentate the ship, which would require about 80% of DREA's meagre budget for this project. It was decided to wind down the last test programmes and retire the ship into long-term storage.

The last trip was made on September 24, 1980. The next day, the preparations for storage were started, with the ST6 turbines being packed away in environment-sealed containers and the entire craft being prepared and sealed. She was shipped across the harbour and into storage in Jetty Nine shed.

As completed, *Proteus* had a broad-beamed, planing hull and canard, surface-piercing foil system. The hull had fine lines forward to reduce wave impact loads, bow wavemaking and wetness. It had a low, full beam and constant 15° bottom deadrise aft for good planing performance and stability. It was sub-divided by four watertight bulkheads into five compartments which comprised (from bow to stern) a small buoyancy chamber, wheelhouse, research instrumentation compartment, forward engine compartment housing the fuel tanks and systems and the aft engine compartment, housing the Pratt and Whitney ST6A-64 turbine for the submerged drive. The airscrew propulsion and second ST6 on pylon originally planned never came about. Construction was of a light $\frac{3}{32}$ inch aluminium shell over transverse frames of 18-inch spacing and longitudinal stringers of 6-inch spacing. The shell was flush-riveted to this frame. The side panel thickness above the chine and deck panels was $\frac{1}{16}$ inch thick. A cutout in the stern was made for the steerable outdrive propulsion and strengthened transom members were fabricated to allow installation of transom flaps.

The bows tapered to two long bowsprits, connected by a cross-beam. These bowsprits were of heavy aluminium members to carry the bow foil unit.

Table 1-7 Specifications, *Proteus* Experimental Hydrofoil Craft

Overall length:	33 feet
Max. hull beam:	9 feet
Max. foil span:	24 feet 4 inches (main)
	7 feet (bow)
Draft of hull: (fl)	1 foot 3 inches
main foil:	5 feet 10 inches
bow foil:	5 feet 3 inches
Keel to marine propeller:	4 feet 6 inches
foil base length: min.	20 feet
max.	24 feet 9 inches
Weight: hull (less foils)	7,100 lb
complete	10,000 lb

Propulsion: 1 United Aircraft of Canada ST6A-64 gas turbine (see engine specifications)
Ratings: Maximum- 550 HP at 2200 RPM
Intermittant: 445 HP at 2100 RPM
Continuous: 300 HP at 2100 RPM
Fuel: JP-5 660 pound overload; 400 pounds normal load.
Endurance: 1.5 hours at 35 knots, 3 hours at 20 knots
Propeller: Newton-Rader, 3-blade, variable-pitch, 17-4 PH steel

Performance: Hullborne, w/o foils-	28 knots
foilborne;	35 knots
Weights: Hull- 2900 lb	
Mechanics & electrics-	900 lb
Propulsion:-	1,500 lb
Foils-bow: 400 lb main:	1,600 lb = 2,000 lb
Instrumentation;	900 lb
Crew (3)-	500 lb
Normal fuel:	400 lb
A, U, W. foilborne-	9,100 lb
A.U.W., planing-	7,100 lb (less foils)

The hull was designed to withstand hullborne slamming and sudden loss of bow foil lift when foilborne. Peak pressures of 30 psi at 35 knots for slamming and 48 psi at 40 knots for foilborne 'crashes' were estimated and designed into the hull.

The non-retractable, surface-piercing canard configuration of the foils is shown in accompanying photos. It was designed to provide a smooth, stable ride, ideal as a high-speed test platform and incorporated variable-geometry to permit research on surface-piercing hydrofoil hydrodynamics and sea-keeping, although this formed only a miniscule portion of her duties, especially in later years. Satisfactory steady running conditions could not easily be achieved at speeds greater than 20 knots without using hydrofoils and higher speeds were needed in most of the scale work envisioned for the craft.

The bow foil consisted of a double 'V' ladder arrangement with a central strut and anhedral upper foil sections. Pin-jointing of connections permitted ready replacement of foil units with others of different geometry and section, although this was not done as DREA divorced itself from hydrofoil investigation after 1971. Alternative locations of the anhedral apex permitted the lower foil dihedral to be varied from 25° to 45°. The bow foil unit was attached to the hull through a dynamometer assembly capable of measuring lift, drag and sideforce. The entire foil assembly could be raked forward and aft by an electric actuator and hydraulic power steering was incorporated.

The main foil was split with the single dihedral and anhedral foils on each side supported on a single strut which was, in turn, attached at its upper end to an athwartship beam. This beam was connected to the hull through a three-axis dynamometer and the main foil assembly could be moved forward and aft on deck rails. This motion permitted bow foil loadings of up to 20% of all-up weight. The entire main foil assembly could be manually adjusted through a vertical distance of 6 inches and raked fore and aft. The main dihedral foil could be easily changed and its angle varied from 10° to 27°. The main anhedral foil structure incorporated provision for ailerons or flaps. Both main and bow foil strut trailing edges were removable to permit their use as base-ventilated sections.

The bow and main dihedral foils were swept, constant-chord planform with 7.5% thickness-chord ratio, flat-faced, ogival (plano-convex) sections. Anhedral foils were symmetrically tapered and employed 10% thick, flat-faced ogival sections. Struts were tapered and had 10% thick biogival sections. These section shapes were chosen for their ease of manufacture and high cavitation inception speed.

Originally it was planned to have two ST6 turbines aboard the *Proteus*. One was to drive a marine screw through a 'Z' drive Hydro-Drive Corporation unit. This unit weighed 960 pounds and allowed for engine growth to 650 h.p. at 2200 rpm. It was attached to the transom in the stern well and was steered by a hydraulic actuator through an angle of ±20°. A shaft brake prevented turbine 'motoring' and interchangeable upper gear sets for ratios of 1:1, 1.46:1 reduction or 1.48:1 step-up gearing.

The second ST6 was to power a Hamilton Standard aluminium pusher propeller, the engine being mounted above the transom in a pod, supported by struts. This would have allowed propulsion of the craft in experiments where the suppression of ship-induced underwater noise was of prime importance, such as sonar research. Maximum speed of the craft was 36 knots with the marine screw.

It should be noted that the bow foil could be dismounted, as well as the main foil assembly. The bow foil could then be replaced by a dynamometer system and strut, allowing testing of models of sonar bodies in the undisturbed water ahead of *Proteus*.[37]

Progressive tests were undertaken into studying the cavitation-induced noise factors of subcavitating and supercavitating propellers in the speed range of 25-30 knots, where noise from both is extreme and efficiency suffers. The intent of these experiments was to find a compromise propeller to reduce or eliminate this problem. As well, propulsion problems were investigated and gains made that will be seen in progressive new ships of the future. However, with the waning interest in the naval hydrofoil research, plus the stunted capabilities of *Proteus*, the craft was retired in 1980, only eight years after she was built.

Where Did They Go?

Massawippi was retired in 1959 and laid about in storage until she was presented to the Maritime Museum of the Atlantic, Halifax, N.S. in October, 1966. Since that date, she has languished in storage in a shed in Mt. Uniacke, N.S., where it is alleged she is too large to display within the new Museum Building. Damage was reported to her upper deck from dry rot in 1982. Efforts are being made to either have her displayed or transferred to the Bell Museum in Baddeck, Cape Breton, but with little success to date.

Baddeck; R-103 was retired in 1970 and has spent the intervening years sitting in her cradle near the Fleet Diving Unit, Atlantic, on the CFB Shearwater waterfront. Her fate remains uncertain, but efforts are currently underway to have her turned over to the Bell Museum as a natural descendant of the Bell-Baldwin genius of so long ago. However, if efforts are not pressed, she might see scrapping yet.

Plucky little *Rx*: the versatile little craft that proved out so many theories in hydrofoil design was declared surplus in the late 1960s and sold to a private individual, unknown. Intending to use the craft as a pleasure craft, *Rx* was placed in a shed for restoration where she burned to ashes one late winter day. Only photos remain . . . plus her sunken bow foil section in the cold mud of Halifax Harbour.

Proteus: born crippled, she was retired in 1980 and now sits in long-term storage, collecting dust and grime in the crumbling, mouldering Jetty Nine Shed. She awaits a NATO partner who might need a hydrofoil research craft . . . or ultimately, the wrecker's hammer.

DREA — Defence Research Establishment, Atlantic is not the bustling building it was during the hydrofoil adventure days. Research efforts have extended into specialized hydro-dynamic fields which are just as important, but far less glamourous to the public. A few research grants to various universities are all that remain of the research efforts of old. The men who helped make the hydrofoil craft happen are older, wiser, more cautious and involved in other fields, looking back at the hydrofoil research period as past history; their youthful history. Only a few of these pioneers are still with DREA anymore; the years and attrition have taken their toll.

Chapter Two
A Possible Solution for ASW

By late 1959, Naval Research Establishment in Dartmouth, N.S., faced a serious dilemma. They had a partially successful 17-ton model (*Baddeck*) of a 50-ton fast patrol boat that with the demise of Coastal Forces in Britain in 1957 no one had a real interest in any more, and a successful research hydrofoil, *Massawippi*. N.R.E. were sure they could redesign the foils for the former to make it satisfactory for rough water operation, but on-going research was proving more and more conclusively that a 'tail-first', or canard configuration, would be necessary to fulfill the potential of the surface-piercing foil system. This would be totally imcompatible with the *R-103* design concept. It was time to assess the lessons learned over the past ten years and propose the route that further research should follow, returning to the original Canadian requirements for anti-submarine warfare vessels.

ASW has become more and more complex since World War Two, with high speed, deep-diving conventional submarines based on captured German knowledge appearing in the Soviet Navy. When *Nautilus*, the USN's first nuclear submarine traversed the North Pole under the ice in August, 1958, it was clear that submarines were now capable of independant unlimited travel under the surface.[1] By extension, it was realized that it would not be too much longer before Soviet technology produced a nuclear-propelled submarine as in fact occurred in late 1959 with the first *November* class SSN.[2]

The major problem in anti-submarine warfare, as far as surface units were concerned, was initial detection. Reliable sonar detection ranges were still very small when compared with the vast area of ocean to be covered. A promising alternative to the direct approach of improving sonar performance was to devise a means of providing significantly larger numbers of sonar platforms economically: the so-called 'small and many' concept.

The basic requirements of ASW demand an extremely versatile vehicle. Initial detection calls for long endurance at slow search speeds. This allows the search or passive sonar to be utilized to its greatest advantage with minimal ship-generated noise to interfere with performance. Once detected, interception and attack require short bursts of speed exceeding possible conventional ship limits. These two opposed requirements had been compromised in all craft up until this time. In the 'small and many' concept hydrofoil warship, this compromise was nearly optimized, with unique top speed, a greater degree of stabilization in the hullborne mode of operation as well as being the smallest, most cost-effective ship capable of operating in the open ocean.[3]

During 1959 at N.R.E., the information gained by the earlier hydrofoil experiments was being married with foreseen and theoretical requirements. The feasibility study undertaken was designated "R-200" and by November, 1959, the study was rapidly reaching completion. The emerging concept was quite radical over past design efforts![4]

Quite apart from the foilborne advantages of the 'tail-first' or canard arrangement, the need for a hull shape optimizing hullborne endurance and seakeeping, and the requirements imposed by sonar towing, clearly dictated other advantages. The fine lines of the bows would enable wave crests to be cut at high speeds without pounding. Heavy components such as the propulsion machinery could be mounted close to the main point of support, where the least range of accelerations would be experienced. This led to a more efficient structural design and more generally the internal layout of the hull could be more satisfactorily arranged. With the advancement of the marinized gas turbine, a craft of greater than fifty tons was feasible, although just how large could only be estimated.

Another important design consideration that was paramount with the N.R.E. study was the avoidance of having the bow overhanging the forward foil unit significantly. This was to prevent the bows dipping deeply or burying into the face of an oncoming wave. More dangerous than the impact would be the abrupt forward shift of the centre of lateral area, which could have led to directional instability, the craft tipping sideways off its foils.

The principal characteristics of the N.R.E.-proposed design were:

Length overall	130 feet (39.6 metres)
Beam of hull	28 feet (8.5 metres)
Depth of hull	14 feet (4.3 metres)
Span main foils	64 feet (19.5 metres)
Foil base length	81 feet (24.7 metres)
Draft displacement	23 feet (7.0 metres)
Draft foilborne	6 feet (1.8 metres)
Foilborne power	16,000 h.p.
Displacement power	3,000 h.p.
Max. foilborne speed	60 knots in calm water
Max. foilborne speed	50 knots in Sea State Five
Normal cruise speed	12 knots (hullborne)
Max. cruise speed	18 knots (hullborne)

In January, 1960 a select group of American, British and Canadian naval experts arrived in Halifax for a tri-partite assessment of hydrofoil research endeavours within NATO. The N.R.E. report was presented at this meeting and N.R.E. was encouraged to continue with the preliminary study. The US were extensively involved with developing the fully-submerged foil system and the British were partial observers; both parties thought the Canadian experimentation with, and development of, the surface-piercing foil system, would fully complement their own studies. Indeed, Canada with a 200-ton craft design would fill the gap within the range of 110-320 tons displacement that neither country was exploring.[5]

The fully-developed report was finally submitted to DRB on January 9, 1960. After study and appraisement in January, DRB began to assess who to approach to undertake a specialized feasibility study to see if such a craft could be built. The requirements of the design study made clear that if it was to be undertaken by a Canadian company, then only the aerospace industry was capable of doing it![6]

The reasons behind this assumption were complex. The necessary craft would have to utilize lightweight metals, systems and engines with the

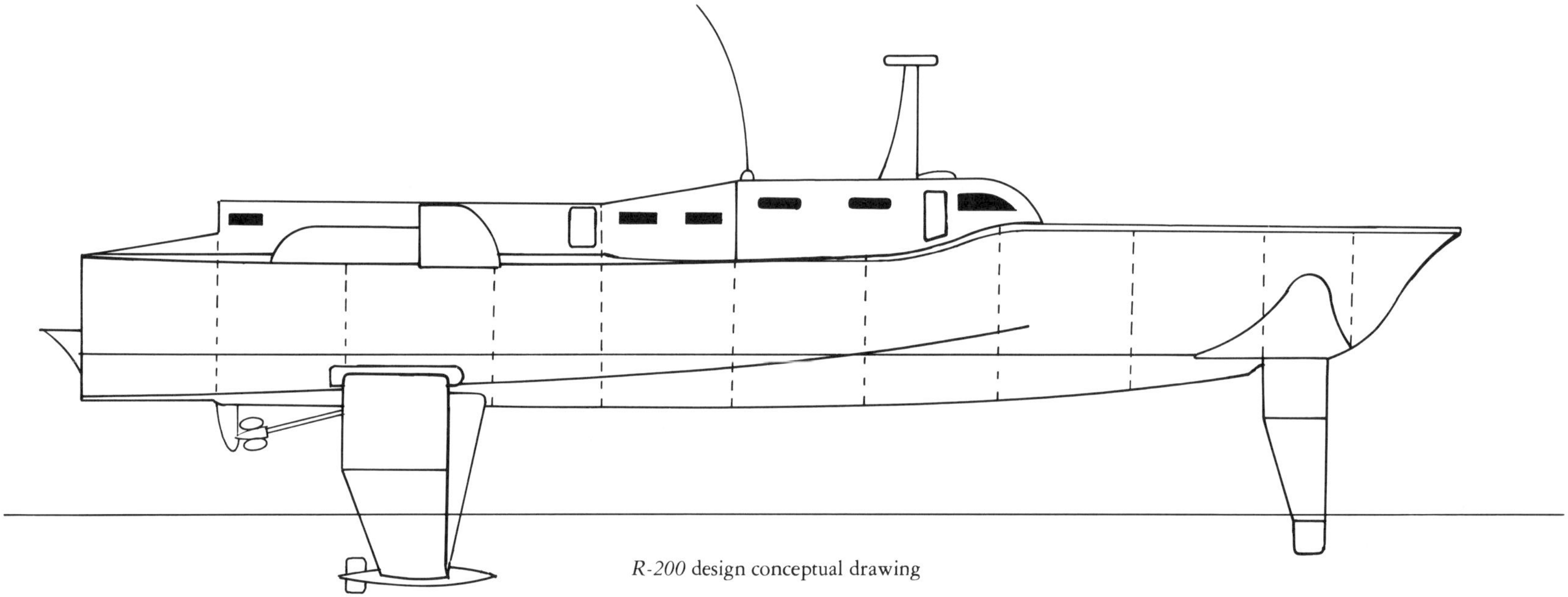

R-200 design conceptual drawing

highest power/weight ratios possible. The necessary design studies were far outside the experience of Canadian shipbuilders, requiring both analogue and digital computers to perform simulated trials to obtain these results before the first piece of aluminium was fabricated or the design finalized. Few, if any, shipyards in the world at that time had an analogue computer. There would not be any Lloyd's Specifications to consult in choosing metal thicknesses and shapes; everything would have to be from calculation.

The aerospace industry therefore was a necessity to meet the high standards and demands of this hydrofoil craft. Further, their experience with lightweight metal construction and fabrication techniques made them the only logical choice. With their computers, a proposed design could be subjected to a major computer study, utilizing criteria gathered by N.R.E. sources as to sea states, wind factors, stress loads, wave impact loads, etc. After several design evaluations this would allow a specific design proposal to be selected for further computer detail study and actual model testing. For 1960 this was a revolutionary procedure in ship design!

In the spring of 1960, a tender was placed for a feasibility study of the N.R.E. proposal. Only one company responded and on August 7, 1960, the Department of Defence Production (DDP), through Treasury Board, awarded a contract to DeHavilland Aircraft of Canada, the sole competitor. The contract, termed Phase I #2BX20-79 had its objectives to examine the N.R.E. concept in depth, pursue parametric studies and to ascertain the engineering feasibility of the proposed design.

The study team was headed up by Mr. R. W. Becker, who eventually became Assistant Chief Designer in the last few years of the *FHE-400* project. The basic equations of motion were written up by N.R.E./RCN personnel and DeHavilland engineers then fed these into the analogue computer, where simulation of the craft in representative seas were conducted, while suitable methods of representing random seas were developed. A separate, but integral study of foil material requirements was initiated and proposed model test series were formulated for the anticipated Phase II contract. DeHavilland was reluctant to undertake the foil material research, which was eventually sub-contracted out to a government agency in Phase II.

During the actual Phase I study, various investigations were undertaken to determine such things as suitable powerplants, weapons suites, sensor requirements, etc. One of the more interesting came about through the complicated foilborne horsepower requirements of the N.R.E. report.

In a report dated October 21, 1960, Captain F. Harley stated that Bristol Aero-Industries thought the required 16,000 h.p. could be met through the use of two Proteus gas turbines and reasonable-diameter air-screw propellers. At a meeting in August 1960, it became apparent that Bristol Aero-Industries had misinterpreted the values shown in the power requirement statement. Using gas turbines with airscrews, it would be necessary to generate 45,000 pounds of thrust, but that could only be done with *four* Proteus gas turbines and 75% efficient propellers. It was countered that the saving in weight, some 30,000 lb. would lower the thrust requirements, but after calculations, it was found that the BAI proposal was still 5,500 lb. short of thrust. Further checking found that the 16,000 h.p. figure was too low as well . . . Good Practice Graphs showed this figure should be 20,000 h.p. Needless to say, it was back to the drawing board for all parties![7]

Meanwhile the suggestion that a hydrofoil craft project review group be set up had come from Mr. G. S. Field, Chief Scientist for the Chairman, DRB, directed to the RCN.[8] This was followed up and liaison officers were exchanged between Canada and the US to co-ordinate information on progress in hydrofoil research in both countries. The first two officers were Captain Fisher, USN and Mr. C. B. Lewis, DRB.

The completed Phase I study report was presented to DDP and N.R.E. in June 1961.

The report tendered concluded that the hydrofoil design conceived by N.R.E. and developed by DeHavilland was technically feasible. In particular, the study confirmed that a canard configuration and a 150-200 ton design weight were optimum to fully exploit the concept. The one grave note was that the calculated stresses could reach 100,000 psi in the foil system, meaning that something special in the line of a high-tensile strength steel would be necessary. At the time, maraging nickel-cobalt-molybdenum steels were just beginning to become available, with calculated yielding strengths of 250,000 psi and further exploration into utilizing this material in a salt water environment would have to be carried out.

The Phase I study clearly showed potential and Treasury Board was approached for further funding. This was forthcoming in Treasury Board Minute No. 57004 on January 26, 1961. The actual contract was awarded on April 14, 1961 under contract #9BXO-72. Funding ceiling was set at $300,000.

This Phase II was concerned with developing a preliminary design for a 200-ton ship for employment primarily in open-ocean ASW roles. An objective was to develop the engineering basis to establish feasibility in detail and produce cost estimates together with proposals for a full-scale prototype ship construction programme. The extensive theoretical and model test programme was to be initiated and consisted of;

1. Resistance measurements on $\frac{1}{25}$ and $\frac{1}{8}$ scale models of the ship at hullborne and foilborne speeds and a qualitative assessment of hullborne seakeeping. These were eventually conducted at the Stevens Institute of Technology, New Jersey, for $33,500.[9]
2. Tests on $\frac{1}{8}$ scale models of the main and bow foils at the National Physical Laboratory, London, England, to establish the basic stability derivatives of the units and pressure distributions over critical regions of the main foil.
3. Tests on representative $\frac{1}{4}$ scale models of the foil system on the *Rx* research vehicle at N.R.E., Dartmouth. These were primarily intended to check the validity of the analogue computer simulation of the full-scale craft at DeHavilland. This involved some $36,949.50 for the design and construction of the initial foil system for *Rx*.
4. A random seaway analogue computer simulation of the full-scale and the $\frac{1}{4}$ scale *Rx* vehicle in foilborne operation. The hull form and its hydrodynamic effects in takeoff and landing were not simulated. The DeHavilland Pegasus computer was used to simulate the non-linear equations of motion of this foil system in six degrees of freedom in random seaways of sea state five conditions. It also accounted for orbital velocities in head, beam and following seas, unsteady flow hydrodynamics, partial ventilation of the foil and strut elements, virtual inertia effects in waves and the onset of local cavitation. A wave pole was developed by N.R.E. to measure wave height and frequency during *Rx* tests in Halifax Harbour. This enabled comparisons between the *Rx* craft analogue simulation and its actual behaviour by means of taped records, later reduced by the National Research Council's Spectral Analysis Centre in Ottawa to suitable data for DHC's computer. These simulations and actual $\frac{1}{4}$-scale tests closely matched throughout the programme, providing proof of the viability of the analogue computer in predicting these motions and performance.

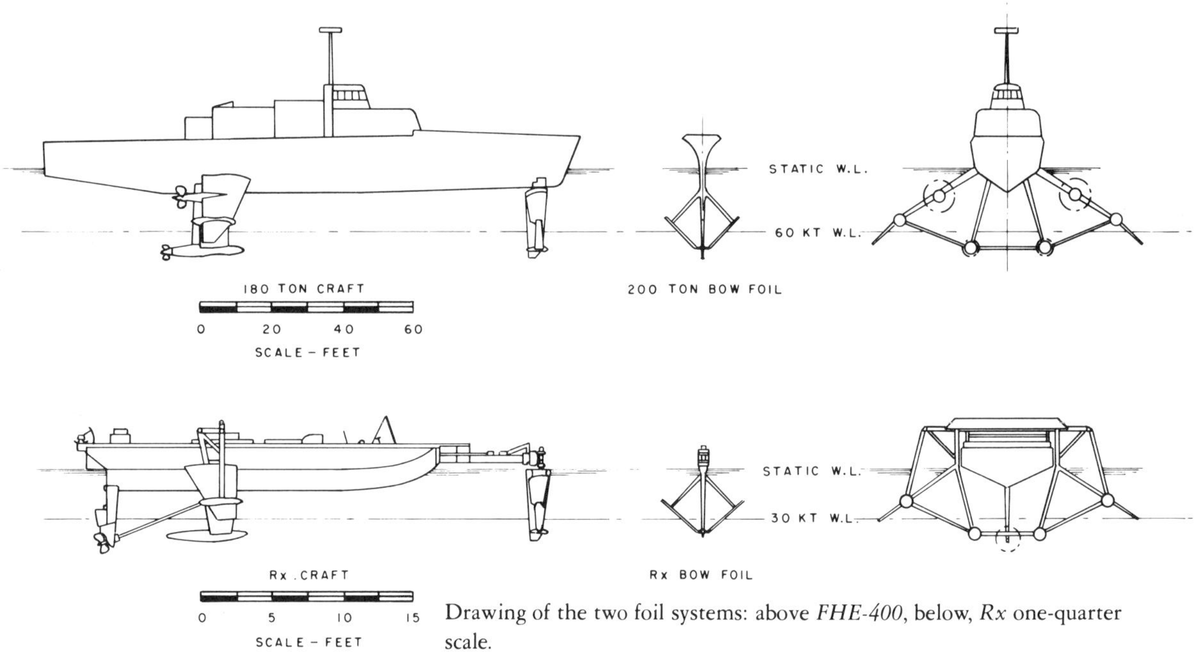

Drawing of the two foil systems: above *FHE-400*, below, *Rx* one-quarter scale.
Credit: N.R.E.

The suggestion of the setting up of a DDP Hydrofoil Project Review Group was acted upon and the first meeting took place on April 12-13, 1961. The terms of reference were summarized as follows;[10]

> "To review development progress with particular reference to the technical aspects and recommend changes as required to ensure that the design meets the existing requirements."

The most outstanding consideration of that first meeting was establishing future references for follow-up programme reports and the discussion of the EDO Corporation report on 'dipped' sonar for hydrofoil craft, released in September 1960. It was agreed that further investigation of this type of sonar should be undertaken by the RCN immediately.[11]

In line with the Phase I recommendation that newer, high-tensile strength materials be investigated for possible foil system manufacture, the RCN awarded a separate materials research contract with DeHavilland. DeHavilland in turn sub-contracted the materials investigation study as covered in Chapter Five.

A number of materials were investigated for various properties in tension, sheer, fatigue, impact yield strength, weldability and for resistance to cracking, warping and residual stress after manufacture. Testing in resistance to normal corrosion and stress corrosion was carried out, the latter showing that unless adequately protected in a marine environment, all considered metals would be highly sensitive to corrosion.[12]

A separate sub-contract study was made on May 9, 1961 to Engineering Research Associates of Toronto for theoretical studies of optimum delayed cavitation foil sections and techniques for computing these. Cost was $25,000, with initial application for the ¼-scale elements manufactured for testing on *Rx*.

The RCN's increasing interest was reflected in its financial arrangements that year. Future funding for hydrofoil research was covered in a memorandum dated July 7, 1961 in which it was proposed that the Hydrofoil Project 1962-63 Estimates be transferred from Priority 1C to Research and Development Estimates (Vote 717). This would be done to gain approval for funding 1962-63, which would not be possible if still in Priority 1C position in Naval Estimates submitted in the Treasury Board Supplement. In these estimates, the following points were made;

1 — An increase in 1962-63 in Research and Development cash expenditure authority of $100,000.

2 — An increase 1962-63 in commitment authority to $200,000.

3 — Analysis of Programme summated in total $8 million.

The *R-200* craft itself to be budgeted as follows:

1 — $200,000 in 1962-63 new programme commitment.

2 — $100,000 in 1962-63 new programme estimated expenditure.

3 — $7,900,000.00 for future expenditure if a decision was made to build a full-scale *R-200*.

Meanwhile, the first ¼-scale foil configuration for *Rx* was delivered in September, and fitted by October 15, 1961. She was pressed into service. This is covered under the *Rx* section in Chapter Two.

Meanwhile, deployment parameters for the ASW hydrofoil craft were now officially being formulated from existing information and current needs. The 'Drift, Search, Dash' régime was mentioned, where the hydrofoil would operate 90% of the time in hullborne mode, trailing her variable depth sonar array and upon acquiring a distant target, dash there foilborne, then attack in hullborne mode once more.

In a December 11, 1961 report authored by Commodore R. P. Welland, RCN, Acting Commanding Naval Officer, Ottawa for general staff circulation, entitled 'Operational Uses of Hydrofoil Craft,' the entire thrust of the hydrofoil programme was covered:

> ". . . would have enormous potential as an ASW craft with substantial savings, as compared with present equipments if in the program the viability of the hydrofoil as a basic vehicle, something that cannot be resolved until a full-scale prototype craft is built. If we proceed in building a craft at the cost of $8 million, and I am of the opinion that we should, the main questions to be answered are:
>
> 1. Will such a craft be able to survive in the North Atlantic in all weather conditions?
> 2. Will the craft be able to proceed at its design speed of 50-60 knots in seas of twelve feet or so?
>
> If these two questions can be resolved through the prototype, other related problems are most certainly within solution. (i.e. an operational design by 1966.)
>
> The submarine detection devices being planned for the hydrofoil are of three types. The main being VDS which is certainly within our capability and within the envisioned time scale, designed to be towed at speeds of up to fifteen knots.
>
> Passive listening equipment of the Jezebel type which will be operated directly from the ship or from Jezebel buoys dropped directly from the ship or aircraft into the sea. Experiments are on-going on the East Coast at this time.
>
> A development, utilizing the hydrofoil, of a very deep sonar system, with detection ranges of 25-30 miles is possible. The hydrofoil craft would not be

able to directly utilize the set itself, but would, with its superior speed and range, allow it to take advantage of these very long range sonar systems. Without hydrofoils, many of the advantages of the sonar system would be denied.

Weapons have been given considerable thought in both Canada and the US and the major weapon appears to be the homing torpedo. Studies have shown that such a high-speed craft would be able to launch a nuclear weapon, if a small ASROC system is employed. Needless to say, the weapon system is not considered a serious problem.

Given the hydrofoil craft proves a viable platform and the necessary sonar can be developed, the ASW hydrofoil should be capable of the following roles:

1. Escorting shipping with speeds up to 24 knots, 'grasshoppering' after fifteen knots.
2. In a variable role, where individual, dependable detection is of prime concern and a large concern is placing a large number of units in the field.
3. In large, close tactical situations where rapid updating of the situation is desirable. In this role the ASW hydrofoil may show a marked advantage over conventional vessels or aircraft.
4. The advantages of a relatively large detection capability and payload with such a small crew as twenty, offers such a pay-off that I feel we cannot ignore."[13]

. . . And this was the general feeling throughout the Planning Department Engineers who were watching the escalating costs of the first as-built helicopter destroyers, the *Annapolis* class.

Meanwhile, the first results were coming back from the model tests. The $\frac{1}{25}$-scale model results were tendered in Stevens Report Number LR-877 on November 28, 1961 and results compared with the computer predictions and *Rx* trials to date. These closely matched in critical areas, further strengthening DDP's faith in the system.

Tests were on-going throughout the winter and spring of 1961-62. These included the $\frac{1}{8}$ foil and model hull tests at the National Physical Laboratory in London. These were giving some vital input into the behaviour of the foil units, coupled with the *Rx* tests results.

The various information pathways were married at DeHavilland's Downsview plant and the design team were busy assembling the final design proposal details. Necessary modifications were made and the design refined again and again. The final report and recommendations were compiled in August 1962 and tabled in October.

This Phase II Report was placed under further study by the RCN on the part of DRB throughout the winter months and it was recommended that the final studies and actual design of a 180-200-ton ASW prototype hydrofoil be undertaken. However, with a change in government in the spring, the final contract signing was delayed until May 16, 1963. The contract, termed 2BX3-244, had a $10 million ceiling placed upon it and was the last hurdle overcome towards the building of the craft.

The following list is of the key members of the DeHavilland team involved in the hydrofoil programme at this time;

R. W. Becker	Project Engineer
B. V. Davis	Chief Hydrodynamicist
G. L. Oates	Simulations, Stability and Control
R. E. Case	Sea State Simulation
A. Stenning	Performance
S. Morita	Stress and Mechanical Design
M. J. Callow	Powerplant and Systems
T. E. Bennett	Foil Design
A. Stonell	Simulation
J. Stewart	Engineering Administrator

As the last bit of loose string in the hydrofoil project, the RCN formally assumed entire control of the programme, making this a purely military-oriented concern in March, 1963.

Chapter Three

Building 'Bras D'or'

The contract (2BX3-244) signed in May, 1963 consisted of three main phases:

Phase A called for design and preparation of contract plans and preliminary specifications for the ship. This design would be based upon volumes I and IV of the DeHavilland Phase II study #9BXO-72. This phase was to be completed by May 1, 1964 and culminated in a final layout and preliminary design conference in the summer of 1964. These results provided specific design drawings that could be issued to prospective sub-contractors. This resulted in a Statement of Requirements on August 25, 1964, which was issued to contractors prepared to tender for *FHE-400* sub-contracts.

Phase B necessarily overlapped Phase A and was essentially a detailed design phase leading to construction, final specification and shore testing. This was to be completed by April 30, 1966 and would then lead to a delivery conference prior to pre-acceptance trials by the manufacturer. It was planned that a final design approval conference be held in December, 1965, when the final design requirements would be 'frozen' and only open to change through subsequent renegotiation.

Phase C consisted of the contractor's sea trials under the responsibility of DeHavilland, acceptance by the RCN, final evaluation and the writing of final reports toward formulating the specifications of a possible, truly operational ASW hydrofoil warship. This would have to be accomplished before 1969, when it was felt that proposed types and designs of warships would have to be made for replacement of the oldest steam frigates.

As will be seen in the rest of this chapter, 'slippage' in delivery times throughout 1964, 1965 and 1966 would see the completion delayed from April 30, 1966 into November . . . with a terrible disaster nearly finishing the project before it saw water.

As an interesting feature of this contract, inclusion of a system of performance incentive points (PERTS) were set up on twenty-one performance items. This offered a sliding scale of points towards additional monetary bonuses if performance of particular elements of the *FHE-400* building programme performed reliably above minimum figures stipulated in the contract and were delivered on time. This was done to encourage sub-contractors to improve on sub-systems such as gas turbine performance, pump outputs, hullborne machinery and propulsion components to obtain near-maximum requirements without compromising reliability. Maximums, minimums and number of points that could be earned were spelled out within the Statement of Requirements. This system was to lead to a mixed-bag of increased performances, but unfortunately reliability limits did suffer with initial items.

It should be noted that even before the Specifications' Statement was released in August, escalating costs were pushing the 1965/66 Allotment of the Naval Development Program to greater heights. Under the proposed Section Vote 717-Primary 22, Field 1 (the *FHE-400* proper), the costs escalated from an estimated requirement of $14,485,000 to $22,437,782. This represented a $7,952,782 increase over the original 1965/66 figures: it was becoming clear that the building of such a state-of-the-art vessel was not going to be possible for the original $10,000,000 projected in 1963. It should also be noted that the fighting equipment was not considered in this increase. Indeed it was a separate contract, escalating from $4,005,000 in 1965 to $7,113,621 in the revised 1965/66 estimates!

Reasons behind the escalations were many: a severe underestimation of the design and engineering efforts, a doubling of the cost of the variable incidence-controlled anhedral tips, inexperience of the contractors in hydrofoil efforts requiring excessive engineering liaison support. Far greater sophistication of tooling in close-tolerance uniqueness of the craft discouraged most Canadian contractors from bidding on 'one-off' items. Research and development on this side was not within their capabilities.

Prior to the contract being awarded in April, 1963, DeHavilland had surveyed potential shipyards capable of handling a major sub-contract to build the actual vessel. This would involve building the hull to DeHavilland specifications and standards, installing sub-contracted sub-systems and being partially responsible to the RCN for adherence to these specifications in the finished product. By the summer of 1963, Marine Industries Limited, Sorel, Quebec had been approached and consented to undertake any possible contract awards.

The building of *FHE-400* was a complex procedure; there were over 715 separate work orders filed with DeHavilland by June, 1965, with an additional 340 orders to sub-contractors in the local area. To give the reader a close-up view of the complexities of the construction of this extraordinary ship the following sections cover components and sub-components and how they came together to create the "*Flying 400*".

The primary sub-contractor, Marine Industries Ltd., of Sorel, P.Q., was charged with the actual construction of the hull, decks, superstructure, plus the overall installation of other sub-contractor's efforts . . . a truly awesome undertaking! Specifications called for a 150-foot long hull with a tolerance of one inch in overall length, ½ inch for the beam and ¼ inch for symmetry. Additionally, over 30,000 detail parts were called for, with cutting tolerances of less than .015 inch from lofted lines and allowances made before cutting for welding shrinkage and erection trimming! Assemblers were asked to fit sections of deck or shell with a maximum air gap of .020 inch so that automatic welding machines could be used at erection joints. The joining of aluminium extrusions and plates varying in thickness from .093 to .625 inches with less than 5% porosity and no cracks, distortion or other welding defects would be permitted.

Firstly, M.I.L. was faced with the fact that the overall dimensions of the finished ship of 151 feet in length, 66 feet wide and 56 feet in height was too large for any erection shop in the yard. Secondly, the hullborne draft of 23 feet 6 inches would prohibit launching of the craft via the normal marine railway.

To solve these problems and to cope with the exacting standards demanded by the contract, M.I.L. management decided the construction of the craft would be entirely independent of other shipbuilding activities and the following organisations and steps were set up;

1 — Formation of the Hydrofoil Production Group.
2 — Construction of a new erection shop.
3 — A new aluminium fabrication shop.
4 — A Hydrofoil Aluminium Welding Program.
5 — Formation of the Hydrofoil Inspection Group.

The hydrofoil production group consisted of several engineers, technicians, draughtsmen and clerks and was independantly set up within the production department. Its duties were to obtain and control all DeHavilland engineering information, to establish and issue fabrication and erection procedures, to define and control material procurement, to design and supervise fabrication of all special jigs and tools and to plan and control production and costs during all stages of construction. This group interacted with DeHavilland by installing a PERT (Program Evaluation and Review Technique) network in the hull construction to allow DHC to keep precise control of the critical procedures, the effects of delays on the overall program and the implementation of corrective action.

After studying the requirements of the contract, it was realized that to achieve consistant high quality welding, it would be necessary to have strict control of ambient temperature and humidity in a suitable shop. The cost of building a shop that was large enough to accommodate the vessel hull with foils and meet the requirements was $1.5 million. The finished shop was 500 feet long, 80 feet wide and 60 feet high, with 50 and 25-ton capacity Demag overhead beam cranes.

The northern part of this large heated shop was used for the sub-assembly of components and hull erection. It contained all the major jigs and tooling, such as the erection bed, 35-foot welder, 36-foot straight-edge router, aluminium cleaning facilities, X-ray shelter, faceplates and field offices for production and inspection staff.

It was found that with this size craft, DHC was able to utilize aircraft 'lofting' practice, where full-size lofting of the entire structure was photo-printed directly on aluminium sheets. These templates were supplied by DeHavilland, one being a .062" working template cut with an accuracy of ± .005 inch. The master loft template of .025 inch was used to check accuracy of components upon inspection. While the working template was used to guide the routing operation of the part, tolerances being ± .015 inch for the finished product.

Management, after determining the space requirements for the 30,000 parts, decided to convert the first floor of the Naval Store into an Aluminium Detail Part shop, having the dimensions of 200 feet by 50 feet by 20 feet and being well heated. Working tables, storage racks and machine tools such as band saws, rotary sanders, and a milling machine were sited here. Additionally, the largest pocketing and profiling machine, a 96-inch Wadkins, was installed. Twenty-six work stations resulted for production, plus field offices for production and inspection personnel.

Fortunately, M.I.L. had a fair scope of knowledge of aluminium welding in the marine field, so determination of requirements for the aluminium hull of *FHE-400* went forward speedily. It was decided to start a new aluminium welding programme from scratch. Careful planning was necessary to minimize warping, distortion and control weld defects. Welders were re-trained to instill these new welding techniques and procedures.

It was decided to use automatic metallic inert gas (MIG) process on single-pass butt welds as often as possible to ensure weld quality, speed, minimal distortion and uniform welds. However, semi-automatic MIG and manual MIG and TIG welders were necessary in some assemblies and locations. More than 247 typical joint configurations were identified and welding procedures investigated. It was found that separate welding procedures were required when variations in amperage/voltage was greater than 5% from one typical weld to another! Checks of welds were made during these tests by dye-penetrant, X-ray, macro-examination and tensile tests at DHC and M.I.L. labs. A total of 75 welding procedures were approved for production by DHC and operators were made familiar with these in classrooms and practical instruction. A total of 26 welders were qualified before production welding was allowed.

Almost 40% of all welding on the hull was handled by a special 35-foot automatic seam-welding machine designed and built by M.I.L. The bed was 42 feet long, so that 35-foot sections of extrusions could be welded together. This eliminated tack welding, as seventy clamps, twelve inches long, positioned about an inch from the seam, held the extrusions in place at a pressure of one ton per linear foot.

The machine weighed 42 tons and had a 3,000 psi clamping height adjustment and a 100 psi system for clamping pressure, the latter being flexible enough to use for the welding of main girders to the main deck sections. A plastic shelter was fitted over the machine to maintain a constant ambient temperature and a dust-free atmosphere.

With a staff of three men, this unique machine performed over 26,000 feet of X-ray quality butt welds.

Welding of D54S aluminium extrusions and plates required extraordinary standards of cleanliness control and inspection, since a particle of dirt could ruin a weld. Hence a 25-foot curtain was erected between the steel and aluminium shop areas. Aluminium workers were required to wear white overalls and rubber shoes. Bottled gas was used to minimize moisture problems and felt pads were mounted to clean the welding wire as it was fed into the torch. Heating air ducts were deflected away from weld areas and the machines were cleaned regularly to control dust and debris.

Automatic welding of extrusions demanded that a maximum air gap between the materials be kept within .020 inch. A special 36-foot straight-edge routing machine was built by M.I.L. to accurately prepare the edges of as-bought extrusions of pre-fabricated strakes. Two gun-lathe beds were bolted together and fitted with a travelling routing head to form a 20-ton machine. A special clamping system held down the material during machining operations.

After the edges were prepared, they were mechanically, then chemically cleaned in a warm acid bath. Then the aluminium was covered by Kraft paper and masking tape. Any edge left waiting over eight hours had to be recleaned before welding. Completed seams were wire-brushed and shaved to within .010 inch of the structure material, then X-ray inspected before being moved to the hull erection area.

The Hydrofoil Inspection Plan called for the formation of a new inspection department. Aircraft inspection procedures were adapted to the marine application, to closely parallel DHC's inspection procedures. A 100% inspection procedure was utilized in loft cutting, detail part fabrication, subassembly of each hull component and each component into the hull. The most important component of this inspection plan was a thorough welding in-process inspection in all important stages of fabrication and assembly. A special X-ray department was set up in the erection shop, including a modern darkroom for developing the film, a radiographer's office and a lead-shielded 40 feet by 22 feet by 8 feet shop area for the protection of workers during shooting. Staff was regularly fifteen men, in three shifts, six days a week. Over 25,000 satisfactory Class A butt weld films were processed during construction. However, this department was instrumental in correcting many hundreds of defective welds, particularly in the earlier stages, that would have passed undetected.

Hull Construction; Since the construction of the hull involved mainly welding aluminium extrusions, plates and sheets, it was decided to build the hull upside-down to maximize the quality of downhand welding. Hence the maindeck was laid first and the hull built up over it. The hull then consisted

Assembly Pattern

FLOWCHART

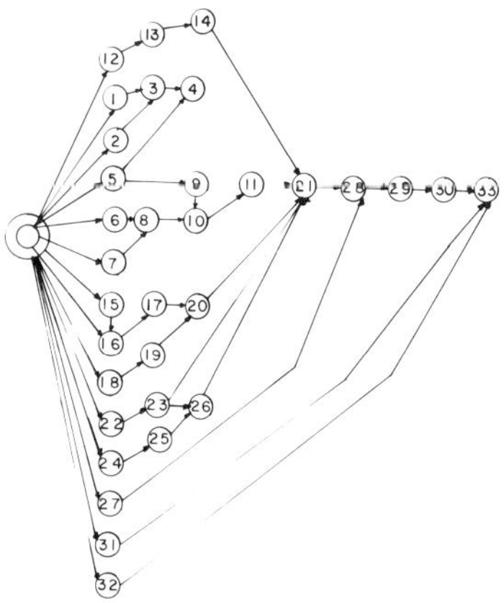

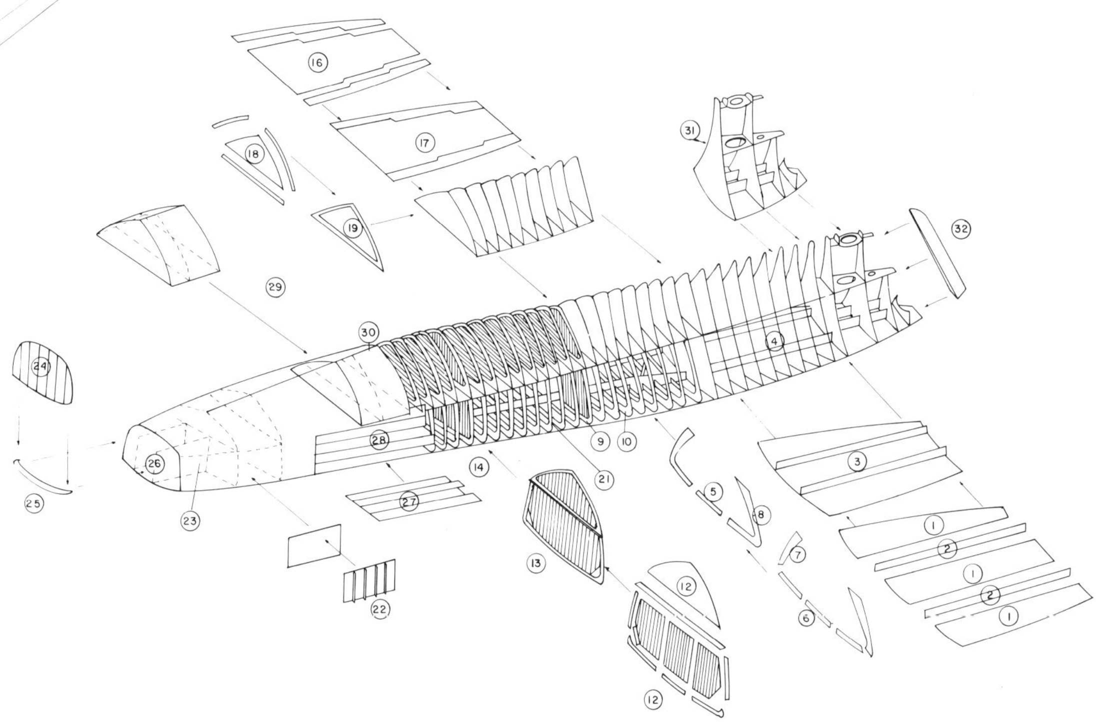

of a main deck, frames, lower deck, floors and skin, with seven bulkheads from keel to main deck.

The assembly and erection of the main hull structure was done on a specially designed erection bed 146 feet long, 20 feet wide, consisting of a formed jig, shaped to the reversed contour of the main deck. The deck was supported under each frame by a transverse beam with wooden linings inclined at the proper slope to insure the exact alignment of decks, frames and keel. The precision of this 25-ton jig was maintained to within one-eighth inch of its theoretical shape throughout its entire utilization by means of an optical alignment method.

The main deck had overall dimensions of 151 feet long 21 feet 6 inches wide made from five sections welded together with staggered erection joints. Deck surface plate thickness was generally .093 inch. Each section included three panels made of welded extrusions and joined together to the main longitudinal deck girders spaced 76 inches apart. The two main deck girders consisted of composite 'T'-beam sections in 30 foot lengths on a special diaphragmed jig with adjustable supports to meet the various forms caused by the different cambers and depths. These girders were then assembled under the 35-foot seam welder to their adjacent main deck panels, to form a full width deck section ready for erection.

The foredeck section was the first unit placed on the erection bed. The transition structure was then assembled and closed with the main deck section number two. The remaining main deck sections were then consequently located, trimmed, fitted and welded on their staggered erection joints using special stainless steel back-up strips attached with welded studs to insure best welding conditions.

The deck stringers were cut in order to permit welding of sections and special bridging pieces were welded on top of stringers over these erection joints. The main deck was pressed against the erection bed by means of thirty 1,000 lb. closing weights. The contour of the main deck was then properly trimmed and prepared for the lap welding of the deck edge extrusion. This deck edge extrusion had to be carefully machined at the foredeck to meet the varying angle of gunwale and deck.

Fifty-eight main deck centre beams of 'T'-beam section were prefabricated and erected over each frame station, normally 30 inches apart. A special frame alignment fixture was designed and built to transfer the frame datum line from the bed to the working surface of the main deck. Each beam was welded across by means of a beam-closing jig.

The 96 outer beams and side frames consisted of variable 'T'-beam sections. Using a grid faceplate and dowelled pins, the outer beams and side frames were located over their master lofts in their proper positions and then the joint TIG welded so the overall contour of this assembly was within the $^1/_{16}$ inch tolerance. These sub-assemblies were then welded exactly over the frame stations aligned, using the frame alignment jig and buttock lines.

The hull was divided into eight compartments by seven bulkheads. The foremost and aftmost were watertight, being collision bulkheads, while the others went up to the main deck girders only. Each bulkhead was in two sections: an upper and lower. Each section in turn was composed of three panels joined by pillar extrusions. The sections were assembled on the 35-foot welder and then trimmed. The complete, inspected bulkhead was then welded to the main deck, held vertically with guy wires.

The lower deck overall 140 feet long 19 feet wide, consisted of eight sections divided by the main transverse bulkheads. Four major portions were at various heights but parallel to the base line. Each section (generally 22 feet by 19 feet) was fabricated from single stringer extrusions welded on the 25-foot automatic welding machine and fitted with butt-welded edge plating to engage the bulkhead landing strips. The sections were then fitted with their respective floors on a faceplate, then moved over the erection bed and aligned three inches above the bulkhead landing strips, using jacks at columns. The frames were then trimmed, the sections lowered to their final position and welded.

The most complex part of the hull structure was the shell. Plating from the gunwale to the keel and from stem to transom consisted of pre-fabricated strakes. Fourteen types of extrusions and various sheet and plate thicknesses were required, the thickest being .25 on the bottom. Where differing thicknesses occurred on either side of a butt joint, the thicker material was chamfered to match the thinner panel. These extrusions were generally 35 feet long, with three to five strakes grouped to form a panel in order to reduce the number of erection joints. These were always made straight and flat and were then formed around the hull framework, trimmed to fit and then welded in place. However, these plates were offered three times over their exact position on the frames and floors before closing and welding took place, since the maximum air gap of .020 inch had to be maintained. A special track to carry the MIG automatic welding machine was set up parallel to the hull seam to be welded.

In order to control distortion of the hull during the 'skinning' operation, the panels and strakes were erected simultaneously on both sides and fixed benchmarks were located on the centreline near the bow and stern, so that movements of the structure during welding could be recorded and corrected.

The transom, being of conical section, was prefabricated in two panels and was erected earlier as landing connection for the shell plating.

The next component was the keel, consisting of a keel extrusion and large triangular keel panels made from stiffened extrusions. These were joined by a complex routed and pocketed fish-tail plate. This largely completed the hull skin procedure.

Right hand rear quarter section of the engineering space. Sixteen years later the aluminium was still as shiny as seen here.
Credit: DeHavilland of Canada

Bow Foundation: forward of the forward collision bulkhead, an integral bow foundation was built. It included the bow foil bearings and guide rail attachment and because of the fine lines of the hull and heavy structure required to take the stresses of this foil, there were additional problems of accessibility. In order to meet the very close tolerances for the erection of heavy pre-fabricated framing and plating, a complex erection jig was used, replacing the guide rails at their exact locations.

The bow foil bearing plate was machined on site, but in case of the bilge strake and its compound curved surfaces these were pre-formed by DHC, shipped to M.I.L. and welded in place with very exacting procedures. The stem consisted of the extreme forward portion of the hull and was fabricated with wrapped plates, breasthooks and stiffeners all assembled in a special jig and welded to the hull structure by external welding as a single unit.[1]

Main Foil foundation consisted of a lower deck section, complete with floors and shell plating of sturdy and precise construction. This, plus the foil attachment fittings were fabricated from 7075 (T3) aluminium forgings and time and again the welds that DHC personnel did turned up defective. This was responsible for putting the construction some thirteen weeks in arrears by May, 1965.[2] However, by June fabrication of the foundation was well in hand and it was delivered to M.I.L. in late August, 1965; but poor welds still plagued the foundation component and it wasn't until December that the foundation sections were finally approved and installed.[3] This installation involved an erection jig, boring fixture and optical alignment instruments. The foundation was fitted with gearbox masters, boring fixture, then moved ten inches over the ship's hull to four supporting pylons, all under DHC personnel supervision. Using the theoretical axes of shafting for foilborne and hullborne propulsion system, the optical alignment of the foundation was finalized after ten lines of sight had been taken. The ship structure was then trimmed to receive the foundation and welding was then begun. Supreme efforts were necessary to keep the accuracy of alignment during the welding process. Eight especially trained welders were used simultaneously to weld the foundation to the hull structure, requiring 600 feet of heavy aluminium butt welding. Optical verification at the end of the weld sequence showed a deviation of .010 inch, well within tolerance. However, this procedure wasn't without problems. An earlier effort had resulted in weld defects that had forced the removal of the foundation and the procedure had to be repeated, resulting in a further two-month 'slippage' in delivery.

The superstructure and bridge were aluminium in construction and assembled in a similar manner as the hull. After fabrication, the operations room was turned over and the bridge assembled atop. The superstructure was then properly braced and made ready for erection on the main deck after the hull rotation.

Rotation: after the major welding was completed in January 1966, the hull was prepared for rotation. Four rings, 25 feet 4 inches in diameter and 11 inches thick, were fitted to the 40-ton hull. These consisted of six plywood sections equally spaced with wooden blocks and bolted together, which were spaced so as not to exert more than the maximum 4,000 lb. per square foot skin loading and were exactly contoured to the hull shape. Each ring was divided into three sections: one covering the main deck and the others covering the hull sides to the keel. Each ring was tested to 20 tons and the outer edges smoothly rounded to minimize friction. The corresponding wooden cradles had their bearing surfaces shaped to accommodate the rings and were heavily greased.

The rings were suitably cross-braced to keep them true in relation to the bearing blocks and each other. The cradles were then shimmed and blocked and the erection bed was lowered and removed from under the hull.

Roll-over is now three quarters complete.
Credit: DeHavilland of Canada

With rotation bearing races and blocks in place the roll-over of the hull could begin. The shackle on the nearest race will be engaged by the overhead crane and its position changed as it nears the top of the arc.
Credit: DeHavilland of Canada

The three aft rings were connected together through a lifting beam to the 50-ton Demag overhead crane. The forward ring was connected directly to a 25-ton overhead crane and bench marks made at each block and ring so that any twisting could be detected during the four-hour long rotation. Radio communication was maintained between the two cranemen, the four

FHE-400 being rolled out from its construction shed at Sorel, Quebec prior to transportation to Halifax.
Credit: DeHavilland of Canada

floor observers and the foreman in charge. Chain blocks were installed to hold back any overriding by gravity during the rotation. The rotation was successfully performed on Saturday, January 22, 1966.

During the skinning process, the elevated bed had been constructed. This 55-ton elevated bed was designed to hold the 200-ton static weight of the ship upon completion. It also allowed access to the foil foundation and allowed 21 feet of clearance for the assembly of the foil system.

Wooden bilge blocking was used at thirteen stations and longitudinal keel supports were fitted between these stations. These bilge blocks were supported by a horizontal beam mounted on three columns, one directly underneath the keel and the other two equally spaced on the outside, the latter also used as the upright staging assembly. Portable stairways and catwalks permitted traffic by workers, temporary services and welding machines.

The port bilge blocking and bracings were removed to allow the passage of the hull to the centre of the elevated bed. The rotation rings were further utilized, as support positions while the cranes lifted the hull, traversed on their beams until the hull was centred over the elevated bed and then gently lowered it onto the bilge blocks. This was accomplished on Saturday, February 5, 1966.

The completed superstructure was lifted and moved above its location on the foredeck, properly trimmed and then lowered and welded into place. This completed all outstanding internal/external welding and the final inspections were carried out.

The major hurdle in the construction of this ship was the installation of the main foils. Under the supervision of DHC, they immediately started a precise, controlled sequence of installation: first, the boring and facing of 64 attachment fittings in the main foil foundation, then the installation of the inboard gearboxes, diesel engine and the FT4 turbine.

Using a universal dolly, the main foil system was erected starting with the left foilborne transmission strut assembly, the left anhedral foil assembly, the left dihedral foil assembly, then the procedure was repeated for the right assemblies. The high-speed main foil was installed between the foilborne transmission pods and the outboard gearboxes and shafting were then fitted and carefully installed complete with their piping sytems. Extreme precautions involving optical alignment were taken by DHC throughout this installation.

Installation of the bow foil assembly was much simpler than the main foil because the various components could be assembled on wooden floor supports. While the bow Teflon-coated spherical bearing and guide rails were fitted aboard ship, the complete bow foil assembly was moved directly below its foundation and then installed and secured in place for its final connection with the trimming and steering actuators.

Transfer of Hydrofoil or "Roll Out": with the final installation of watertight doors, escape scuttles and pilot house windows the completed ship was painted and readied for roll out from the erection shop.

The weight of the ship was transferred from the bilge blocking on the elevated bed to specially designed main pod and forebody supports. The ultimate design loadings of these supports was 142,500 lb. forward and 641,250 lb. at each of the foilborne pods. When the main pod and forebody supports were in place, the elevated bed and steel erection gear were dismantled and removed from the erection shed. The actual hauling of the ship was via the shipyard transfer system. This consisted of a straight haul of 900 feet from the erection shop, followed by a side haul of 100 feet to No. 5 Berth via a specially-designed two-way transfer carriage. Since the move necessitated the entire emptying of the erection shop, it was scheduled during the summer holidays and it was performed on July 21, 1966.

From here *FHE-400* was fitted out with the auxiliary machinery, piping and interior furniture; the anhedral foil controlled-incidence tip was installed and tested. Over 400 equipment packages were devised, planned and supplied by various sub-contractors and installed at Sorel. Each was the product of thoughtful planning, designing by DeHavilland as prime contractor and had been painstakingly simulated in the full-scale wooden mock-up at the Malton plant. Here they were checked for interface, accessibility, non-interference with other systems and for general fit within the hull space limitations.

Pre-delivery tests began in September, 1966 of some systems and the major machinery tests began in the latter half of October, 1966. On November 5, 1966 disaster struck . . . something that almost cancelled the entire *FHE-400* Project before it saw water.

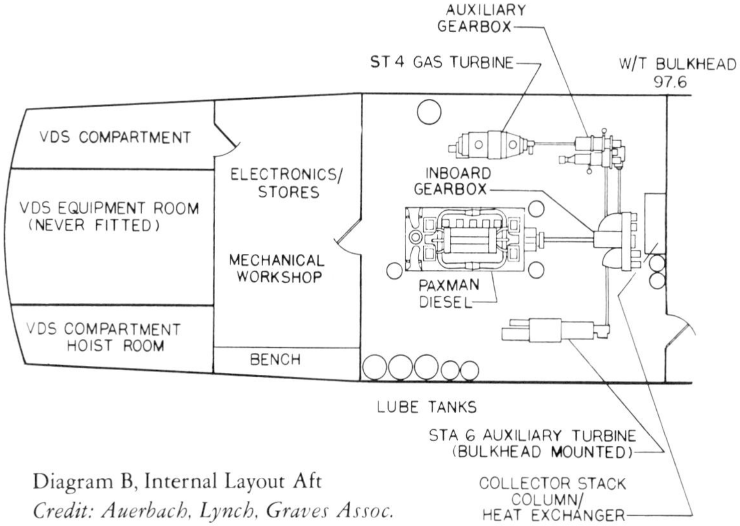

Diagram B, Internal Layout Aft
Credit: Auerbach, Lynch, Graves Assoc.

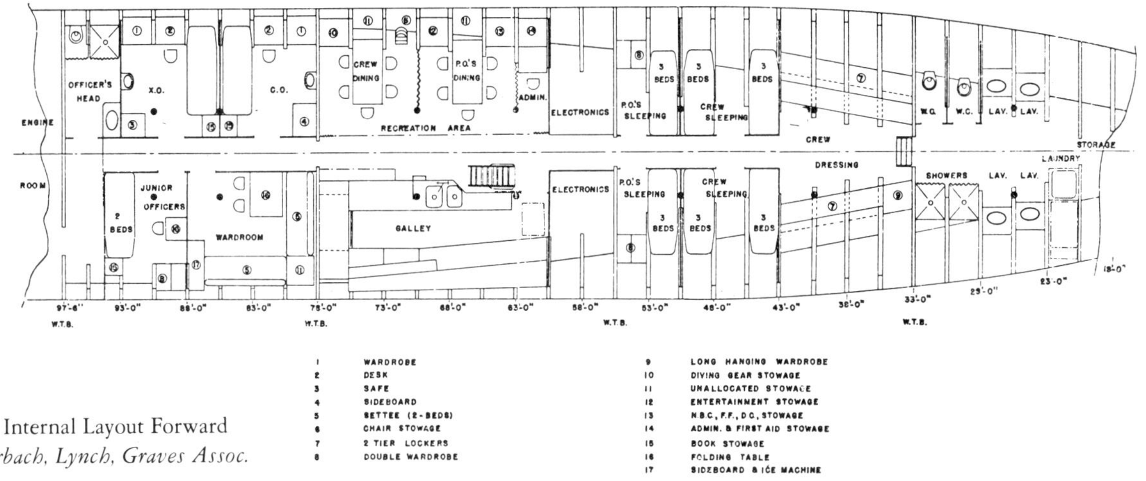

Diagram A, Internal Layout Forward
Credit: Auerbach, Lynch, Graves Assoc.

Chapter Four

A Jet-age Puzzle

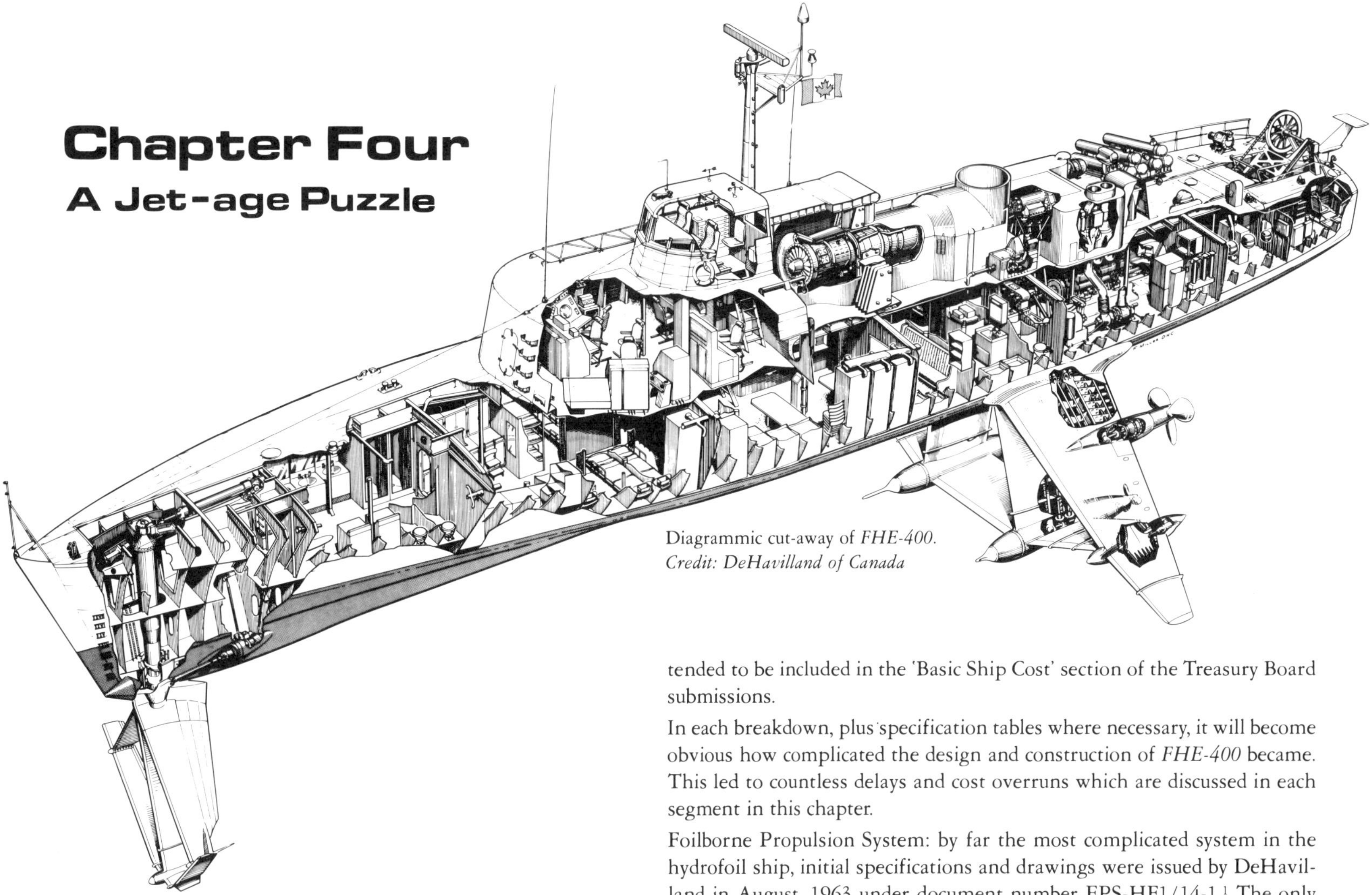

Diagrammic cut-away of *FHE-400*.
Credit: DeHavilland of Canada

Because of the complexity of *FHE-400* and it's construction, it has been broken down into sub-systems to give the reader a better understanding of the engineering marvel this ship represented in her time.

Where possible, contract dates and sub-contractors, plus cost are mentioned. However, before the establishment of the Hydrofoil Project Office in 1965 and the later Joint Management Review Board in 1967, DeHavilland sub-contracted on a job-basis. Amounts, especially smaller items, tended to be included in the 'Basic Ship Cost' section of the Treasury Board submissions.

In each breakdown, plus specification tables where necessary, it will become obvious how complicated the design and construction of *FHE-400* became. This led to countless delays and cost overruns which are discussed in each segment in this chapter.

Foilborne Propulsion System: by far the most complicated system in the hydrofoil ship, initial specifications and drawings were issued by DeHavilland in August, 1963 under document number EPS-HF1/14-1.[1] The only contractor interested had been contacted earlier in the year and the bid entered on behalf of the parent company in the US, General Electric of Lynn, Mass., by Canadian General Electric Co. The US parent had previous experience with hydrofoil propulsion through the USN's *Denison* and the AG(EH) Program. This contract was awarded in November, 1963.

The CGE contract called for three phases:

Phase I included the design report, vibration, strength, weight analysis, contract drawings, specifications, estimated time-cost details for Phase II and III, all within four months of accepting the initial contract. The first overrun by this company occurred here, with Phase I taking six months to accomplish.

Phase II A detailed time, weight, cost, strength analysis required and revised monthly. A comprehensive design report to be provided twelve months after acceptance of a Phase II contract.

Phase III Construction of the transmission, to be delivered to DeHavilland eighteen months after acceptance of the Phase II and III contracts. Subsequent events were to prove how naive both parties had been in time estimation for such a pioneer engineering effort.

Referring to drawing #5-1, the complexity of this system can readily be seen. With lined struts and anhedral foil, and the deflection of these struts of up to 4.9 inches, laterally, at 50 knots under normal loads, shafting and bearing support was vastly complicated. Hollow shafts were opted for in all cases as a weight-saver, allowing for the considerable torque-twisting of the shafts under initial thrust, without shearing.

The demands of foilborne power requirements required that a marinized turbine engine be adopted. At the time of planning, only the recently-released marinized J-75 derivative, the FT4A-2, was suitable for use. Purchased from United Aircraft of Canada, the FT4 delivered far more horsepower than required by *FHE-400*, but at this early date it was the only turbine engine that would fulfill the requirement without pairing.[2] Delivering 25,500 s.h.p. continuous and 21,500 rpm normally, the FT4 was mounted on the main deck, abaft the pilot house. Coupled by direct shafting with the GE-built foilborne transmission, the FT4 drove twin shafts per side, 30 feet down through the struts to the foilborne outboard transmission pods at the bottom. These shafts were geared up 1:2 to allow reduction in

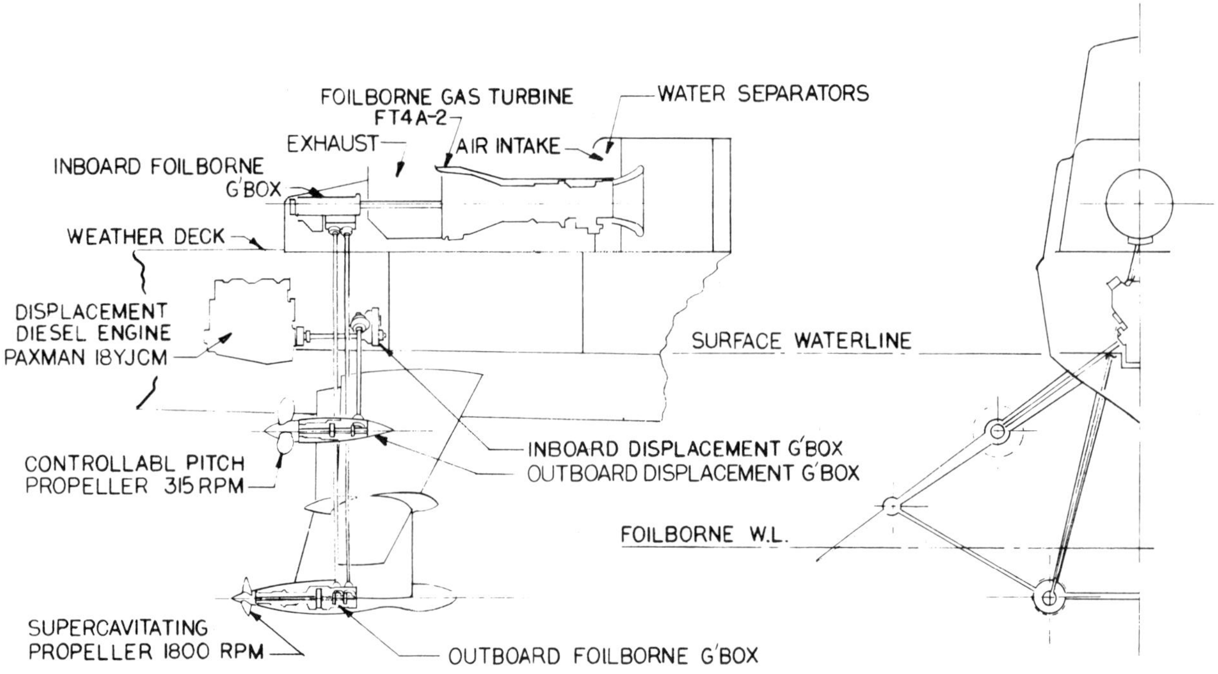

Propulsion system layout

shaft diameter and strain. The pod-mounted outboard foilborne gearboxes turned the thrust 90° back to the horizontal and provided a 4:1 down ratio to the foilborne propellers, giving a net 2:1 reduction ratio from the engine. The fixed-pitch, three bladed, super-cavitating propellers of 48-inch diame-

Completed FT4A-2 installation and housing.
Credit: DeHavilland of Canada

ter were jointly developed by DeHavilland and the Ship Division of the National Physical Laboratory, London and manufactured by Ladish company of Milwaukee from Iconel 718 stainless steel.[3]

As well as the complex components listed above, an overruning clutch system allowing the propellers to 'windmill' during displacement operation, plus a brake was required. Virtual inaccessability of all gearboxes and shafting required specialized design and components for long life without maintenance. Overshadowing all these requirements was the severe limitations on weight and space. The designer's success can be measured by the fact that the system weight was less than eight tons or ¾ pound per shaft horsepower transmitted and the system worked. However, it didn't make it in the first attempt. In fact, the transmission production turned out to be a development programme in its own right.

The fixed-pitch, three-bladed, supercavitating propeller.
Credit: B. V. Davis

The production of the transmissions, plagued by underestimation in required engineering effort and time and production delays, first underwent testing in September, 1966. After four hours at full speed and torque on the test stand, the test was terminated with a fractured bevel gear shaft, originating at a stress raiser weld. The stress raiser was eliminated by redesigning the shaft, using a solid forging. However, at the same time, severe wear in the inboard helical gear had been discovered and was attributed to the mating of a non-nitrided gear with a nitrided pinion. A nitrided replacement gear was fitted.

By June 1967 the foilborne transmission was ready once more for shop testing. After eighteen hours at full speed and torque, severe vibration of an outboard gearbox was encountered and the test terminated. There had been a massive failure of the compound star train. Its cause was traced to severe fretting of the journals of the star pinion inner roller races, with similar fretting evident elsewhere in the system. Correction involved redesign to incorporate journals with integral races and improved lubrication.

The completed transmission finally arrived in Halifax on October 30, 1968; five years after the initial contract was signed. It was installed and completed on December 19, 1968.

However, fretting of the star train remained a problem throughout the ship's life, albeit one that could be lived with. The very concept of a thirty-foot separation of engine and propeller strained technology to the limits and coupled with the weight and material limitations (no aluminium or titanium) resulted in a highly-stressed component with attendant reliability problems.[4]

Alternatively, the hullborne propulsion system was a marvel of reliability. The inboard transmission was situated just forward of the Paxman diesel engine, hard against the forward engine room bulkhead. It was connected to the diesel by extension shaft and through an interconnecting shaft, it drove the auxiliary gearbox which supplied electrical power, cooling water circulation, and hydraulic pressure. Utilizing an overrunning clutch, the ST6 auxiliary turbine could be made to drive the ship in hullborne mode in case of diesel failure.

Drive output from the inboard hullborne transmission was effected by single shafts per side, routed through the hollow anhedral foil elements. Each downshaft was of two sections with a remote-control, air-powered clutch for propelled disengagement from the power source when in the foilborne mode. This allowed the hullborne propellers to rotate when feathered, if struck by a wave, thereby minimizing impact loads and reducing drag.

The displacement propellers were built by KMW of Sweden and were variable, constant controlled-pitch items, 84 inches in diameter and three-bladed. Being situated thirty feet apart, they allowed for great versatility in manoeuvering of the ship at slow speeds and in confined waters where the bow foil steering was not sufficient.

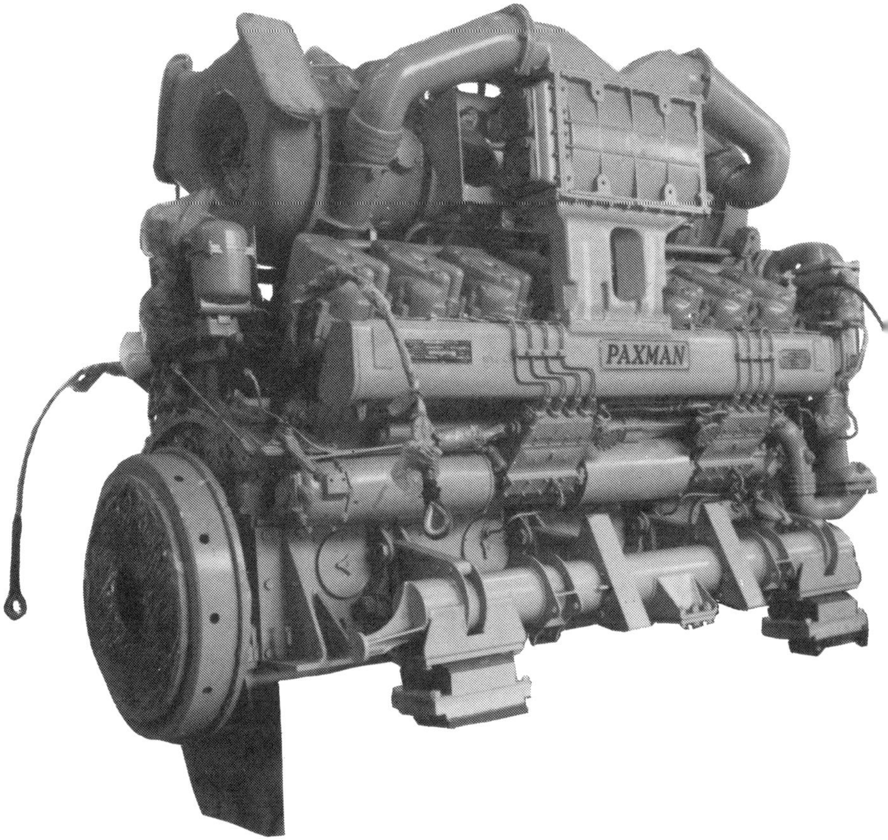

The Davey Paxman Ventura 16YJCM diesel engine for hullborne propulsion.
Credit: DeHavilland of Canada

The chosen displacement engine was the Davey Paxman Marine Ventura 16YJCM diesel, distributed in Canada by Ruston-Paxman of Montreal. It was chosen to provide reliability over long hours of service, to provide fuel economy and reasonable noise factors, but unfortunately it was to plague the ship throughout her trials' time.

The diesel suffered from a reputation for unreliability without constant maintenance. Problems with the mechanical governors were rampant,

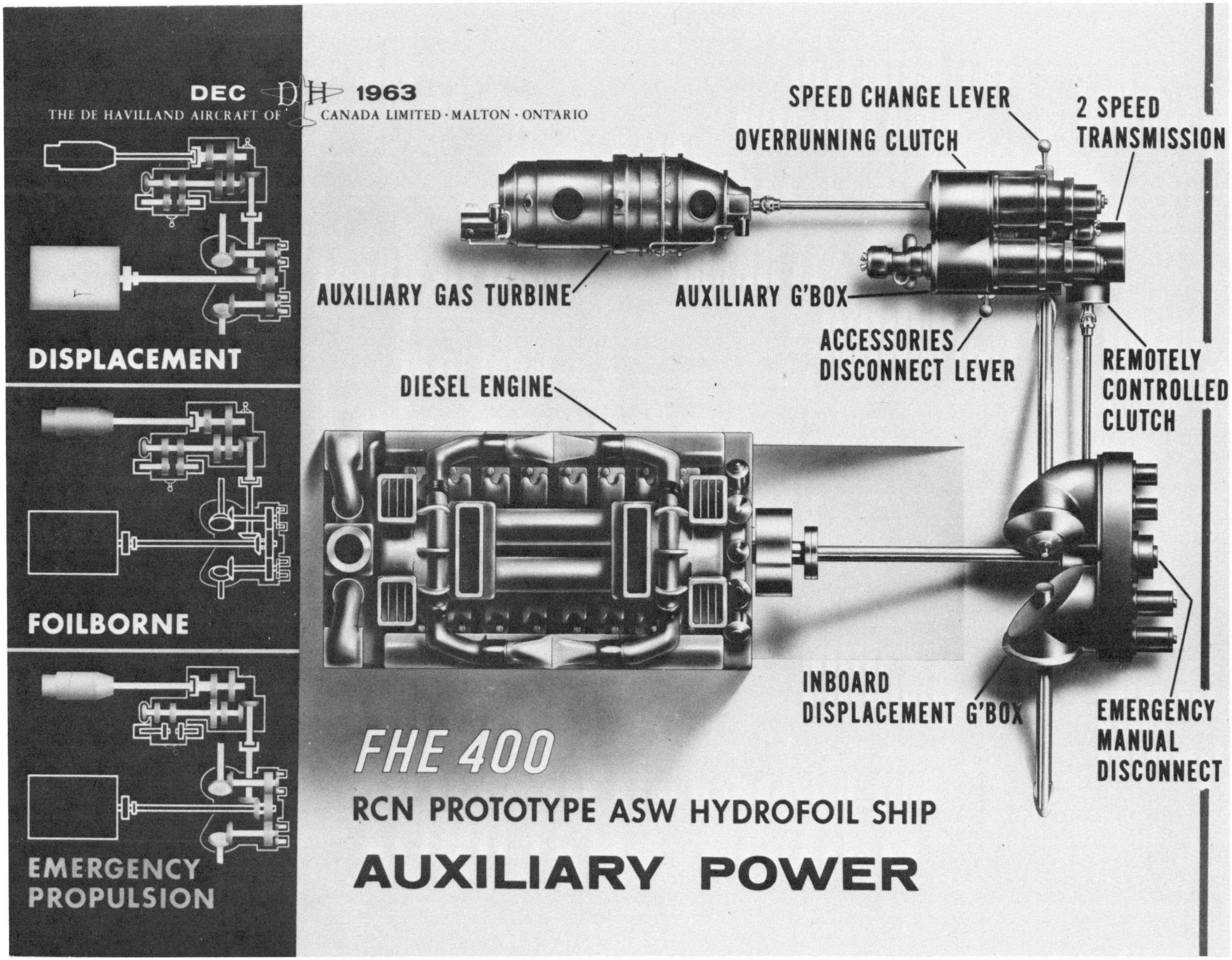

Diagram of auxiliary propulsion system and different propulsion modes.

never allowing the engine to develop its maximum horsepower. It continually leaked oil and gasketing was a constant nightmare. Failures in critical components very nearly ruined the last, most successful Halifax-Bermuda-Norfolk-Halifax trip in 1971. Details of this engine are found in Appendix B.

Auxiliary Systems: as mentioned, hydraulic, electrical power and cooling water circulation was provided by the auxiliary gearbox, driven by the diesel in the hullborne mode. However, during foilborne operation or in harbour where electrical and air service were not available, the ST6A-53 gas turbine drove the auxiliary gearbox, situated to port in the engine room and in the foremost quadrant. No matter what motive source was utilized, the auxiliary gearbox drove the seawater pump and gearbox lubrication pumps.

The ST6 was also capable of boosting the diesel engine output in a combined drive arrangement, or replacing, at half speed, the diesel as the displacement propulsion unit in case of failure of the latter. This was only possible when the diesel over-running clutch was manually engaged in the inboard hullborne gearbox in the first case or disengaged in the latter case and the auxiliary gearbox changed to reduction gear without load.

The accessory load could be eliminated when the ST6 served as motive power, by disengaging the shift lever while both engines were shut down. However, the lube pumps and circulation pumps would continue to function at a reduced rate.

The peak duty pumps for the hydraulic system were engaged by a magnetic clutch automatically during the initiation of the foilborne mode or manually by the Engineer's Console if necessary. The two-speed gearbox remained engaged in low ratio except when the ST6 was being used to propel the ship. Then the gear change was affected manually by changing the gearbox lever without load. The first ratio was 1.715:1 increase; the emergency propulsion mode ratio was 1:1.226 reduction. The auxiliary gearbox was built by Western Gear Corporation.

Services provided by the auxiliary gearbox can be summed up as follows:

1. 3,000 psi hydraulic pressure
2. 115 vAC, 400 cycle, 3-phase electrical
3. 28 vDC (for most electrical sub-systems and pump accepting DC current)
4. Input seawater cooling pressure to heat exchanger 60 psi
5. Maximum flowrate cooling seawater 50 gph.
6. Emergency propulsion in hullborne mode.

GTCP85-291 Emergency Turbine: to supply essential power requirements for the ship in an emergency, such as hydraulics, electrics, via an AC generator and firefighting via a seawater pump. The GT85 could supply low pressure air to be used in starting the FT4A-2 in case of failure of the regular system. Output was either via shaft power or bleed air flow. The turbine was mounted on the starboard deckhead, above the flood line, abreast the diesel. Lubrication was via an integral oil system, with DC starting via the ship's batteries. The unit was controlled from the Engineer's Console. The turbine turned the AC alternator via the gearbox shaft output shaft, with two hydraulic pumps and the seawater firefighting pump driven by this gearbox output too. The generator was a 60 Kva unit, delivering 115/200 vAC, 400 cps, three-phase current.[5]

Foils: the bow foil unit was intended to carry only 10% of the gross 475,000 lb (212 tonne) weight of the hydrofoil craft. The foil unit forward used superventilating sections with upper surface spoilers to encourage and sustain ventilation over the widest possible range of angles of attack, immersion and speed. The low lift curve/slope of these sections gave the bow foil unit the required characteristics of light damping and sensitivity to depth change, but had a comparatively low lift/drag ratio.

Total stress through multipath was estimated not to exceed 80,000 psi. The bow foil was steerable and acted as a rudder for both modes. Rake was adjustable, a total of 20°, enabling the best angle of attack to be selected.

The bow foil was basically a diamond form, with a vertical strut and short, horizontal bridge-pieces of delayed cavitation section at the lower apex. The dihedral foils were pin-jointed to the bridge-piece and to the anhedral foils at the outboard intersections, but the upper ends of the anhedrals were bolted rigidly to the strut. The mounting shaft pivoted at a spherical bearing in the forefoot and the upper bearing traversed through an arc, fore and aft, to provide a rake angle adjustment of −15° to +5°, combined with a steering angle range of ±15° (restricted to ±5° when in the foilborne mode). These bearings were teflon lined to ease friction.[6]

The steering actuator was located at the lower end of the bow foil shaft to avoid torsional oscillations. However, this was a redesign: during the early construction stages, the Jarry Hydraulics steering actuator failed and suffered a malfunction when the feedback nut seized, allowing the feedback loop to be by-passed and the actuator going to full activation. This severely damaged internal components taking three months to repair, while a way to prevent this happening again was devised. Luckily, this had been a bench test, but it was frightening to think what could have happened if this had occurred at sea in a foilborne trial. The unit, in going to full activation or full extension, would have forced the bow foil to turn a full 15° to starboard, with the hydrofoil craft probably falling or side-slipping off its foils, at the very least injuring or shaking up the crew severely.

A bronze split nut was substituted for the stainless steel one to decrease friction on the steel feedback screw, plus the realization that the split (providing the feedback hydraulic fluid) would, without proper filtration, collect foreign material and tend to freeze the nut. Hence more stringent filtering was called for and close watch kept on particulate matter in the fluid.

The steering actuator had been planned to couple with the foil post at the top. However, testing cast some doubt on the rigidity of the structure at this height and the position was re-designed to place the actuator at the bottom.

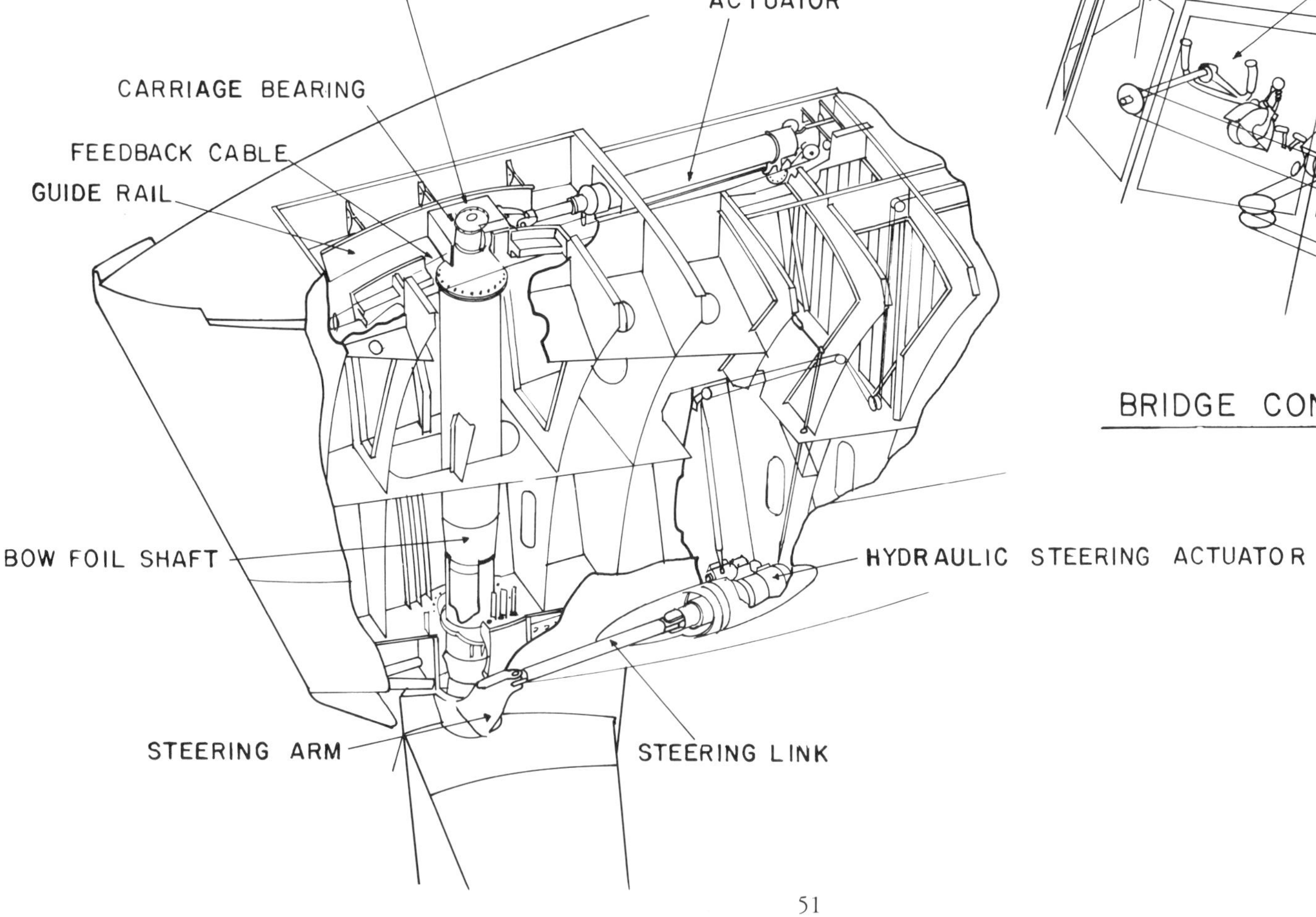

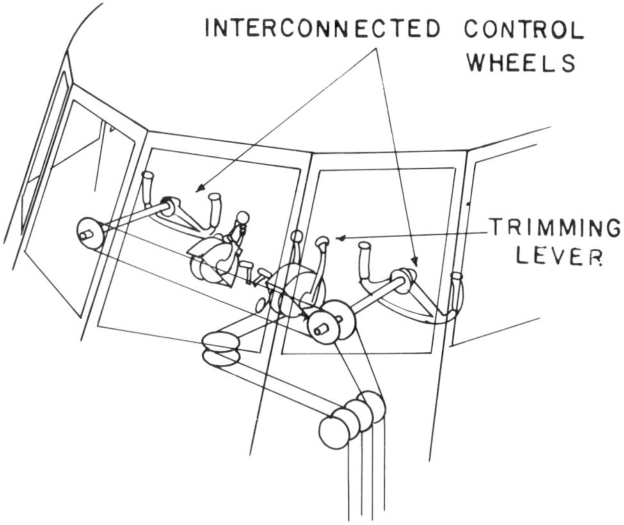

BRIDGE CONTROLS

Steering could be maintained automatically by utilizing the Bendix Eclipse Pioneer auto-pilot and gyro compass input.[7]

By May 21, 1966, DeHavilland admitted they could no longer keep pace with the intended production schedule.[8] DeHavilland had encountered problems in the design and manufacture of the foils, plus enduring a devastating strike between August 25 — September 27, 1965 and this, coupled with a lack of communication between DeHavilland's Production Branch and the Executive, had allowed the company to become placed in heavy penalty situation without management's knowledge. Expenses were out of hand and DeHavilland were experiencing difficulties in welding the nickel steel selected for the ship's foils without warpages and broken welds outside tolerances. Facing the situation, a new slate of executives were appointed and 70% of the foil manufacture was placed on contract with North American Aviation, Los Angeles Division. North American first undertook a production cost study for the necessary elements; both main anhedral foils, the anhedral tips, the starboard main strut and the bow foil strut and both anhedrals. They also assisted in solving the problems DeHavilland were encountering with welding of the 18% maraging steel. There was a $100,000 disbursement by DDP to cover the initial month of N.A.A.'s contract while additional funds were re-allocated. Meanwhile, the finished bow foil dihedrals were manufactured by Ladish of Milwaukee and shipped to Malton for assembly.[9] There persisted in the minds of many a doubt that DeHavilland could produce the remaining elements, but produce they did. The anhedrals for the bow foil were shipped on April 15, 1966 to Marine Industries Ltd., Sorel, P.Q., for final assembly. However, North American had done quite a crude job in contouring the anhedral tips for the main foils and it was necessary for DHC to refinish and then fill in the low spots with neoprene coating. The assemblies were then shipped to M.I.L.

Main foils: the unusually large hull clearance and projected high speed led to an estimated stress figure approaching 100,000 psi maximum in the foil structure.[10] This presented very difficult structural design and fabrication problems for DeHavilland. However, a new steel alloy, 18% maraging steel appeared to meet and exceed this need and it was decided to fabricate the foil surfaces from this 18% NiCoMo steel plate, plus forgings for the foils.

To keep stresses and dimensional changes as small as possible, it was decided to machine and grind the plates to the proper curvatures, a very expensive method with wastages approaching 80% of plate material in some cases. However, the 250,000 psi yield strength, plus the low temperature heat treatment without quenching were the deciding factors in selecting this metal. The problems of using maraging steel in a marine environment were not fully understood or appreciated at this time and DeHavilland were not interested in undertaking a study themselves. Instead, they immediately sub-contracted the study out to the Department of Mines, Energy and Resources, a government agency! Although a thorough study was made, the final results were not proven conclusively until it was too late to switch materials.[11] However, by 1965 the Department of Mines, Energy and Resources suggested that with the test results and the realized stress maximums of less than 80,000 psi, a lower tensile strength steel, with less aversion to salt water would be advisable on any follow-on hydrofoil craft.[12] Unfortunately, complications arose during the trials and evaluation portion of *Bras d'Or*'s lifetime that were to play no small part in dooming the vessel.

All foil surfaces were treated to a coat of neoprene, about one quarter of an inch thick. This was done after the test results of the Mines, Energy and Resources were made known, showing that 18% maraging steel was subject to severe corrosion problems in a saltwater environment if not properly protected. Coating investigations had begun in 1963, with the field rapidly narrowed to a polysulphide/polyurethane method and a cold-process neoprene coating. Investigations led to practical testings, first carried out on the 'A' brackets of the RCN destroyer, *St. Croix* in November, 1965. This showed loss of adhesion in two areas of the neoprene coating, whereas the Almatex polyurethane coating only detached in the 'feathered-off' areas at the bearing housings. However, the latter coating was judged too complicated and expensive for the time remaining before the foils would be required by M.I.L. and the neoprene coating was further tested, surviving some 200 hours battering on the foil of PC(H) at Boeing's test facility in May, 1966.[13]

Accessible areas within the hollow foils were treated with a zinc 'sacrificial' coating and on flatter surfaces a neoprene matting was secured to control movement of minor seepage. The idea was sound, but the massive leaks that developed in 1969 and 1971 overwhelmed the zinc coating and attacked the steel itself. Faults resulted from improperly sealed access panels, which in turn caused cracks in the structural panels through combined stress corrosion and attendant hydrogen embrittlement. Later investigations after the second bout of cracks in 1971 showed higher residual stresses than anticipated after heat treatment, especially near welds, which contributed greatly in defeating the metal's soundness. Both of these cracked units were the main high-speed centre foils, although cracking in the struts and

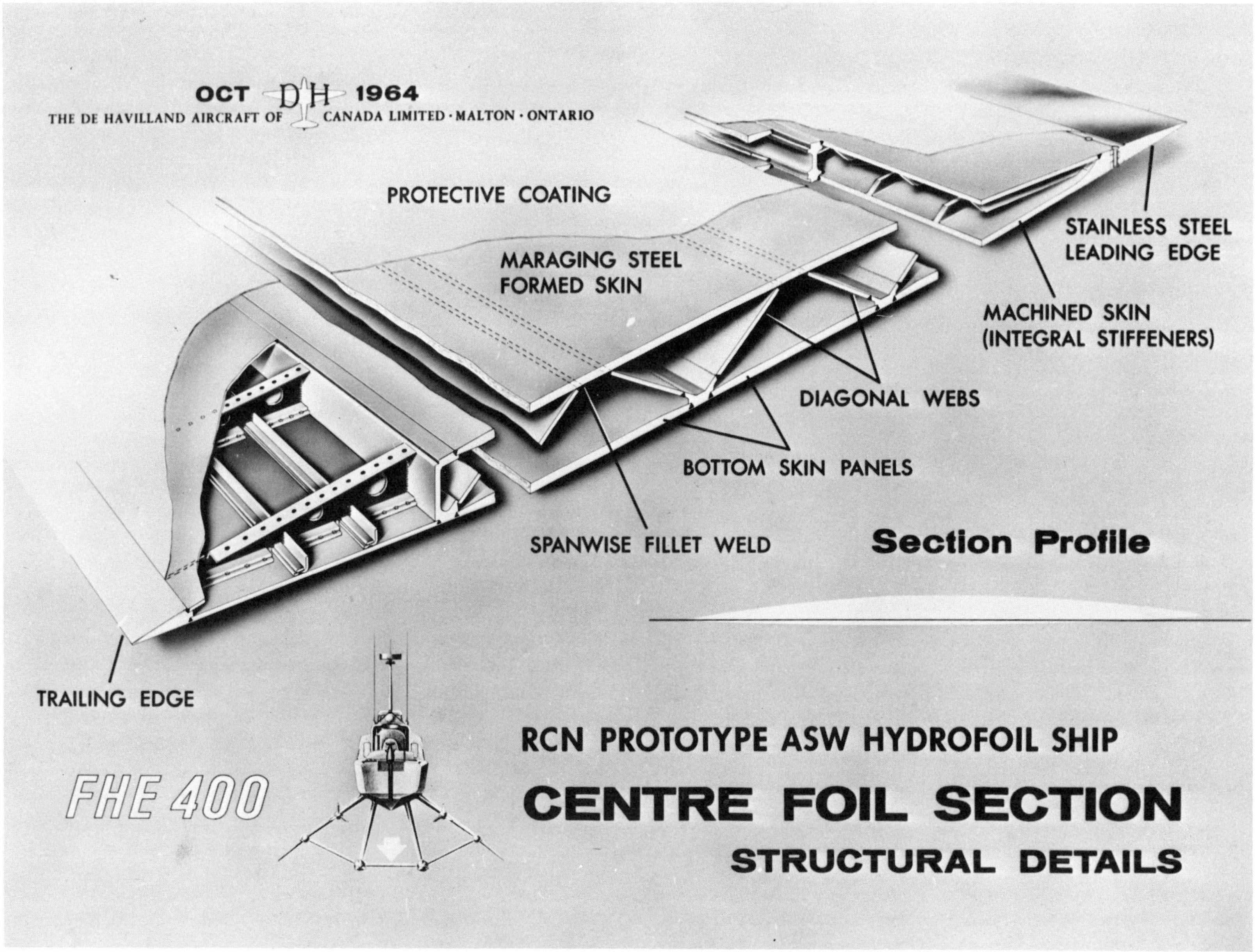

Section profile of the main high-speed foil.

dihedral foil elements were identified in the 1971 episode. At no time did these cracks constitute a hazard to the ship. Indeed, several runs were made in 1969 before the cracks were discovered and the long-distance 'Triangle Run' in 1971 was made with the centre high-speed foil completely filled with water!

DeHavilland and North American Aviation shared in the final assembly of the main foil elements as outlined previously. The first foil surface was completed and subjected to proof-loading in the test frame at Malton on November 15, 1965. The first strut and foilborne pod skeleton was welded together on the same date and 'skinning' began in November as well. All foil units were delivered to M.I.L. by May 11, 1966.

Early in the model and computer simulation tests, it was shown that with slow (20-30 knots) variable depth sonar towing speeds, there might exist an inherent instability. Although scale models and simulation showed this, it was not known whether this would be manifested in the actual full-scale craft or not. It was decided in the December 20, 1963 meeting of the Research Control Committee in Ottawa that although the proposed incidence-controlled anhedral tips might not be needed, the very nature of *FHE-400* as a 'prototype' would dictate that these be fitted to investigate their influence in aiding roll control and assisting in turns. Although in trials these indeed did do these two functions quite well, there remained the thought that these heavy, two-ton, moveable anhedral tips added a further one million dollars to an already runaway budget. By 1971 it was conceded that some re-engineering of the foil system would do away with any need of these tips in a follow-on class.[14]

The main dihedral foils used delayed-cavitation sections with six-inch fences to prevent uncontrolled ventilation. The foils were of surface-piercing type and were non-retractable. Although this increased hullborne draught to twenty-three feet six inches, it gave *FHE-400* the stability of an average frigate without the top hamper roll and pitch when hullborne in rough seas. The entire foil arrangement was significantly different from systems adopted by the US and European navies. The canard arrangement did away with the excessive overhang as seen in the AG(EH) *Plainview* in the US. The main foil arrangement carried 90% of the ship's weight, which meant a centre of balance further aft than any other comparable craft. It also allowed for a finer-lined hull, since the propulsion equipment was situated aft, over the main foil arrangement. This was a decided advantage in the open North Atlantic where the hydrofoil was intended to operate and set *Bras d'Or* apart in the military aspect of its design.[15]

A central, submerged, horizontal foil made this a heavily-damped and efficient unit and was supported by two nearly vertical struts. Outboard of these were intersecting dihedral and anhedral foil elements and at the end of the latter, the incidence-controlled anhedral tips. Fences on the struts, near the foilborne propulsion pods, incorporated ram inlets for saltwater cooling water pick-up. The horizontal and dihedral foils were pin-jointed and each forged end-fitting of the anhedral foils and struts were bolted to the foil foundation by sixteen bolts. These fittings were in turn streamlined by large fibreglass fairings to the foil and strut surfaces and the hull.[16]

The leading edges of the foils were replaceable, being external from the coating and were made of stainless steel, except those of the main anhedral foils, which were plastic.

Quite naturally the foilborne pods figured into the foil assembly, since they joined the dihedrals with the centre, high-speed foil. The hullborne pods, as previously noted, were faired into and formed part of the anhedral foil unit.[17]

Hydraulics: the main hydraulic system operated at 3,000 psi and was supplied by two sets of three pumps originally; a continuous-duty set and an intermittent duty set. All six were mounted on and driven by the auxiliary gearbox. A fourth peak duty pump was used to supplement hydraulic power during foilborne operation. All the main pumps were supplied from a 42-gallon (US) reservoir, pressurized by air at 60 psi from the pneumatic system. Hydraulic system isolation was made manually to contain leakage within one particular system or branch. Hydraulic accumulators were installed in the system at the steering actuator and on the supply line to each actuator in the anhedral foils.

A self-contained emergency hydraulic system was supplied by two pumps driven by the GTCP-85 emergency turbine. The emergency system reservoir was the same as that used in the main system and the emergency system could be cross-connected as required. The lines were of stainless steel and aluminium alloy with flared end fittings.

Hydraulic services were many: the pumps and scavenge pumps for lubrication were powered by Vickers-type fixed displacement motors. The anhedral tips, bow steering and rake were hydraulically actuated. The controlled-pitch propellers utilized by hydraulic pressure to change and maintain pitch (see Table 4-1).[18]

Most of the pumps were ABEX Corporation units, supplied by Jarry Hydraulics. Bendix acted as a consultant to DeHavilland in getting the hydraulic system sorted out in late 1965-early 1966. Indeed, in January, 1966 the

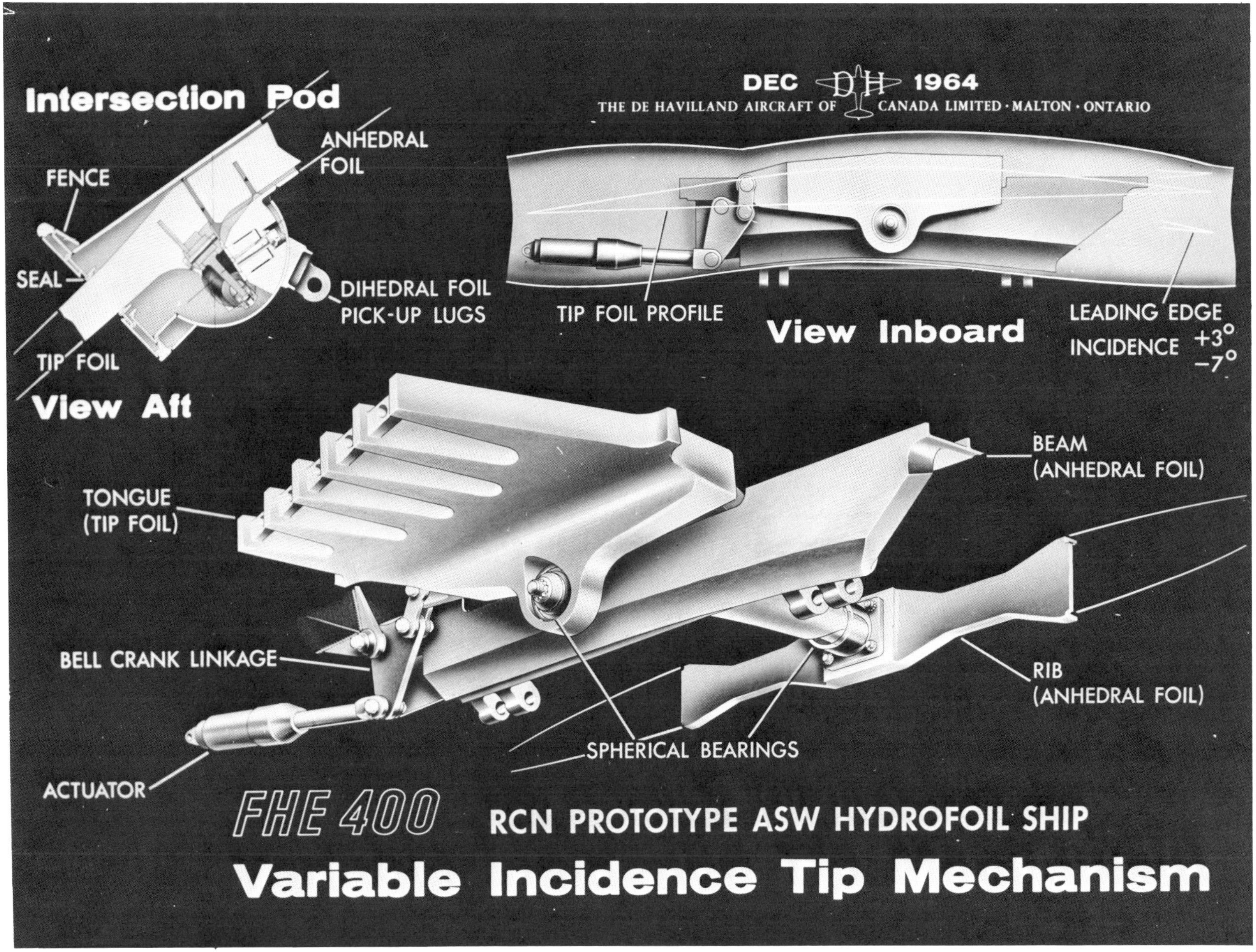

Diagram of variable incidence anhedral tip mechanism.

hydraulic system became the pacing item in completing the ship systems, with problems in installation packages, connections, pumps and actuators putting the system behind schedule.

The arrangement in pump duties was changed in 1970 to better utilize the risks of failures. Continuous duty chores were taken over by one set of ABS-AP6US pumps and one new ABS-AP12(31B) 'super-pump', used to augment flow while foilborne. Pump failures had occurred in both the AP6 and AP12V units used previously. Scoring of the bearing surfaces and material failure of the cylinder group assembly were noted as well, failure being blamed on marginal strength in the AP12V, compensation of one pump over another and aeration of hydraulic fluid in the AP6 units. Finally in December, 1970, ABEX admitted the hydraulic pumps supplied were marginal for this intended use and suggested that their new ABS-AP12(31B) be substituted for a just-failed AP12V, the flow rates being 45 versus 30 gallons per minute respectively. Additionally, the price per unit dropped to $1,400 per unit and these proved far superior in performance for the last seven months of *Bras d'Or*'s operational lifetime.[19]

Fuel: a common fuel was used to supply all four engines and was controlled from the fuel control panel on the Engineer's Console. JP5 was the normal fuel, but JP4 or marine distillate diesel fuel was acceptable. Fuel was stored in four tanks, numbered one through four, from forward to aft. These were below deck number two and transferred fuel to the engine supply line by centrifugal pumps. Fuel was normally drawn from tank three and the fuel level in this tank maintained by pumping from the three other tanks. Two coalescing filters paralleled in the engine supply line, capable of passing maximum flow singly in case of clogging. Flowmeters controlled fuel flow to each engine and were opened or closed from the Engineer's Console. Each tank vented into a common tank, which in turn vented overboard. Refuelling was by a single point on the main deck, aft of the FT4 transmission housing (see Table 4-2).[20]

Pneumatic System: pneumatic or compressed air at 3000 psi was supplied by two hydraulic motor-driven air compressors, with a capacity of 8 cubic feet per minute. After passing through moisture separators and dehydrators, the compressed air was stored in 3000 cubic inch reservoirs. A separate 900-cubic-inch reservoir provided an emergency air supply for diesel engine starting, in case of complete air or electrical failure. The high-pressure air leaving the main reservoirs was pressure-regulated according to requirements as noted in Table 4-3.

The two main air compressors formed part of a package that was suspended from the deckhead, between stations 118 feet and 120 feet 6 inches in the engine room, aft of the auxiliary turbine. Included in the package were the following; vacuum switches, moisture separators, chemical dryers, filters, high and low shore charging connections. The three reservoirs were housed in the port side workshops, aft of the engine room proper.

Air conditioning: the grab-all name is misleading, since it also covered the heating plant. It was designed to maintain a pre selected ship temperature within the hull, with a relative humidity of 50% and to ventilate critical areas such as the engine room and electronics bays. With ambient temperatures of −10° to +85°, the compartments were temperature controlled to the following values; accommodation areas 70-85° F, store areas 50-100° F, engine room 50-130° F . . . at least on paper.

However in practice the temperature control was found wanting, especially in the accommodation areas. Crew areas forward were found to be 10-15 degrees cooler than areas aft of the cafeteria. This was judged to be the fault of lack of zone heat or cooling controls. All heat was controlled from a centralized area and was found to be too inflexible for individual areas. The only method of control was to cut off the vents in the too warm areas, which then invited dampness.[21]

Air was taken in through the intake on the foilborne inboard transmission housing aft and fed into a heat exchanger by the intake fans. Heat normally came from either the diesel or ST6 exhaust ducts. Hence up the two main ducts went the heated air into the crew-combat spaces. For air conditioning the heat exchanger was by-passed and the air passed into the air conditioner plant directly, where it was cooled, dehumidified and fed into the main fore and aft supply ducts. A centreline return duct, powered by the return fan, returned stale air to the conditioning plant and the cycle was repeated. Humidity was maintained between 40-50% by the use of the dehydrators or water mist injectors.[22]

The inadequacies of the air-conditioning plant became all too apparent on the July, 1971 trip south. Half-way to Bermuda, one conditioner motor burned out, leaving the other plant to try and carry the load. Temperatures were high inside throughout the entire trip, with the limited conditioner ability directed to the trials instrumentation area to maintain a reasonable electronic equipment temperature. A major redesign of the system would have to be done for future trips and future craft.

Fresh water: for domestic use water was supplied by two means; the first was three 75-gallon freshwater tanks and the other was the Maxim Model HJ20 distillation plant. The tanks were pressurized to 35 psi for domestic

Hydraulic System — Pumps, Locations, Duties, Lubrication. Table 4-1

Component or Pump	Location	Remarks
6 (size 1) ABS-AP6VS	On auxiliary gearbox On GTCP-85 Emergency On GTCP-85 Emergency	1 continuous duty, three intermittant duty 1 emergency, variable delivery, pressure-compensating type, 15 US gallons/min. at 3750 rpm 1 foilborne operation.
3 (size 2) ABS-AP12V	On auxiliary gearbox On GTCP-85 emergency	2 continuous duty 1 emergency. Variable delivery/pressure type, rated 29.9 US GPM at 3750 rpm continuous or 47.8 GPM at 6000 rpm intermittant. One AP6 can be tandemed with a AP-12 on continuous duty if req'd.
2 Hydraulic reservoirs	port side, eng. rm., stn. 98′ stbd. side, eng. rm., stn. 100′	42 US gallon, pressurized by air at 60 psi.
3 Accumulators	port side stn. 109′ stbd. side, stn. 104′ bow foil cmpt., Stn. 14′2″	2.5 US gallon for port tip, pressurized by nitrogen to 1500 psi. 2.5 US gallon for stbd. tip, pressurized to 1500 psi. 2.5 US gallon for bow foil steering, rake.
2 outboard displacement g'box scavenge	on gearbox (All pumps for lubrication)	pumps driven by Vickers type fixed disp. motor #MF006. Flow 1.29 GPM @ 3000 rpm. Regulated at 2900 psi motor inlet, 100 psi back press.
2 outboard disp. g'box wetdown pumps	port and starboard	pumps driven via Vickers type fixed disp. motor #MF008. flow 1.739 GPM at 3000 rpm. same press.
2 f'bne pod scavenge	port and starboard	pumps driven by Vickers F.D. mtr. GMF-016. Flow rate 3.47 GPM.
2 f'bne pod bilge	port and starboard	pumps driven by Vickers F.D. motor. flow 15.47 GPM. Tandemed with scavenge by regulator.
1 f'bne feed and wetdown	port and starboard feed	two pumps in series, Vickers GMF-039, variable flow, 1000 rpm, ½ flow of 2.26 GPM; 8.10 GPM @ 3000.
1 disp. and f'bne inbd. feed and wetdown		Vickers type MF-032 motor, pump del.2.26 GPM at 1000 rpm; 8.10 GPM at 3000 rpm.
3 inbd. f'bne g'box scavenge	three areas of FT4 inbd. g'box	All three driven by Vickers F.D. motor MF-039 which was speed limited.

Table 4-2 Tank and Pump Specifications

Component	Location	Features
Pump P1-3, AC 115v	submerged in tanks 4, 2, 1	15,000 pulses per hour at 26 psi for fuel transfer, emergency displacement mode or in pairs with P9-10 for foilborne mode.
Pump P4	bolted to aft end of tank 3	1500 pph at 10 psi for sludge pumping and fuel sampling.
Pump P5 28 vDC	bolted to aft end of tank 3	1500 pph at 10 psi for normal displacement mode supply of diesel.
Pump P6 115 vAC	bolted to face of vent tank	25,000 pph at 20 psi for discharge.
Pumps P7-8 115 vAC	in engine room adjacent aft face of bulkhead 97 feet 6 inches.	15,000 pph at 26 psi for foilborne, displacement. Operates in pairs with P7 or eight.
Filter/water separator	engine room, aft face, fwd bulkhead	filters water and +30 micron dirt particles.
Tank #1	From station 33′ to 55′6″ (foremost)	4,850 US gallons.
Tank #2	From station 55′6″ to 78′	8,150 US gallons.
Tank #3	From station 78′ to 88′	4,150 US gallons. Normal feed tank.
Vent Tank	From station 108′ to 110′6″	vent fumes, overflow overboard.
Tank #4	From station 120′6″ to transom	9600 US gallons — two compartments, valve between.

NOTE: all tanks were internally baffled to minimize fuel surge. Provision for gravity feed between all tanks provided.

supply and there were two hot water tanks, one 35-gallon tank in the galley and and a 75-gallon one in the crew washroom.

Distillation: this consisted of the Maxim distiller, a heat exchanger, chlorination package, distribution pump, salinity cell and shore connection. Heat was provided by the hot saltwater from the diesel engine jacket, which passed through the heat exchanger. Here, a combination of heat and vacuum caused the seawater in the tubes to boil and the vapour (being free of salt) was condensed and collected. It was chlorinated and then pumped into the freshwater tank, after passing by the salinity cell. If too high a salt content contamination was detected by this cell, say from a defective condenser, the water would be rejected and voided over the side, rather than being allowed to contaminate the freshwater tanks.

Water from the distillation plant was erratic because of insufficient feed pump capacity and it wasn't until 1970 that the plant was finally sorted out. Production soared from an erratic 20 gallons per hour to 30-50 gallons per hour.[23] However, throughout the three and a half years the hydrofoil craft was in service, showers were either prohibited or restricted because of the limited freshwater capacity of the distillation plant.

Seawater: intake for heat exchangers, fire hydrants, distillation plant, oil conditioner cooling, cooling in the air conditioning plant, diesel intercoolers and electronic equipment bay cooling was constant. Seawater was taken into the ship through inlets in the hull at stations 118 feet 20 inches to port and starboard of the ship's centreline when in the displacement mode and through ram nozzles near the bottom of the main foil struts at station 102 feet when foilborne. These inlets could be closed manually by hand-operated sea cocks. Water from the inlets was stored in the sea chest, abaft the diesel at station 117 feet and from there it was transferred through a strainer to a main supply manifold. The water was moved by a impeller type pump at 45 psi hullborne and 60 psi foilborne. This impeller-type pump was driven by the auxiliary gearbox. The GTCP-85 emergency turbine drove a fire pump which in turn supplied the fire hydrants at 150 psi, if necessary. Additionally, the fire pump could transfer seawater from the sea chest to the main supply manifold in case of main system failure. After use, the cooling water was dumped overboard through valve-controlled hull outlets.

Bilges: four compartments required bilging. These were formed by the hull skin and were compartmentized, with no. 2 deck forming the upper containment. These lay between the following stations and were bilged by a 28 vDC Jabsco self-priming pump.

Bilge #1 — stations 10 feet 6 inches to 33 feet.
Bilge #2 — stations 88 feet to 97 feet 6 inches.
Bilge #3 — stations 97 feet 6 inches to 108 feet.
Bilge #4 — stations 113 feet to 120 feet 6 inches.

Each bilge compartment was outfitted with a float switch, which activated the pump when raised high enough. The pump would then draw bilging through the interconnecting tubing and vent it overboard, port side, below the gunwale. The tanks were atmosphere vented.

Sanitary Systems: heads were flushed directly overboard. This proved troublesome in rough weather, since if the toilet was flushed as a surging sea encountered the hull in hullborne mode, it overcame the built-in check valves causing some spectacular reverse venting into the crew's washroom!

'Grey' water disposal was automatic, collecting in three collector tanks, which when filled were pumped overboard through ¾ inch discharge ports below the waterline. Pumping was automatically controlled by two pressure switches.

Furniture Fits: since *Bras d'Or* was the first warship in Canada of this type, it was logical that an aircraft firm would be approached to build the various

T. Lynch — Table 4-3 Pneumatic System

Services Tended	Pressure Required and Regulated
Diesel engine normal and emergency prime/start	325 psi
Displacement transmission shaft clutches	128 psi
Diesel fuel rack stop actuators	128 psi
Diesel governor speed control	60 psi
Main gas turbine high pressure starting	750 psi
Auxiliary turbine fuel atomisation (cold weather)	60 psi
Seawater intakes and sea chest blow down	35 psi
Fresh water reservoir pressurization	35 psi
Hydraulic reservoir	60 psi
Lubricating oil conditioner, condensate pump	35 psi
Windshield washer tank pressurization	60 psi
Air whistle	100 psi
Compressor wash tank pressurization	128 psi
General workshop use	100 psi
Weapons charging provision (not used)	2000 psi

NOTE:
Hydraulic requirements by compressors was 4.9 gallons per minute at 3600 rpm.

pieces of furniture required (outside of crew bunks). Timmins Aviation was approached to build and lay out the furniture according to specifications set out in an N.R.C. study into hydrofoil craft accommodations. Because of the specifications that all NCO's and Officers' settees be dual purpose, these pieces of furniture were unsatisfactory. When the settee was folded down into a bed, it lost approximately one-third of its width. Additionally, they were found to be hard to work, binding easily.[24]

Timmins was also responsible for the galley and did an admirable job given the small space available. There were two microwave ovens at chest level, a flat-top griddle at the stern end of the galley against the starboard side, a floor level oven, two freezer units, a refrigerator, a dual hot plate, two electric sauce pans, a coffee maker and toaster, the last four items being counter-top appliances. However, it was found that because the hot cooking surfaces were so handy to the freezer and refrigerator these items ran continuously, contributing further to the heat in the galley and cafeteria areas.

Bunks were laid out athwartships, rather than fore and aft as in most conventional ships, largely because of space limitations. At no time did these cause any more inconvenience to the crew than did the more conventional layout and were judged acceptable. However, the fixed reading lights were found wanting, since they could not be trained so as not to bother others if one wished to read in bed. Additionally, the clothing closets were judged too narrow and no space had been allowed for shoe storage. However, this was what *FHE-400* was to do . . . identify defects so they could be rectified in a possible follow-on class of hydrofoil warships.

Cathodic Corrosion Protection System: introduced into the *FHE-400* project at a later date, this was awarded to Hydronautics Incorporated in 1965 and used a continuous cathode strip down each side of the ship, just below the displacement waterline. As with most cathodic systems, the cathode strip was mildly charged and corroded faster than metal in the ship structure. However, it was powerless to stop the corrosion within the damaged foil sections in 1969 and 1971.

Lubrication: there were two systems of lubrication for the hullborne and foilborne modes. The pumps were driven by the auxiliary gearbox in the hullborne mode. These provided lubrication oil to the displacement gearboxes and displacement downshaft bearings, the latter being adjustable by needle valves in the engineroom. The foilborne transmissions were prewetted during the displacement mode, or just prior to foilborne transition. During the pre-wet, the pumps were increased from one-third to full flow at 1325 rpm automatically via a speed switch on the FT4 transmission gearbox. The hydraulically-driven scavenge pumps continued to run in conjunction with the gear-driven feed pumps until another speed switch on the FT4 transmission cut them out at about 2825 rpm on the turbine. When returned to the hullborne mode, the process was reversed, other than the hydraulically-driven pumps being restarted at 2675 rpm and the gear-driven feed pumps reverting to wet down mode at 1175 rpm. Lubricating oil to each set of down-shaft bearings and propulsion pods was 17.4 gallons per minutes at 20 psi, with operating temperatures of between 100°-210° F. There were definite problems with lubrication to the lower pods during hullborne operation in cold North Atlantic waters. The temperature of the oil dropped below 60° F on occasion, allowing pressures of 100 psi to build up because of the thickened lube oil. This was remedied by the installation of heaters in the lube oil tanks that could be engaged when oil temperature returning from the pods fell below 80° F.

All lubrication oil was contained in three 170-gallon (US) insulated tanks and two 35-gallon tanks. Two of the larger tanks supplied the outboard foilborne pods and the other served the inboard gearboxes. The two 35-gallon tanks served the displacement outboard transmissions and bearings.

All lubrication oil went through the Bowser conditioning plant, but only one tank at a time could be conditioned. The plant was brought into play when the sensor detected excessive particulate matter in the oil flow. Filters were changed at 200 running hours maximum or sooner if required.

Electronics: although a comprehensive sensor fit was planned and built for *FHE-400*, only the Phase I fit was ever made. This included a communications fit, intercom, radar, gyro-compass, Decca navigator and echo sounder.

Communications: there were two single-sideband, high-frequency transceivers and one ultra-high frequency set fitted aboard. Destroyer-type whip antennae were found to be too short for the higher frequencies of the HF set, causing the antenna-match couplings to work at maximum levels. The HF antennae were replaced in April, 1971 after corrosion made the old ones nearly useless. The Fleet communication fit of radio-teletype and second UHF set was not made. These sets were supplied by Collins Radio Co., on February 15, 1966 at $17,946.

Radar: selection of an appropriate radar began in 1963, with searches conducted in the UK and the USA. However, nothing quite meeting the criteria of the ship was found in these countries. Weight was a prime factor, as well as performance, resistance to shock failure, robustness of the scanner head, versatility and availability of parts. It was finally decided in

1965 that the best of the two finalists was the NV Hallandse Signaallppar-aten, Hengelo, Netherlands, Type 8GR300-03A X-band surveillance/navigation radar. Without modification, it was purchased for $82,000. Modifications were made by Canadian General Electric to allow the integration of the AIS fit, including the provision for repeaters on the bridge and Action Information Centre, but the latter was not fitted. The radar performed admirably, with only minor clutter of the screen during rough weather and the near-loss of the scanner head in 1970 when the mounting bolts sheared.[25]

Navigation: a Decca Navigator with Mk.23 repeater on the bridge was fitted aboard the hydrofoil, giving satisfactory fixes until the late months of 1970, when errors of one mile threw serious doubts onto the reliability of its bearings. However, this was ultimately traced to interference. The echo sounder was fair, but the acoustic 'window' was masked by underwater wash above four knots, making it only suitable for spot checks. A pelorus on the bridge made visual navigation easy during the day, swinging up out of the way against the bridge's deckhead, just abaft the windows. However, night navigation was limited by the bridge structure supports towards the stern and when foilborne, FT4 stack effluent masked the whole stern horizon and made astral fixes a joke. Hence, navigation was largely done by Decca and the radar; there were no provisions for lookouts, clearly showing that a seaman or serving officer hadn't been consulted in the design phase!

Fighting Equipment: all the following entries were slated for Phase I and II fitting of the *FHE-400* fighting suite. This was intended to evaluate the performance of the equipment and their integration aboard a high-speed hydrofoil ship.

As in most cases with this ship, only one company showed an interest in competing for this particular contract. This was Canadian Westinghouse Co. Ltd., Hamilton, Ontario. They were awarded a contract worth $233,850 on October 4, 1965 to conduct a fighting equipment design study. It should be noted that this was a separate contract awarded by the Department of Defence Production and Treasury Board, with only system integration consultation with DeHavilland.[26]

The design study contract covered the design criteria of a computer-controlled Information Centre that would process sonar and radar contacts, solve ballistic and ASW torpedo firing angles, while accurately updating the tactical 'picture' to both weapons and AIS crewmembers at their respective stations. This was no small task, as computer equipment would have to be as lightweight as possible, be resistant to shock and temperature variations, be extremely reliable and versatile.

Severe problems were encountered in both this and the subsequent detail design and construction contract. The capabilities of the system, coupled with the lightweight construction and reliability factors required, clearly called for a lot of design work.

However, the package began to come together in 1966, with only the continued plague of problems in the IBM 2402 programme computer holding up the installation of the Programme Generation Centre at C.W.C.'s Hamilton facility. The projected date of April, 1966 was slipped accordingly and the Centre did not begin work until July 1967. This was not a calamity, since the hydrofoil could not be delivered until mid-1968.

Phase I of the Fighting Equipment called for the installation of the radar, navigation equipment and intercom, all of which were provided in late 1966.

Phase II called for the installation of the Action Information Centre, software, integration of the AN/SQS-507 sonar, Phillips radar into this system, fighting equipment package integration (ASW torpedo ballistics computation, arming, etc.)

As noted, Phase I saw numerous uses throughout the trials of 1968-71, but the Phase II equipment never made it past the Maritime Warfare School. The completed Canadian Westinghouse contract for $7,171,305 was finally re-negotiated on October 15, 1968. The completed AIS system was installed at the Maritime Warfare School by Cameron Windows Ltd., under a contract dated April 30 1968 for $3,843.[27]

Additionally, the AIS Hughes display equipment was purchased from the USN at a cost of $594,700 under a contract dated July 3, 1968.

Sonar: with an established need for a lightweight variable depth sonar, it was only natural to turn to Canadian Westinghouse for assistance in design, since they had been instrumental in the nearly-finished design and construction of the AN/SQS-504 and 505 VDS sonar arrays for conventional frigates and destroyers.

N.R.E., with their up-to-half-scale high-speed towed body research facility, *Baddeck*, had been instrumental in designing the shaped towed bodies and had devised a faired cable profile that had seriously reduced 'kiting' of the body at high speeds. *Baddeck* successfully towed half-scale bodies to the to-scale speed of 40 knots.

The electronics, transducer and energy storage were very similar to the

AN/SQS-505 (*DIANA I*) VDS, with 70% of the drawings identical. However, the transducer was scaled down to fulfill the task and meet the weight and space limitations. Fleet Manufacturing Ltd., was then contracted to produce a lightweight version of the VDS handling gear then being tooled for the steam frigates. Contract was completed and delivered on January 22, 1969 at a cost of $557,500. The high-speed VDS bodies were produced by Hawker-Siddeley in 1965 for $66,766.[28]

Torpedo tubes: orginally four groups of three Mk.32 lightweight torpedo tubes were to be installed. This was later changed to two fits of triple tubes with Mk.46 torpedoes, angled at 90° to the ship's centreline and angled downward. A limiting sensor was developed to inhibit firing a torpedo when ship roll made the torpedo entry-angle too oblique, since the Mk.46 would then broach. This system although complete, was not fitted.

Overall this was an entirely separate programme from the actual hydrofoil ship and as such should not be included in the Basic Ship cost, although this has been done in the past by politicians, reporters and other misinformed persons. This accounted for $8,749,946 of the contract totals.[29]

The last item, for which no provision had been made in the original design was a 'slave' dock. It was realized in late 1965 that the Syncro-Lift facility then under construction in HMC Dockyard, Halifax would not be finished in time to accommodate the hydrofoil ship during refits or other underwater modifications or repairs. A contract was let for a steel dumb barge, capable of being flooded. After submersion the hydrofoil could then be guided over it and then the barge pumped out, lifting the craft clear of the water. Ferguson Industries of Pictou, N.S., were successful in their bid for an approximate $700,000. This barge was delivered to Halifax in late 1966, since it was planned that the hydrofoil ship would proceed to Halifax under her own power, hullborne, after final systems checks. However November 5, 1966 changed all this.

Chapter Five

The Great Fire

Slippage continued in the completion of *FHE-400*, largely through continued problems with hydraulics and delayed delivery of the foilborne transmission system. September and October passed and November arrived, with pre-launch system checks being conducted six days a week. However, it was realized that it would not be possible to deliver *Bras d'Or* until after the spring break-up of the ice in the St. Lawrence River . . . ice was forming early that year, further up river.

Saturday, November 5 was a bright, cold day, presaging the more bitter weather to come shortly. DeHavilland personnel were in the yard to test various systems for certification. As a result of the hurried pace of testing of the past month, paperwork had fallen behind and half the certificates of proof-testing and approval were still to be had; no one was quite sure which sub-assemblies of each system had been tested or certified. Each inspection team found that they were approving both sub-assemblies and systems in some cases, which was dangerous and time-consuming.

At about 14:30, a DeHavilland test team moved on to begin testing of the 115/200 vAC generation system. This necessitated the running of the ST6A-53 gas turbine to run the auxiliary gearbox, which drove the generators. As an incidental, the hydraulic pumps were also being run to provide proper loading of the auxiliary gearbox. The engine room was filled with the high-pitched scream of the ST6 and the whine of the gearbox as the lone DeHavilland technician moved about the engine compartment, checking electrical connections and testing AC output.[1] The test had been going on for some eighteen minutes when the technician, being near the ST6 corner, port side, observed a narrow stream of hydraulic fluid, micro-seconds before being hit in the face and eyes, unable to raise his hands to ward off the hot fluid. As the technician reeled blindly back, the same stream sprayed over the ST6 body and stack. The chamber casing only reached 400° F when running and only acrid smoke resulted, but the highly-volatile fluid found the uninsulated joint in the exhaust stack, which had reached 1000° F and the fluid immediately ignited. This was closely followed by a flash fire that spread along the deckhead, burning the chest and arms of the DeHavilland employee. As he staggered toward the forward bulkhead hatch, he was met by the stand-by technician, tasked with turning on the partially-installed fire suppression system. Faced with the choice of doing his duty or saving his friend from the fire, this man chose to preserve life and helped the badly burned man to the upper deck. Meanwhile an intense secondary fire had taken root, fed by a ruptured coupling in the hydraulic line. The ST6 continued to run, turning the auxiliary gearbox and pumps, feeding the ever-spreading conflagration more hydraulic oil through the original leak and now burned-through hydraulic hoses. The fire roared louder and began to attack the aluminium ship structure, which began to sag under the intense heat. The remainder of the ship filled with choking, black, oily smoke.

Meanwhile, the four M.I.L. firemen on duty, arrived within five minutes of the outbreak, at 15:20. They immediately set up, donning Scott breathers and began to fight the fire with available equipment. However, within minutes it was realized that the intensity of the fire was more than they could cope with and the Sorel Municipal Fire Department was called in at 15:25. Battling the stubborn fire and dense choking smoke, the fire was smothered into extinction by 16:00.[2]

The picture *Bras d'Or* presented to the hastily-assembled Fire Investigation Committee two days later was a dismal one. The deck and hull, particularly to port was burned through and buckled in other places. Entering the ship, everything reeked of unburned hydraulic oil, hydrocarbons and everything else was covered with a thick, gritty layer of soot. Entering the engine room, remnants of firefighting foam and pools of sooty hydraulic fluid, sodden insulation and charred rubber were underfoot, while electrical wiring, tubing and pipes drooped from the deckhead. The hydraulic tanks, auxiliary gearbox and ST6 were blackened ruins, while overhead, deck beams sagged downwards, attesting to the intensity of the fire. It looked like the hydrofoil project was at the least badly delayed, and more than likely cancelled.

Reconstruction of the fire immediately began with depositions from all parties on or near the fire scene. The filthy mess in the engine room was probed for surviving bits and pieces and the fire's progress mapped out by the degree of severity of damage. The sifting went on and the reconstruction results were handed over to the Fire Investigation Committee, who in turn completed their findings on November 25, 1966. These, after deliberation, were turned over to the Chief of Naval Staff, Ottawa and hence to the Minister of Defence.[3]

In one of the best stone-walling efforts to be mounted in recent years, the government quashed any controversy over the incident in both the House and publicly. It wasn't until the March 11, 1969 Minutes of Proceedings and Evidence No. 23, Standing Committee on Public Accounts, 1st Session, 28th Parliament, that the public gained any access to the truth surrounding the fire. And by then . . . who cared?

The results of the DND/DDP and DeHavilland investigations were fairly close in fact. The most probable cause had been a hydraulic leak in a flex hose and clamp connection, used in large quantities in the low pressure (60 psi) side of the hydraulic system. Evidence pointed to the fact that some of these connectors were improperly installed and there was no record to indicate that certain of these connections had been inspected by DeHavilland personnel prior to the November 5 testing!

Other conclusions reached were that the accident had not been the result of negligence on the part of the test crew, that firefighting provision and organisation had been inadequate to cope with a fire of this magnitude and that inspection records did not afford proof that the hydraulic system had been fully inspected. Documentary evidence of quality assurance was incomplete and worst of all, that the Naval Overseer's Office had not been extended the courtesy of notification of testing planned on November 5!

Recommendations of the Committee were as follows:

1. That firefighting provisions and organisation be improved.
2. That improved fireproof fluid couplings be used in lieu of the hose and clamp connections where risk of fire was great if a leak should develop.
3. That flammable fluid be isolated where practical from potential ignition sources.
4. That DND Overseer's Office, Sorel, be informed in writing, in advance of any testing.
5. That investigation continue to determine other areas of design where potentially dangerous or inadequate for intended purpose faults might exist.
6. That quality assurance requirements be made more stringent and explicit.

Now that a cause had been found, members of the 1969 Public Accounts Committee began a witchhunt with DND/DDP representatives, led by Mr. Lloyd Crouse, M.P. It is not the purpose of this account to quote remarks, but some of the points made at least partially explained what had gone wrong.

1. DeHavilland and other sub-contractors had been issued with a cost reimbursement type contract with built-in performance cash awards. These contracts had allowed the contractor to develop this hybrid naval craft, for which there had never been a parallel in Canadian shipbuilding, with minimum RCN input. Thus they had been allowed to specify systems, designs and construction materials without submitting drawings and specifications for approval of the Naval Engineer's Office or the Department of Defence Production. The unique performance and requirements, so in common with aircraft practice had been entrusted to DeHavilland and quality assurance to people more familar with aircraft than a hybrid ship. DND and DDP were at fault here, allowing assurance, certification of performance and specifications to be laid out and in some cases, allowed to become marginal. In the case of systems testing in the fall of 1966, DeHavilland had allowed certification and proof-testing records to become haphazard to the point where no one was sure what had been tested and if tested, had it been tested in entirety? Apparently not, since a fitting tested to 300 psi failed at 60 psi through improper installation.

2. That DND and DDP had been lax in not foreseeing the possibilities of problems of this nature because of ill-defined procedures of specifications' safety margins, compliance to specifications and quality control of the finished product. Too much blind faith and responsibility had been placed in the manufacturer who, by past performance, had shown a propensity for getting into contractual tight corners and technical problems beyond their ability to solve.

3. That a lack of communication between the DeHavilland personnel and the Naval Overseer's Office at Sorel had allowed potentially dangerous testing to be done without the knowledge of that Office, although liability of any damages was with the Crown.

4. The latter finding bears a bit of explanation and background history. Self-insurance by the Crown dates back to a 1881 decision by the government of the day which decided that in view of the large amount, varied character and widely separated positions of property in the Dominion

belonging to the Crown, it was wise economy for the government to underwrite its own risks on all moveable or immoveable properties.

From that time for the next fifty years or so there were very few exceptions made. One was made in the case of the Supreme Court Library: because of the very high value of the books authority was given to privately insure the steam boilers because this led to automatic inspection by the insurance companies. Additionally, External Affairs was given the privilege of third-party insurance in foreign countries where Crown self-insurance would be unacceptable by the host country. Another exception was National Revenue on outgoing shipments of stamps.

In 1952 when the Department of Defence Production was formed, they were about to write standard contract forms, so they referred to Treasury Board to have them confirm or change for future use, the policy of self-insurance. Treasury Board directed DDP to put into all standard contracts on plant equipment, machinery, jigs, fixtures, dyes and tools of all kinds that they have no insurance on any parts, equipment, government-furnished property, raw materials, work in progress, finished goods or anything that the Crown owned, except in the case where it was impossible through a co-mingling of Crown and contractors-civilian production requirements to determine what was Crown owned and what was not, and in that case they directed DDP to allow the contractor to carry insurance.

One of these cases happens to be the shipbuilding and repair business, which are normally of short duration. Where a Crown-owned ship would occupy space for a month or two with a civilian or privately-owned ship in proximity, Treasury Board directed DDP to allow the contractor to carry liability insurance, such as Marine Builder's Risk Insurance. *Bonaventure* was so covered when a small fire broke out in 1968.

The other two types of ship construction were reviewed in 1952. Most contracts were cost-reimbursable at this time, so Treasury Board instructed DDP not to insure them; the Crown would self-insure. These were the regulations when the *FHE-400* contract was drawn up. Since DDP/Treasury Board assured the contractor that the Crown was self-insuring the ship, the Justice Department informed DDP, Dehavilland and M.I.L. that indemnification had been given the contractors by DDP. This was the same as under the Builder's Risk policy, thus making the Crown completely liable for any damages. This indemnification took the place of an insurance policy. This was the second type of ship construction: cost-reimbursable.

In the case of firm price new construction, which became DDP policy after the fire, DDP were looking at these cases with DND to see if third-party insurance would be advantageous on a case-by-case evaluation. The *DDH-280* ship was the first major ship construction to be considered under this new policy.

However, the fact remained: based on the Treasury Board decisions made in 1952, DDP had let this unique ship be constructed under the Crown self-insuring, cost-reimbursing contract. Paradoxically the standard practice of submission of all specifications and design were waived since it was thought that the greatest latitude granted the manufacturer would produce the best product. In all fairness the other side of the coin must be examined. Testimony presented at the Public Accounts meetings showed that in examining the fire losses DDP had experienced in the thirteen years previous to 1969, it was found that losses totalled some $5.7 million, including the $3.25 million real loss figure for the hydrofoil ship. These real costs did not consider potential losses to programmes. If DDP had insured in these cases with a third-party, it would have cost $1 million per year for new construction, whereas it had cost $400,000 a year in fire losses, averaged over the thirteen years. Hence, theoretically, the Crown saved at least $500,000-$600,000 per year by self-insuring or a gross saving of $8 million for this period.

Getting back to the question of who was responsible or at fault, the simplest answer is everyone.

1. DeHavilland for allowing shoddy inspection practices to enter the construction programme at so late a date. Also for not co-operating more fully with the Naval Overseer's Office at Sorel.
2. DDP/DND for not insisting that the Crown self-insurance contract be more closely examined by Treasury Board as a high-risk, high-loss, unique proposal and insuring accordingly. Terms of quality control and specifications should have been more stringent. Mandatory submissions of design specifications should have been made before construction and formed part of the performance package of the contract.
3. M.I.L. for not identifying the serious fire risk that DHC personnel were courting in their piecemeal inspections and tests, providing the necessary fire precautions closer the hydrofoil craft at the very least.
4. The Naval Overseer's Office for not keeping a closer liaison with DHC and effectively overseeing their activities. They then would have been aware of the risks DHC were running in an effort to complete this seriously-delayed ship.[4]

Meanwhile, during the investigation, a Ship Review Committee had been set up. Ship design review began on December 2, 1966, after the fire investigation was completed. The redesign recommendations of the Fire

Investigation Committee were incorporated as much as possible, although the removal of the hydraulic tanks proved impossible. Instead, a hydraulic fluid with a far higher flash point was discovered and utilized. Other suggestions on strengthening the hull in the engine room area were incorporated as well, with the fate of *Bras d'Or* hung in the scales.

From November, 1966 until March, 1967 the Minister of Defence withheld the decision to proceed or scrap, pending completion of the investigations and formulation of new procedures to be implemented if the program was resumed. Finally on April 13, 1967 a submission was made to Treasury Board to continue the hydrofoil ship project, with a ceiling of $50,006,000. However, this was a whole new situation since DDP/DND had redefined and renegotiated certain aspects of the contract. Major points affecting the contractor were:

1. Government inspections over and above manufacturer's/contractor's inspections.
2. Improved engineering, production and quality control by DeHavilland and government participation and surveillance in all matters.
3. Better integration of management procedures with those of government to control costs and improve cost-effectiveness.
4. Improved fire and safety standards.

The contract was re-negotiated on a new pricing basis in April and duly received Treasury Board approval. The contract was divided into three elements;

Element 1 — Covering the period from 1963 to the date of the fire and including a fixed fee settlement in lieu of the best available performance estimate of what DHC had earned under the cash-incentive programme (PERT), had not the fire occurred, minus late cost penalties (since it was proven the hydrofoil ship couldn't have been made ready until the summer of 1967). The final net total to DeHavilland was $180,000 based on the approximate $27,150,000 worth of work, a profit margin of two-thirds of one percent of total value.

Element 2 — Covering the cost of repairing the fire damage and completing the ship construction up until delivery. This was estimated at $7.5 million, the contractor to receive a fixed fee of $281,000 for this portion.

Element 3 — Covering post-delivery work, fixed time rate basis. This remained unchanged from the original contract.

A Joint Management Review Board was set up in early 1967 to oversee the entire programme, comprised of the President and three Vice-presidents from DHC and senior representatives of DND and DDP, meeting every six to eight weeks while the ship was at Sorel and with the same frequency after the ship was delivered to Halifax. For the first time cost and delivery schedules came into line and increased costs could be anticipated, rather than showing up as an after-the-fact surprise at budget time. However past performance left tender spots, easily bruised when unforeseen costs cropped up, such as the foil cracking in 1969 and 1971.

Meanwhile in March of 1967, it was tentatively known that the Minister of Defence was going to allow construction to continue. DeHavilland and M.I.L. began to remove the damaged machinery on March 31 and each piece was sent back to the respective sub-contractor for rebuilding where possible.

After the contract was signed in April, the green light was given on starting structural repairs starting May 1. This involved cutting out damaged structural members, deck beams and ship skin, sectioning in new members and 'reskinning' the affected area of the hull. Unsubstantiated reports claim that additional strengthening in the engine room area were carried out at this time, since this area had been found to be marginally rigid enough.

The recommendations of the Fire Investigation Committee were taken to heart and the Ship Review Committee had studied various improvements to the ship's systems with the view of incorporating added safety measures, reducing fire hazards and improving systems where possible. All connectors of the type suspected of starting the fire were eliminated, improved hydraulic components, including the troublesome actuators from Jarry were installed, as well as hundreds of smaller items throughout the ship. These review and improvement schemes were completed on April 30, 1968. Design review procurement was completed May 31, 1968 and installed immediately. Repaired machinery had been returned to M.I.L. by January 12 and installation completed by Feburary 15 1968.

Testing of propulsion/emergency machinery began on March 31, with completion of the ST6 function trials. Diesel functions testing was done on May 3 and GT85 functions verified and passed on the 9th.

The last items delivered and installed before the ship was to be delivered were the Jarry Hydraulic units. They were only four weeks behind in delivery and final tests were completed on June 22, 1968. By this time all ship systems were certified, with only the final seal and pressure tests of the pods and struts to be completed on July 4. Of course the foilborne transmission system was not yet installed.

The ship was transferred from adjacent no. 5 berth, on to the slave dock and readied to leave Sorel on July 12.

Summarizing the effects of the fire upon the hydrofoil programme, the time factor was the most crucial. In order for DND to consider hydrofoil craft in their 1969 new equipment procurement programme (the latest date that DND could tolerate in defining new-replacement ship types), *Bras d'Or* would have to prove itself capable of all design criteria *before* 1969, now an impossibility. The foilborne transmission system, plagued by mechanical failures, arrived too late to see the *first* foilborne trip until mid-1969 and indeed pre-acceptance trials were not completed until early 1971!

Clearly, *Bras d'Or* had been robbed of any consideration as a replacement class by the fire in part, but the great leap in technology necessary to produce a complete ship of this type proved too great in too short a time frame. Most authorities in Defence Procurement to this day claim a period of at least eleven years for a new weapon or ship type is necessary; Canada tried it in five and a half years and failed . . . but not by much.

Chapter Six

Gremlins, Headaches, Frustrations ...but boy it flies

July 12, 1968 was a bright, typically humid and hot St. Lawrence River Valley summer day when *Bras d'Or* was coaxed out into the river by the tugs *L'Aiglon* and CFAV *St. Charles*. Once clear of the M.I.L. marine railway, *L'Aiglon* yielded her place to CFAV *Riverton* and the pair started the long tow to Halifax on the thirteenth.[1] Because of the delay in the delivery of the foilborne transmissions, only the variable-pitch propellers hinted at the hydrofoil's power.

Finally, after a tedious and sometimes dangerous trip, dodging occasional storms that nearly capsized the YBL 465 slave barge, the trio arrived off Halifax on July 17, 1968. They were met and escorted by smaller *Ville* class tugs and *Baddeck*, now utilized as a high-speed towed body test facility. *Bras d'Or* was gently nudged into position in Dockyard to await access to DOSCO's floating dry dock.

July 23, the *Bras d'Or* was ready to meet the Atlantic waters at last! Prior to the move, in a brief ceremony on the 18th and attended by the Fleet chaplain, Commander 'Tino' Cotaras and his wife, plus interested Naval and DREA personnel, *Bras d'Or* was christened and commissioned into the RCN by the smashing of a bottle of champagne by Mrs. Cotaras over the foil pod.[2] This simple ceremony heralded the beginning of the most exciting and controversial 28 months in Canadian Naval history.

Commander Constantine 'Tino' Cotaras, RCN was no newcomer to the hydrofoil programme. Appointed the Commander Designate of *Bras d'Or* in January, 1966, Cotaras had worked with the Project Management Office in Ottawa since late 1965. He sat through the teething problems in production and construction, underwent Phase I hydrofoil familiarization training in 1966, only to see his hopes dashed by the November fire. While *FHE-400's* fate hung in the balance, he was posted as Senior Staff Officer at Maritime Command Headquarters, Halifax and then posted as Captain of *HMCS Ottawa* to round out his operational command time. Finally he had been re-posted to *Bras d'Or* in early July, 1968, in time to meet the hydrofoil craft in Halifax.[3]

A basically moderate man Cotaras, born on March 15, 1929, was a graduate from Royal Roads Military College. Between stints at training establishments in Britain and Canada, Cotaras had served and later commanded minesweepers and frigates, mainly on the west coast. In August, 1963 he had been assigned to Ottawa as a Flag Lieutenant to the Chief of Naval Staff and later as a Staff Officer in Naval Operational Requirements. Cotaras, however, was now delighted to return to the project as Commanding Officer. He was pleased to find that 75% of the designated crew of 1966 had been gathered together once again and were ready to man the hydrofoil. Problems were expected with this craft and it seemed the best possible team was ready to meet these head-on.

One point must be made here to keep the record straight. Although *Bras d'Or* was 'commissioned' into the RCN, she remained the property of DeHavilland until the pre-acceptance trials were completed. No one foresaw that this would not happen until February, 1971. DeHavilland maintained a crew of 30 expert technicians in Halifax to oversee these trials. The Navy did nothing more than man the vessel during this trials' period.

The ship, on its slave dock was moved to DOSCO's floating dry dock, just north of Jetty Five, and for the first time *Bras d'Or* stood poised to feel the salt water of the Atlantic as the slave dock was slowly submerged within the sunken dock. The waters rose until *Bras d'Or* shivered and floated free of her cradle for the first time. The tug, *Parksville,* towed *Bras d'Or* clear of the dock, while the NRE research craft, *Rx,* made several passes sporting the ¼ scale canard configuration foils that had been so instrumental in proving *Bras d'Or*'s foil system.

The hydrofoil was then gently towed down the harbour to Jetty Three where she was berthed alongside a service barge with specially-built rubber

July 23, 1968, *FHE-400* is towed out of DOSCO's floating drydock. *Rx* passes showing the one quarter-scale replica foil system.
Credit: DREA

stand-offs and fenders. Over the next few days, preliminary system checks would begin.

Function familiarization began with the crew immediately, with testing, calibration and the setting up of test equipment going on well into August. First, alongside testing occurred on August 10 and 16, in which the displacement machinery, hydraulic systems, emergency systems were made functional. On the 23rd the first "flight test", the measurement of diesel torsional vibration, proved inconclusive with the diesel suffering a malfunction. Luckily this was done along-side, or it would have necessitated the whistling up of a tug for a tow home, something only too common in later 1968-69 tests.[4]

The next signs of difficulties with the ship occurred during diesel function set-up on September 15 to establish diesel speed/governor air pressure relationships. The instruments noted a high differential pressure across the port displacement lubrication filters of 58 psi. The filters were removed and large deposits of metallic particles were found in the cleaner elements and casings, pointing to severe problems in the port displacement pod, with possible duplication of the problem in the starboard.[5]

The ship was docked that week and a more thorough investigation begun. Upon removing the inspection panels on the hullborne pods, it was apparent that wear damage was extensive. The pod transmissions were pulled and upon the recommendation of the DeHavilland Trials Team, General Electric Canada was asked to assess the damage done.[6] Meanwhile, problems with the autopilot, tip and steering actuators, bow foil Teflon bearing and hydraulic pumps were tackled.

The autopilot had been coupling with hull high-frequency vibrations while hullborne, inducing serious errors in navigation. This was solved by isolating the unit from the hull with rubber mountings. In addition rates of roll, recovery rates set up within the autopilot were wrong, and the autopilot was fighting ship movement at the wrong times, necessitating recalibration to more closely conform with actual ship motion.

The tip and foil actuators were also over-sensitive. The gain on the anhedral foil tips was recalibrated and gain control turned away down during this refit. Initial trials showed the tips to be far more effective, hullborne, in making turns or manoeuvering than previously predicted by computer simulation. The bow actuator likewise was found sensitive in steering and trim, and needed adjusting .

However, the Teflon lining in the spherical bearing on the bow foil was found to be extensively scored. It was necessary to remove the bow foil and reline the bearing, which showed up the problem of Teflon adhesion to aluminium structures.

The first of the AP-12 hydraulic pumps had failed during the initial testing, something that plagued the hydraulics system right up until the last six months of operational life.

The eight-week refit to the foilborne transmissions dragged on until March, 1969. The hullborne pod transmissions, examined by C.G.E., Hamilton, in October, showed the port planet cage had suffered severe gouging of between .05 — .080 inches in depth. The planet gear after end was severely scored. The planet gears, interfering with the cage, caused by improper assembly at the plant, had placed the planet gears offset one half pitch aft. This condition still gave smooth tooth mesh, but was disastrous to the cage. The starboard ring gear teeth were badly abraded, to the point of showing rolled-over edges. The port ring gears showed slight signs of scoring in the same areas. This was caused by a lack of clearance between the internal teeth and mating external teeth. Proper clearance should have allowed relief of the internal teeth height so that the mating teeth could retract cleanly.[7]

Nothing needed replacing, but the necessary machining and cleaning up delayed the shipping of the hullborne pod transmissions back to Halifax until November 6, 1968. The entire propulsion system was reinstalled by December 19, including the foilborne propulsion systems.

Nothing much happened over the Christmas period, other than work as mentioned above. However, by January 10, 1969, limited system reactivation was underway while the ship was still in drydock. This was on-going, proving each system or sub-system, patiently and with minor set-backs. However, on February 16, while loading up the inboard auxiliary gearbox, the main seal blew out, allowing gearbox lubricant to leak all over the deck and spray over surrounding equipment. This necessitated the teardown of the gearbox and replacement of the seal.

Finally the ship was judged ready to resume pre-acceptance trials in March. First trials occurred on the 15th and once again the gremlins struck. Another of the AP15 hydraulic pumps packed up while testing the foilborne machinery, in turn causing all machinery to be shut down. Disgusted, Commander Cotaras was forced to whistle up a tug and suffer the indignity of being towed back to Dockyard.[8]

Trials resumed on the 24th, with continued testing of the foilborne machin-

Crew, 1968. Rear, left to right: L/S MacAuley, PO Walters, L/S Burnett, L/S Hargraft, PO Gould, PO Gaines, not identified, L/S Pelletier. Second row: Lt. Cdr. R. E. Bowkett, PO Clarke, PO Jenkins, PO Cooper, PO Henderson, PO Lynch. Front row: PO Valleau, CPO Smith, CPO Howles, CPO Fraser, Cdr. Cotaras, PO Costello, Lt. Hodgson, Lt. Cdr. McMunagle.

ery in hullborne mode. Initial, partial trials of 'running up' to transition speed were done on the 31st and the 1st of April.

The dawning of April 9, 1969 was no different than any other to the average Haligonian: sunny, cool, as extensive fog off the coast gave way to sea haze. *Bras d'Or* slipped her moorings and proceeded to the test area off Chebucto Head. The Captain and crew were slightly apprehensive: today they were to attempt to become foilborne.[9] The ship was ready and all that was left to do was the actual deed. After testing and warming up the foilborne propulsion system, the ship was given the go-ahead, as various Naval photographers stood by on one frigate and other harbour craft. All waited with drawn breath; this could either be *Bras d'Or's* finest hour of achievement or disaster.

Cotaras and his helmsman, CPO Barry Howles, sat tense in their seats in the tiny bridge as the speed mounted. The foilborne super-cavitating propellers were being slowly brought into play while the hullborne machinery pushed the vessel to 14 knots. A sudden tremor and transitory vibration went through the ship, giving many overwrought nerves a jangle they really didn't need and then disappeared. Faster and faster the throttles were advanced past their maximum performance at 14 knots and the FT4 turbine's power began to be felt. The bow foil was raked to -7° and the turbine allowed to reach 2,000 rpm while the craft stabilized with the bows trimmed up. Turbine speed was then increased to 2500 rpm, bow foil rake selected to 0° and the ship 'popped' up on level flight as the main foils increased their lifting capability. The time; 12:43 PM. *Bras d'Or* tore off down course at 35 knots, streaming a trail of faint black smoke, a banshee wail and a trail of sparkling spray and mist. The crew could breathe now; they were foilborne![10]

Perched in the wheelhouse over forty feet above the sea's surface, Cotaras was experiencing the exhilaration of finally seeing *Bras d'Or* 'fly'. The sight was beautiful and personally fulfilling.

During the afternoon, three take-offs and landings were conducted, while preliminary foilborne handling trials were carried out. The procedures and sequences of raking the bow foil, increasing power, negating foil rake were changed minutely, while monitoring such items as sea chest float levels and diesel engine intercooler temperatures during 'flight'. The captain and crew returned to dockyard, tired but in the very best of spirits. Their greatest enemy at this point, as Cotaras well knew, was over-confidence and expectations in the future. Total foilborne time: thirty-one minutes.

During the subsequent tests on April 26 and 28, further transition speed combinations were tried, aimed at finding that elusive optimum take-off procedure. The transient vibration was found to be caused by the interaction between the supercavitating propellers as they gained a 'bite' in the water and the twisting of the long foilborne drive shafts. Later, it was found that these shafts were twisting over 135° under initial thrust and the shafts were deflecting appreciatively, causing the vibration and tremor. Total foilborne time; 1 hr., 10 minutes on these dates.

During the winter refit, a modified casing shaft had been fitted on one side of the downshaft transmissions. Tests of the previous summer and fall showed alarming rises in the temperature of the lubricating oil in these downshafts and from the inboard foilborne gearbox to the foilborne pod gearboxes below. It was decided that in the next refit that the other three shafts would be replaced too. It was later determined that centrifugal force

Interior of the bridge with the Captain's position on left and coxswain's on right.
Credit: DREA

was preventing the lube oil from filtering downwards, plus shaft bearing deflection which prevented metallic 'sludge' from draining away, accelerating wear in the flanges and bearings. From the above it can be seen that the evolution of the CGE propulsion systems was an on-going affair. In June modified spline casings were shown to improve spline life. One had been fitted to each of three downshafts, with the starboard aft downshaft left with the original spline as a control element to compare wear.

Testing on June 14 and 19 saw the longest foilborne flight to date; 1 hour 43 minutes on the 19th. Speeds were advanced to 42 knots, but testing of stability was limited by short, steep ground swells and approximate sea state three.[11]

During the early part of July, *Bras d'Or* was tested with weights ranging from 456,566 lb All Up Weight (AUW) to 474,966 lb. This was done by carrying concrete blocks to simulate the weight of the fighting equipment. Total foilborne time was 15 hours 52 minutes by this time. However, the most spectacular event occurred on July 9, when *Bras d'Or* exceeded her designed 60 knots by two knots. These speeds were determined by Decca fixes in mild sea states of 3-4 foot waves. However, everything was not rosy. Back in June, it was noted that there was saltwater seepage into the starboard foilborne propulsion pod and starboard anhedral foil. By July 9, the time required to pump out the pod had extended from 2 minutes to 44 minutes, indicating that the leaks were increasing. It would have to be watched closely and investigated in the fall during normal lay-up.[12]

Testing of co-ordinated turns, using the incidence-controlled anhedral tips in conjunction with the bow foil occupied July 10 and 16th. Rates of turn up to 3.5° per second were accomplished with co-ordination and 3° per second

HMCS *Bras d'Or* exceeding 60 knots, July 16, 1969, near Halifax.
Copyright: W. R. Carty

in flat, unassisted turns. Ship speeds varied from 35-50 knots. During these tests, the press was given free reign to photograph *Bras d'Or* in both hullborne and foilborne 'flight'. Although 'stills' had been shot back as early as April of foilborne trials, this was the first time that commercial video-tape and cine-cameras were allowed to record this remarkable feat.

After the press went home, it was time to take stock. *Bras d'Or* had lived up to predictions as far as hullborne and initial foilborne trials were concerned, but the pumping times on the starboard pod now exceeded 50 minutes, clearly indicating that the situation was becoming critical. Therefore, it was decided to dock the hydrofoil ship on July 18 to see if the persistent leaks could be located and repaired; no one was prepared for what lay ahead.

Upon examination, it was found that there were cracks in the anhedral foil intersection with the starboard strut, cracks in the strut and worst of all, the centre high-speed foil. The neoprene coating was stripped from the affected areas so that the extent of damage could be determined. Fortunately the cracks in the strut and anhedral members were repairable, but the high-speed centre foil was cracked beyond repair. The foil was removed and shipped to DeHavilland's Downsview plant to fully investigate the cause of this cracking.

DeHavilland, working with representatives of Energy, Mines and Resources and Defence Research Board, set about finding the causes. Through extensive testing done by Energy, Mines and Resources a few years previously, the detrimental effects of saltwater on NiCoMo 18% steel were fully known. It was determined that seawater entering an improperly sealed plug in the end of the centre foil had attacked and overwhelmed the zinc 'sacrificial' coating on the interior and had given rise to hydrogen embrittlement and stress corrosion, particularly around welded joints. Further, it was determined that with the very nature of the metal used in the foil system that cracking would occur in the future, but with careful monitoring it would be possible to repair 'in situ', other than the centre foil element.[13]

Some controversy arose within the Investigative Committee as to the source of the leak. DeHavilland contended that the occurrence of leaks showed the greater majority of cracks arose after first cracks, therefore the material was failing through other causes. However the majority of available evidence showed otherwise and the joint findings of the committee were entered in the records.[14]

Meanwhile there was still the problem of what to do with the ship? The answer was two-fold; first a tender for a new centre foil element would be let and awarded after the New Year of 1970. Secondly, a mild steel dummy centre foil was fabricated and fitted on December 5, 1969 to allow hullborne trials to continue while the new foil element was fabricated.

The first was accomplished when Treasury Board accepted a bid from DeHavilland on January 9, 1970 for the new centre element, valued at $460,000. Delivery was not until late summer, so the mild steel foil was fitted and the ship relaunched on January 16 to begin systems re-activation between January 21-28.[15] However, the first hullborne trials on February 2 and 5 were a total loss. The unfaired junctions of the temporary foil set up such a vibration problem within the hull that it was deemed necessary to redock *Bras d'Or* on the 11th to fit fairings over the exposed joints. The ship was relaunched on the 19th and hullborne trials began on the 24th.[16]

The outstanding problem of this period was with the diesel engine. Governor malfunctions were chronic and apparent pressurization of the crankcase was causing various leaks around gaskets and fittings. This was eventually traced to an improper lubrication oil level being specified by the manufacturer's dealer in Canada and when lowered, seal 'blow-by'was eliminated.[17]

Once again hydraulic pump problems arose in March, necessitating a replacement of the port prop pitch boost pump. This situation persisted throughout the year and into the early months of 1971 when newer, higher-capacity pumps became available.[18]

Getting back to the DeHavilland construction of the high-speed centre foil, things were progressing on schedule. However, somewhere in the fabrication of the foil section, conformity was lost and it was discovered that the leading section was 'cocked-up' over what it should be. This necessitated cutting this section off, resectioning and rewelding to the rest of the foil element. The delivery time was then set for September 30, 1970.

Hullborne trials were hindered by rough weather in April, but significant testing was done, with propulsion tests, practice turns, optimum 'take-off' settings investigated and emergency propulsion exercises. Once again the diesel governors were found defective and maximum hullborne speeds were impossible to determine.

Bras d'Or was docked in mid-May for a full refit. Here, the ship was treated to full maintenance procedures. The ship was launched to begin system reactivation during the September 18-October 8 period.

Meanwhile, Lt.-Colonel 'Tino' Cotaras, in his second year of command of *Bras d'Or*, was told he would be relieved in July, 1971 to further his staff career training. Cotaras, a cautious man, normally referred to as a 'cruiser man' by fellow officers, would have been only too glad to move on from the heart-breaking task of trying to 'prove' the *FHE-400* hydrofoil design. False indicator reports and alarms had frazzled nerves for the past two years and after the emotional 'high' of the foilborne tests in April, 1969, it had become a never-ending litany of failures and delays. He frankly told his successor, Lt.-Colonel Gordon L. Edwards, that he strongly felt that Edwards would never make an overnight cruise nor undertake any rough water or extended cruise testing of the ship — a frank admission of his low state of spirits! He told Edwards that it was kind of fun, but would probably not amount to much. Clearly a change was needed by both Cotaras and *FHE-400*.

Chapter Seven

A Zoomie in Command

When Gordon Edwards was notified that he was to assume command of *Bras d'Or,* he was not too pleased. *Bras d'Or* was somewhat of an oddity, forever being towed in from sea and it was considered a lame duck by most officers, especially on the ladder of successive commands. His interview with Cotaras only went that much further to deepen his conviction that there were serious problems with the project, not the least being low morale after the setbacks of the past year. With his upbeat character Edwards decided to make the best of the situation, after being told that the perfect captain for this 'ship that flew' was naturally a naval aviator or as most sailors know them, a "Zoomie". Through some obscure chain of thought Naval Headquarters had arrived at this conclusion and fortunately were proven right!

When Lt.-Colonel G. L. Edwards assumed command in July, 1970, he found a ship that was deeply involved in a summer-long refit, with key ratings on vacation or conducting stand-by duties while DeHavilland personnel pursued seemingly endless defects and glitches. From their emotional high of 1969, the crew had withdrawn into a determined group, bent on finishing their tour of duty and surviving the experience. There was talk in the local press that with the difficulties encountered and escalating costs that Ottawa was thinking of curtailing or completely cancelling the project.[1]

Although there was little truth at that time in the latter, it was a great morale loss to the crew. Nothing undermines the morale and determination of hard-pressed, hard-working men than uncertainty that the job you are doing may not be worthwhile. This was the situation that Edwards inherited.

Edwards, born in Medicine Hat, Alberta in 1931, had joined the RCN in 1948 and had served aboard HMCS *Athabaskan* in the Korean War in 1950-51. He received his commission while aboard the HMCS *Crusader* and after further training, was shipped to the UK to learn to fly Sea Hawk jets from HMS *Illustrious.* Returning to Canada, he flew piston-driven Sea Furies from HMCS *Magnificent* and in 1956, Banshee jets from HMCS *Bonaventure.* After serving as a jet pilot instructor, he had served as an exchange pilot with the USN, flying from USS *Independence* and *Intrepid* from 1958-1960. After further RCN flying, he served as Operations Officer in HCMS *St. Croix,* Executive Officer in HMCS *New Waterford* and assumed his first command in HMCS *Assiniboine* in July 1967.[2]

Outgoing, generally well-liked, Edwards was a perfect choice as a captain for the ailing *FHE-400.* One of his first moves to restore morale was to disprove the 'scuttle-butt' about the project being abandoned. Secondly, he declared that never again would the hydrofoil craft be towed into harbour! Emergency systems were there to propel the ship if the main systems broke down and be damned if they would not be used to return the ship to port! A new wind was ablowing from the commander.

However, when the ship was undocked in mid-September, it seemed it was ready to tackle Edward's determination from the beginning. On the 18th the auxiliary ST6 turbine auto control system malfunctioned, aborting the displacement transmission run. Additionally, the Cardan shaft back-turning lock on the auto gearbox refused to engage, aborting the auxiliary systems testing. These were finally resolved in Flight Three but were a less than successful commencement of a command.

Once again on October 8 testing was curtailed when the diesel engine runs aborted through over-speed conditions brought on by faulty engine control rigging. This, however, did not call for a tow as previously; the defect was corrected and Flight Six took place the same day with satisfactory results. October 15 test runs in Bedford Basin were cut short when the ST6 went into over-speed mode through the failure of the output shaft speed governor. This problem persisted throughout the month until October 22, when a new unit was installed, borrowed from DREA.

Consecutive series showing *Bras d'Or* becoming foilborne in Sea State Four.

However, by the 22nd, *Bras d'Or* appeared to relent, allowing full systems activation by the 26th, when the first foilborne flight of 1970 took place.[3] Foilborne operations were executed during sea state four, the first rough water foilborne trials of the year. However, it was not until October 28, 29 that rough water hullborne/foilborne trials were attempted. After a period of demonstrations for the press in foilborne mode, a series of take-offs were carried out in Bedford Basin to establish auto-pilot control roll gains. These were terminated when a lube oil leak developed in the starboard foilborne pod. After repairs, an overnight trip was attempted but aborted after an inboard AP12 hydraulic pump on the auxiliary gearbox continuous duty set failed. The ship returned to port with the GT85 supplying emergency services, while the diesel drove the ship. No tugs for *Bras d'Or*!

October 29 got off to a dismal start when a hydraulic line burst in the early morning activation. However the ship undertook displacement trials with the anhedral tips locked at -7° that afternoon, a practice soon discontinued after very large roll angles developed during turns.

But late afternoon *Bras d'Or* and crew were as ready as they ever would be. For the first time without a consort vessel, she slipped quietly down the blustery harbour and out into the grey seas. The vessel, in sea state four conditions of six to eight foot waves and large swells, proceeded hullborne at 12 knots with only the odd bit of water reaching the bridge. However a cyclic noise in the hydraulic system heralded the end of another AP12 hydraulic pump and necessitated the shut down of the entire propulsive system. The ship was dead in the water for some 12 minutes while systems' changeover was made. The ship developed a slight list, attributed to a shifting of fuel oil from tank to tank, the surging fuel overcoming the one fore and aft baffle in the fuel tanks.

The hydraulic system was switched over to emergency mode and the GT85 emergency turbine brought on line, supplying emergency electric and hydraulic services. Then the ST6 auxiliary turbine was brought on line with the auxiliary gearbox, the diesel started and the ST6 shut down. The ship returned to Halifax in six hours using the GT85 emergency services and the diesel providing propulsion and operating the main seawater cooling pump. The offending AP12 was removed during the trip back, making it possible to re-engage the main hydraulic system, but this would have necessitated a further 'dead in the water' change-over.

Findings of the first overnight rough water hullborne trails were encouraging. In the head-on, quartering and astern sea, *Bras d'Or* behaved like a much larger frigate of 3000 tons without the attendant ship roll and pitch caused by conventional ship top hamper. In great part this was because of the submerged foil systems which acted as a huge damper to lively ship movements of the relatively small hull.

For the personnel however, the relatively-uninsulated wardroom and officers quarters were noisy, even with just the diesel running. This was borne out in following tests, making acoustical insulation of greater thickness a must in any follow-on hydrofoil ship at sea longer than twenty-four hours. Further, the nominal 28 capacity sleeping accommodation was taxed to the limits with a 37-man crew during the tests, with fifteen DeHavilland personnel sandwiched into the quarters. Six were accommodated in sleeping bags, a totally unacceptable arrangement.[4]

Next testing was on November 6, when displacement cruising tests at maximum continuous power ratings were carried out in ten-foot swells with one-foot chop, with seas from 180°. Runs were made so that seas approached from all quarters and were successfully concluded.

The ship was docked later in the month and the delayed centre high-speed foil was installed. Undocked on December 9, the ship immediately began alongside activation on the 10th, proceeding to sea on the same day for displacement cruising. On the 11th foilborne activation was attempted but aborted when it was found that lube oil lines on bearings number one and two on the forward and aft starboard foilborne downshafts had not been reconnected during the November refit. All four downshaft bearings were damaged, necessitating the installation of four new journal bearings in these locations.[5] December 15 was spent in displacement mode with the foilborne transmission engaged to 'run-in' the new bearings. On the same flight, foilborne operation was achieved for seven minutes, while discrepancies in the foilborne downshaft supply pressures from port to starboard side were investigated unsuccessfully.

On December 19th, while conducting auto-control gain settings, the outboard starboard gearbox started losing oil pressure and the lube tank level rapidly diminished. It was determined that the five-year old outboard gearbox cartridge boot had failed. This failure was followed by the failure of the port boot on Flight Eight that same day. An improved version was installed, but the problem was repeated until it was discovered that the gearbox vent systems had been cross-connected in error during the November refit.[6]

Bras d'Or was laid up during the Christmas period and not re-activated until January 7, 1971. It became apparent that the performance of the mechanically-driven scavenge pumps in the outboard starboard foilborne gearbox was inferior in performance to that of the port one. This was indicated by the lower level of lube oil in the tank for the starboard side and the pump was working longer than its twin on the port side. This situation became worse with increased pressure in the foilborne mode, clearly indicating a worsening state of operation of that pod gearbox scavenge pump. This pressure gradually reached 4-5 psi on January 11-12 in 35-knot runs (the limit being 5 psi for this system). When foilborne on the 12th, the pressure reached dangerous levels but by turning the ship to starboard or at the end of a run, turning the ship alternatively port and starboard, the pressure was relieved. This clearly showed performance of the scavenge pumps was reaching minimum requirements. To combat this on a temporary basis, the N3 switch was moved to hydraulic valve EV2 to remove the 'shut-down' operation of the outboard gearbox hydraulic scavenge pumps, allowing these to operate continuously, rather than shutting down at N3(2,650 rpm). In this way, excessive oil was pumped back to the lube tank and filters.[7]

January 14 saw operations with Fleet units in the test vicinity, with measured mile speed calibrations at 35 and 50 knots and wake-crossing trials with a destroyer at 20 knots. Wakes of 3-4 feet in height affected foil performance only marginally. On January 19, two press parties were laid on with the CBC film crew and the RN Senior Officer, West Indies aboard. Photographing and straight runs were successfully carried out.[8]

It was now decided that *Bras d'Or* should carry out a Fleet exercise overnight on January 20, 1971. This trip was reluctantly aborted when yet another hydraulic pump failed and *Bras d'Or* was forced to return to Halifax to replace it. The next attempt was on the 22nd, with bow foil optimisations carried out in sea state five. Testing continued throughout the last week of January, with a ominous feature re-appearing . . . the starboard foilborne pod pumped for forty minutes and the port one for five minutes. Clearly salt water was entering the starboard pods, both foilborne and displacement, through cracks or seepage.

Flight 7 on the 29th was devoted to demonstrating the vessel for the Under-Secretary for the U.S. Navy. A planned sea trip for him was cancelled at the last moment when the Captain's heated window shattered. The ship returned to port, where during the shut-down procedure, an overspeed occurred on the ST6 auxiliary gas turbine, attributed to a faulty output shaft governor.

The next big event slated was a planned 48-hour test for February 8, 9 and 10. The ship was prepared and sailed in company of the frigates *Fraser* and *Saguenay*. Immediately on exiting the harbour, conditions were far worse than expected. Head seas of 10-15 feet on large swells were encountered the full forty miles to the test area. During the early periods when the seas were shorter and sharper in coastal waters, green water was shipped over the bridge. Minor leaks were encountered around deck hatches, flanges of exhaust outlets from the ST6 and GT85. However, the diesel was a continuing difficulty. The inlet manifold on the port bank of the engine cracked on the underside and when the engine intakes took in a small amount of water, it leaked from this crack onto the engine. Several small oil leaks developed and the diesel jacket water high temperature and high temperature oil warning switches were triggering at low settings even though they had been newly calibrated.

During the first day, sea states reached seven, with wave lengths of 250 feet and some waves 25 feet in height for over five hours. Winds were in the 50-60 knot range. Perhaps the best description of the day was contained in a message from HMCS *Fraser*, who was in company for most of the time;

> Weather conditions were considered most unpleasant, heavy seas and 15-20 foot swell, wind gusting to 60 knots, ship spraying overall with upper deck out of bounds most of the time. *Bras d'Or* appeared to possess enviable seakeeping qualities. She was remarkably stable, with a noticeable absence of roll and pitch and apparently no lack of maneouvrability. The almost complete absence of spray over the bridge and fo'c'sle was very impressive. Of some 250 people aboard *Fraser*, 15-20 percent were sea-sick during the period.

It should be noted that *Bras d'Or* had 35% seasick the first day, but this difference could be attributed to the facts that *Bras d'Or* personnel had not been in rough weather for a long time and that *Bras d'Or's* count occurred during the first day, whereas *Fraser's* was an after the fact estimate.

Some idea of *Bras d'Or's* superior manoeuvrability in this weather can be illustrated by the fact that *Fraser* had revolutions on for 6-8 knots, while *Bras d'Or* only needed revs for 4-5 knots to maintain station. Indeed, to maintain sufficient headway, *Bras d'Or* was forced to steam in continuous figure-eights about *Fraser*, while visibility deteriorated to less than two cables for over twenty hours!

Since some concern was expressed at the last of this trip that salt water immersion of the foilborne machinery might have had detrimental effects on performance, it was decided to try and become foilborne for the last hour as the weather abated. So on February 10 the foilborne FT4 and ST6 were examined and brought into operational status. Other than some shorted sensors on the FT4, everything appeared normal. The ship was then made

Foilborne off Chebucto Head, N.S. May 1971

foilborne in sea state 4-5 and carried out passes at 40, 45 and 50 knots. The anhedral tips were used in automatic mode, travelling +5 to –5 degrees and greatly controlling pitch and roll. HMCS *Saguenay*, part of the escort, sent the following message after being close-at-hand witness to a couple of these high-speed passes;

> Performance of your ship when foilborne in seas of three feet with swell about ten feet was impressive. You looked more comfortable at 40 knots than *Saguenay* at 18. Maximum sensible speed of a DDH in these conditions, without straining the ship would be about 22 knots. Your motion appeared smooth, both in pitch and roll. Ship seemed to be borne entirely by the foils, although forward foil did come clear of the water on occasion.

Bras d'Or then proceeded back to Halifax where a complete engine wash was carried out after shut-down.[9]

Bras d'Or entered drydock on February 12 for routine refit of five weeks, in which an inspection of the foils was carried out. A new set of spoilers was installed on the bow foils to further decrease re-attachment of flow to the foils, thus improving response and softening the ride.

The ship was undocked April 6 and the month was taken up by an inspection of the bow hydraulic actuators, re-activation and hull/foilborne trials. By April 15, *Bras d'Or* had accumulated 352 hours 28 minutes at sea of which 43 hours 29 minutes had been spent foilborne. After February 1, a plateau of reliability was reached, allowing frequent sailings to be scheduled and carried out without cancellations due to mechanical defects. Turning circles of 500 yards at 50 knots and 600 yards at 40 knots were recorded during this period, utilizing the anhedral tips in co-ordinated turns.

April 29 testing was disrupted by excessive vibration and noises in the inboard foilborne transmission. Prior to this on the 28th, during routine inspection, several spline coupling bolts in the inboard gearbox/downshaft spline couplings were found to be loose. These had been re-tightened, but when opened up on the 29th, it was found that three of the coupling bolts on each side had sheared, due to fatigue fractures resulting from the bending. This in turn was caused by distortion of the coupling flanges. Custom-fitted steel dams were installed with the bolts and the problem of flange flexibility was resolved. However, these failures had resulted in a great deal of debris being washed down the shafting. The shafts were removed and cleaned, and the shaft spaces flushed. It was discovered that the housings for the shaft bearings contained small hairline cracks, attributed to manufacturing material problems. New units were installed in the worst cases and a review of bearing specifications called for in the future. The hydrofoil ship returned to service on May 4.[10]

Although heavyweight flight tests in various sea states occupied the greater part of May, the greatest emphasis was placed on an ambitious long-distance run. Shore staff were defining the necessary facilities needed in foreign ports to service the hydrofoil ship and a short list of possible destinations were nearly complete. The Department of External Affairs was asked to stand-by to assist in making arrangements.

The up coming event for the month though was a 'shop-window' demonstration with other elements of the fleet in Bedford Basin. The ship cruised, hullborne in the Basin, demonstrating her hullborne manoeuvering abilities before becoming foilborne and proceeding down the harbour at 35 knots. Reaching Chebucto Head, the ship came about and returned to Dockyard, fully foilborne until just off Jetty Two, where she gracefully settled into the water with very little disturbance to surrounding craft.[11]

Another two-day cruise was carried out on May 25-27 in which further hullborne trials in sea state three were carried out at 12 knots with seas approaching from ahead, astern and from the starboard side. Foilborne times in the same sea state were carried out on the 9th. Total foilborne time until June 10 was 79 hours 35 minutes. The ship then entered a brief maintenance period where everything was checked and rechecked . . . . the extended cruise was on!

The proposed route was ambitious to the extreme; 2,500 miles, unescorted. It was planned to proceed with HMCS *Preserver*, a naval replenishment ship and four frigates to sea for fleet evolutions and then, about half-way to Bermuda, *Bras d'Or* would detach and proceed to Hamilton, Bermuda alone. There it would carry out a series of demonstrations and trials before proceeding to Norfolk, Virginia for another round of demonstrations for the USN and Coast Guard, both of whom were evaluating hydrofoil craft for their respective services. From there it would be back to Halifax, attempting to intercept the NATO Squadron and carry out a mock attack. This would be the first experience for NATO ships with a high-speed hydrofoil ship in the North Atlantic and hopefully some clues to detection and handling of such vessels would come out of the encounter.[12]

June 15th was a sunny, warm day in Halifax as *Bras d'Or*, *Preserver* and four frigates of First Canadian Destroyer Squadron slipped from the harbour for the open Atlantic. Maneouvers with Fleet units made plain that *Bras d'Or's* 12-14 knot normal diesel speed was a severe constraint on maintaining station with conventional surface units. *Bras d'Or* would either force other units to reduce speed or she would have to operate semi-detached.[13]

On June 16th, the first at-sea replenishment was carried out, with fair weather making the transfer relatively easy. Sea-keeping was first practised and then a jack-stay was rigged to transfer solid stores. After completion, a $2\frac{1}{2}$ inch hose was transferred and secured to a recently-installed tripod on the stern deck, allowing the transfer of JP5 to begin. A full load of fuel was transferred in less than thirty minutes, but it required close co-operation and co-ordination in opening interconnecting valves and constant two-way communication was necessary for safety and speedy transfer.

Bras d'Or detached from the conventional ships late on the 16th and proceeded to Bermuda, taking $15\frac{1}{2}$ hours to reach port. Only three hours were spent foilborne and this to guarantee their estimated time of arrival. The only trouble on this leg of the trip was a fractured lube line that delayed the ship a half hour. Heavy seas on the morning of the 18th with 10-12 head seas and reduced visibility of one mile afforded a chance for more hullborne rough water trials, before Bermuda popped up on time in the radar scope. The ship became foilborne to enter the narrow channel in gradually improving weather. A demonstration of foilborne travel was made to several thousand appreciative islanders in Murray's Anchorage. The tricky part of South Channel passage was navigated hullborne, then DunDonald Channel and Two Rocks passage made foilborne at 40 knots, landing spectacularly in front of the Princess Hotel. The ship berthed alongside a borrowed barge at Flagpole Jetty. There were no difficulties with this berth, other than a lack of shore based power. Hence the GT85 emergency turbine was run for the entire four-day stay to provide essential power requirements. This was a bit irksome, since watchkeepers were necessary and the incessant scream of the GT85 was apparent both within and without the hull. Several thousand people visited the ship during an 'open ship' on the 20th and many others came and asked questions at the reception with dignitaries of the Island that evening.

On Monday, June 21 a demonstration was carried out with the Governor and eleven other dignitaries aboard, plus members of the press. The visitors were discharged onto the Port Admiral's barge off Port Royal. *Bras d'Or* then proceeded to a barge at Port Royal, where she took on 12,000 gallons of JP5 in twenty minutes. She then prepared for sailing on the afternoon tide.[14]

Bras d'Or quietly slipped away from her berth and departed Bermuda . . . destination — Norfolk, Virginia. Proceeding towards the U.S., *Bras d'Or* encountered USS *Marble Head*, 135 nautical miles (155.36 statute miles) from Bermuda. Edwards, always one to put the Navy's best foot forward with friendly ships, became foilborne and proceeded to do a couple of figure-eights about the USN ship, then haring off for Norfolk, leaving only the Roadrunner-like "Beep, beep!" of the ship's horn lingering in the air.

On the 22nd, a rocker arm in cylinder number five failed, necessitating a shutdown of the diesel. Luckily, the offending cylinder could be disconnected or *Bras d'Or* would have been forced to proceed foilborne for the rest of the trip, placing her in Norfolk sixteen hours too early! A new rocker arm of modified design was rushed by air from Ruston, Montreal and fitted while in Norfolk.[15]

The ship became foilborne on the 23rd while still miles outside Hampton Roads Channel, encountering a USN destroyer squadron in Formation One, in rainy, foggy weather. She approached the nearest destroyer at forty knots, catching the squadron flat-footed, not aware that *Bras d'Or* was in the vicinity! *Bras d'Or* made the entire twenty mile transit of Hampton Roads foilborne at 40 knots, arriving hours ahead of the destroyers. A pass was made at Pier Seven in Norfolk and the ship was berthed stern-first, with a stern board for access.

On June 24th, five 20-minute briefings, followed by 45-minute demonstrations were successfully carried out for seventy USN and foreign officers, as well as fifteen members of the local and international press. On the 25th three separate briefings were given by Lt.-Col. Edwards, followed by more detailed tours of the ship with special emphasis on systems and propulsion.

However, on Saturday morning, June 26, in anticipation of the 13:00 demonstration for Admiral Duncan, USN, the systems were prepared and the ST6 compressor given a fresh water wash before shut-down. However, when a restart was attempted five minutes later, the ST6 cut out with high turbine inlet temperatures indicated. Checks showed little out of the ordinary, another try was made and again the ST6 aborted. A five-hour instrumentation test was initiated, precluding Admiral Duncan's trip and this could not be rescheduled due to Duncan's busy schedule.

Rather than delay sailing for home while a more comprehensive check was done, the ST6 was switched to emergency mode, negating all safety cutouts. In this mode, turbine cut-out temperature was raised from 1730° F to 1900° F. Starting, the ST6 temperature peaked at 1850° F. As soon as the hydraulics were loaded and the diesel started, the ST6 was shut down and secured. *Bras d'Or* then proceeded to sea, homeward bound.

It had been hoped that *Bras d'Or* would be able to intercept the NATO Squadron then enroute to Norfolk on the 27th. However, since the NATO ships could navigate twenty miles closer to George's Bank using Decca coverage rather than *Bras d'Or's* direction ranging, this could not be done. The NATO ships were spotted on radar twenty miles off the port beam, slightly astern the hydrofoil craft and it was deemed too great a stern chase, especially given the shape of the propulsion machinery.

To finalize this tale of woe, the diesel again packed up at 22:45 on the 28th, losing power rapidly. It was discovered that when the new rocker arm had been installed in Norfolk that the fuel injectors had not been properly readjusted, permitting fuel to contaminate the diesel lubrication system and subsequently overloading the injection pump drive. The injection pump drive for bank 'A' failed, leaving the ship with only a bank of eight cylinders on the starboard side of the diesel. This bank was isolated and blanked off to prevent oil leaks and the GT85 started to pressurize the systems. They were less than twelve hours from Halifax.

Within minutes another crisis arose with the sounding of the high temperature alarm on the case drain and lube system of the GT85 and rapidly reached maximum permissable temperatures. Before all systems were lost, the ST6 was brought into play in emergency mode and the GT85 shut down. Temperatures on the ST6 stabilized at 1600° F under load. The ship was then brought into foilborne operation and the ST6 ran until arrival in Halifax. The ship arrived off Chebucto Head at 04:00 on the 29th, where she hove to until 08:40 when she transited the harbour, arriving in Dockyard at exactly 09:00, foilborne. The whistles blew and the Royal Canadian Regiment Band supplied suitable martial airs, as the half-bank diesel was run up to provide maneouvring power at the last moments. The excessive motions of the engine suffering from this imbalance fractured the starter air supply line, but she was safely home. Later Edwards commented that eight cylinders didn't sound that much different from sixteen!

Presenting a brave face to the attendant press, Edwards and the crew never let on about the problems of the thrice-cursed diesel engine and emergency power turbines. However, they had proved one thing; *Bras d'Or* could cover vast distances all on her own, in sea states of five and greater and overcome more emergencies in fourteen days than the average destroyer in fourteen months!

In the following days, the ST6 was thoroughly tested and stripped. No over-temperature damage had been done and the guilty culprit was found to be a shorted igniter plug and partially-plugged washer ring. The failure in Norfolk was determined to be the short plug and a dirty fuel path, with a brown sludge partially obstructing the line.

Outside of the propulsion problems, there had been a fractured hydraulic line on the Halifax-Bermuda leg and the thoroughly inadequate performance of the air-conditioning plant. At ambient temperatures greater than 70° F, the plant continually lost ground with rising temperatures. The first air conditioner in the package gave up the ghost to a burnt armature motor on the Halifax-Bermuda leg and the other was totally unable to carry the load. Clearly a revised air-conditioning plant and insulation of the hull from outside heat would be necessary before further warm-water cruising.

In addition, the bow foil steering had developed a distinct 'clunking' sound between Halifax and Bermuda. Once again the bow foil spherical bearing had worn until the clearances were excessive. However, this was an identified problem area dating back to 1968 and was easily repaired. However, the biggest problem existed in the foil system once more. The ship had suffered a seawater leak in the port foilborne propulsion pod on the way back from Bermuda, although pump times had been increasing since that spring. This leak was found to be the result of an improperly sealed door at the pod base. There were some minor cracks in the struts and in one intersection pod. However, it was noted that when the ship was hauled out of the water that water was flowing over the upper surface of the centre high-speed foil and running down to the Syncro-lift surface. It was coming from what turned out to be a crack a few inches long, across the corner of the upper skin at the leading edge. Obviously, the centre foil was flooded once more through this crack.

Further inspection however showed a long crack on the lower skin of the main centre high-speed foil. The crack was in the forward side of the leading edge spar, running about six feet in the athwartships direction. The eventual cause was traced to unexpected residual stress introduced when the foil profile was corrected by cutting, bending and rewelding in the course of manufacture in 1970. The high residual stress, superimposed on the load stress was considered sufficient to cause this failure, but it was thought that seawater leaking in through the crack in the upper surface initiated a corrosive attack that was the straw that broke the camel's back. However, the re-convened committee from DeHavilland, DND, DRB and Energy, Mines and Resources determined this foil could be repaired by welding. This would be followed by heat aging, shot-peening plus flushing of the interior and careful re-inhibiting.[16]

The refloating was delayed while the investigation was carried out. While the ship was waiting, it was moved to it's slave dock at Jetty Two. It was decided that the ship would remain there until DeHavilland's leave period shut-down ended in August.

However, in the real world, *Bras d'Or* had been in trouble politically since 1970 and the press had joined the pack actively criticising the programme. Armed by open opponents in Ottawa with often misleading or incomplete information or figures, plus the very real problems that existed with the craft, the press were conducting a witchhunt that sold papers.[17] With only a bare glimmering of the programme's aims and advantages, the press and Members of the House were using the hydrofoil craft as a way to embarrass the Liberal Government, although the programme had been initiated by the preceeding Conservative Executive![18] The Liberals, looking for obvious ways to chop defence expenditures further, were busy undermining the credibility of the programme so that it would be easier to drop in due course, as soon as the Minister of Defence could deliver his long-awaited White Paper on Defence in August. Everyone knew the project was doomed . . . they just didn't know when the axe would fall.

To further muddy the picture and demoralize the crew and members of DeHavilland based in Halifax, it was announced that Gordon Edwards would be transferred to the NATO Defence College in Rome on August 26 and worse yet, there wasn't a replacement. This was a bittersweet posting for Edwards, since he was sure that despite the sniping going on in Ottawa and the newspapers, the Navy would carry on with the Phase II evaluation with the fighting equipment aboard. In the meantime he recommended that his Executive Officer, Lt.-Commander Ian Sturgess be given temporary command while a decision on *Bras d'Or's* fate was being made.[19]

Edwards departed and Sturgess began his thankless task of routine refit and maintenance checks. The entire foil system was stripped of the neoprene coating and the cracks were repaired in other than the centre foil. The ship was as ready as ever to proceed, once the foils were repaired and recoated. Sturgess still felt the Navy would continue with Phase Two; hadn't they paid for the Action Information Centre and weapons systems already *and* accepted delivery of *Bras d'Or* in February?

The long summer days wore on, with crew members transferred ashore to undergo training courses and take some well-earned leave. Hope was soured with the DeHavilland personnel though, with lack of decision or clear-cut direction from Downsview. The golden days of September went by with the ship ready for re-coating, but the order to do so never came.

Lt. Col. G. L. Edwards

Finally on November 2, 1971 the axe fell. National Defence Headquarters knew that the project would be chopped, but hadn't informed the ship's officers or men until less than twelve hours before the announcement was made! Ian Sturgess remembered vividly the shock of the announcement to himself and the crew. All summer they had been preparing the ship for the last five hours foilborne and twelve hours hullborne in sea states four and five to complete the entire Phase I trials package. It only made sense to continue the trials and fit the fighting equipment. In sheer incredulity Sturgess listened to the announcement . . . *Bras d'Or* was to be laid up for a five-year period.

In the House of Commons on November 2, the Minister of National Defence, Donald S. MacDonald, rose and in a complete hush, informed the Members that in light of the August, 1971 release of the Defence White Paper and a switch from anti-submarine warfare to sovereignty protection for Canada's Armed Forces, the high-speed hydrofoil warship would no longer be needed. Further, with the cost of the hydrofoil ship in production, there was no potential for off-shore sales. Additionally, Maritime Command's needs would have only been ten hydrofoil warships at a cost of $28 million per unit without weapons systems. A further 4.7-6 million dollars would be required to complete Phase II testing over three years, with possible escalation of close to $20 million, above the $52,700,000 already spent on the project. Hence the ship would be stored for a period of five years at a combined cost of $1 million for maintenance.[20]

The House reacted with pandemonium after the first paragraph. Everyone in Defence in Ottawa had expected it, but it still was a shock. Reading between the lines, anyone could read the message . . . the *FHE-400* project was dead, permanently . . . R.I.P.

Cotaras wasn't surprised. His confidence in the craft had never recovered after his command of the vessel and he had expected it to be cancelled long before it actually happened.

Gordon Edwards in sunny Italy at the NATO Staff College, was appalled. The sheer waste of cancelling the project far offset any savings that would be realized in the next few years after the cancellation. A fully-functional lightweight sonar system and lightweight, computer-controlled Action Information Centre costing $10 million to develop, would not be utilized.

However, nothing would change the picture now. The die was cast and *Bras d'Or* would languish on for twelve years, a constant reminder of another Canadian development chopped off before it could prove its real worth.

Chapter Eight
They Clipped Her Wings

With the project now effectively cancelled and the Naval and DeHavilland personnel reeling in shock, National Defence Headquarters rapidly made plans to finish the task. Lt.-Cdr. Ian Sturgess was given orders to begin posting the crew ashore for retraining and to other ships in the fleet. The remaining crewmembers would be utilized in preparing the ship for it's five year 'hibernation'.

Starting just after the New Year, 1972, the pace of preparation accelerated. The turbine engines were drained and inhibited against corrosion and weathering. The fuel tanks were drained and steamed clean of sludge; the hydraulic systems were drained and sealed. Electrical circuits were coated and slowly the electronics were sealed against dust by wrapping in plastic and duct tape. The thousand and one small things to be done in the dying ship were tackled by the subdued crew.

By May 1 the major inhibiting efforts were complete. In a final mocking ceremony, the ship was officially decommissioned. A small group of officers and men trooped aboard the hydrofoil ship, perched atop her slave barge, basking in the afternoon sun. Facing toward the mast, they watched as the Canadian flag and the small commissioning pennant were slowly lowered for the last time, accompanied by the shrill squeal of the bosun's pipes. In a moment's silence after the flag was lowered and being folded, the only sound was the shuffling of feet, plus the lonely cry of harbour gulls in the background. The party faced forward and briskly stepped off over the brow in single file. All that was left was a demoralized Lt.-Cdr. Sturgess to answer questions for the CBC film crew and after they had left, only the hydrofoil, basking in lonely splendour in the setting afternoon sun.[1]

Even after the decommissioning, the preservation procedures continued. After the ship had been thoroughly inhibited, the ship was vacuumed to clear as much dust as possible from the hull. Then the ship was evacuated by air pumps to lower levels of dust and moisture to as low as possible. The ship was carefully re-entered with Shell VPI-260 crystals in bags to give off a preservative gas. The hatches were then sealed and tamper-proof seals applied to the dogs to prevent entry.[2]

The bow foil was enclosed in a climate-controlled enclosure of plywood and shingle. The anhedral foil tips were removed and crated, as were the propellers. Then the entire main foil structure and FT4 housing were enclosed in a climate-controlled shelter and the ship on its barge was moved to Jetty Nine, the farthermost corner of Dockyard, to await her final outcome.

She sat, neglected, in this position, her only visitors being CFAV watchkeepers, until 1976. By this time it was known by all that the ship would never be re-activated and the ship was unsealed. Slowly items disappeared, to be declared surplus and handed over to Crown Assets for disposal. Over 1500 spare parts were inventoried and declared surplus and sold for scrap value. The super-cavitating propellers which had cost nearly $750,000 to design, build and use were sold as scrap.

The author saw *Bras d'Or* in 1979 just after a CTV television crew had been aboard to film her present state. Bunks, microwaves, freezers, radios, and electronic gear had been stripped and sold by this time. The Paxman diesel had been removed years before in 1971. Neglect was everywhere.

Shortly thereafter, *Bras d'Or* was moved to Jetty Six, the old Naval Armament Depot Wharf in Dartmouth. Here the dismantling began in earnest in 1981-82. The turbines were spirited away to DRB facilities in Quebec. By April, 1983, the destruction of the ship's interior was in its last stages, with the engine room a mass of tangled stainless steel piping, slippery with red hydraulic oil, making the ship appear to have bled to death.

It had been stated that *Bras d'Or* had been offered to various museums over the years. However, the estimated cost of $1 million to set up the ship as a practical exhibit had scared off any potential takers.[3] The Maritime Museum of the Atlantic hadn't the room.[4] *Bras d'Or* was claimed to lie outside the mandate of the Alexander Graham Bell Museum at Baddeck, N.S.[5] *Bras d'Or* was an engineering marvel that had failed in most people's estimation and was, therefore, a leper.

By 1982 it was plain that Maritime Command had only one choice . . . it would have to declare *Bras d'Or* surplus and watch it scrapped. Most were resigned to watching this unique experimental hydrofoil warship disappear under the cutter's torch, to exist only in memory and pictures like the *AVRO Arrow*. All seemed lost to those actively working to save her.

However, a new museum entered the picture, eager to acquire the ship. This was the Bernier Museum of L'Islet-sur-Mer, Quebec, who immediately began to investigate acquiring the hydrofoil craft. The negotiations dragged on until it was announced on May 25, 1983 that these talks had been successful . . . the *FHE-400* hulk now had a new home.

June 6th was one of the first sunny days of the month in Halifax as I waited at Jetty 6 for *Bras d'Or* to be towed away. The 10:00 AM departure time passed, with the tow postponed while the Salvage Insurance Inspector did

Towing *FHE-400* out of Halifax harbour on her slave barge, en route to the Bernier Museum, in Quebec, June 6, 1983.
Credit: Thomas G. Lynch

his last once-over after some defects had been corrected. Finally, the departure time was announced as 14:00 and after lunch, I returned, like other members of the press to witness her leaving.

Finally at 15:05 the tow rounded the end of Jetty 6, with the Montreal-based *Techno Venture* in the lead position, assisted by the Ville class tugs, *Parkville* and *Listerville*. (Many thanks to Captain Paul Brick and Captain John Barkhouse for the chance to witness the departure from close-up.)

Bras d'Or was last seen by Haligonians just off the Herring Cove Light at about 17:10 as she disappeared into the fog that had been threatening the city throughout the day. The last thing to disappear was the ship, on her slave barge, being towed backwards out into the Atlantic where she had so gracefully raced less than twelve years before. Adieu, *Bras d'Or*.[6]

But the story doesn't end here. The two arrived without incident at L'Islet-sur-mer on June 18th and were met by a very large bulldozer, which proceeded to tow the barge inland into a marshy basin that had been excavated to accept the ship. Here, six concrete pylons will be constructed and three steel strong-backs placed under the hull. The barge will be placed between the pylons at high tide and the strong-backs will come to rest on the pylons as the tide recedes. As the barge falls away, it will be towed clear and *Bras d'Or* will be secured fast.

However, in a brief ceremony, the Museum was presented with the crest for HMCS *Bras d'Or*, plus the title of the ship. When properly secured, the ship will be open to public viewing, a reminder of the near-greatness the ship represented and hopefully, a harbinger of the future for the Canadian Navy.

What went wrong with the *FHE-400* Project and why was it cancelled? To quote the various reasons given by differing sources is indicative of the confusion that exists surrounding the project and its aims. Let's examine these more closely.

1. Change in role for Maritime Command from a priority of anti-submarine warfare to sovereignty protection is the first and most quoted. However, examining the term "sovereignty protection", we find that this role has been one of the functions of the Canadian Navy from its very inception in 1910 with only one addition; fisheries protection patrols. The patrols and inspection of foreign fishing vessels within the 200-mile economic control zone has placed an enormous strain upon the fabric of Maritime Command, necessitating the grouping of all the helicopter-equipped frigates on the east coast and denuding Maritime Forces Pacific. It calls for the use of one operational destroyer or frigate year-round and makes little sense. Utilizing a 3700-4000 ton warship for this chore is extremely cost-inefficient; somewhat like using a howitzer to swat flies. *Bras d'Or* had proven capable of operating in sea states greater than five and with the recommended reduction in top speed to fifty knots, a follow-on series of hydrofoil craft would lend themselves to distinct classes for specific duties with a common hull. The role of fisheries patrol lies with the Federal Department of Fisheries and only this department's lack of suitable sea-going ships necessitated the tie-in with Maritime Command. A class of lightly-armed hydrofoil craft would have nicely fulfilled this role, with the high-speed 'dash' ability to pursue violators of the ICNAF agreement.

The retort to this answer usually suggests that hydrofoil craft haven't any northern water capability. However, one sad fact appears to elude such persons; the Canadian Navy hasn't an ice-capable warship to cover northern waters! True, the Canadian Coast Guard are admirably suited for this work, but are civilian and therefore unarmed.

Maritime Command, through it's sub-organization, Maritime Air Group, are only capable of aerial surveillance by Tracker and Aurora aircraft of northern waters and land masses.

This acquisition of the CP-140 Aurora long-range aircraft is given as another excuse for cancellation and is one of the few concrete explanations. However, with the time-spread of the acquisition of the Aurora, it would have been possible to still continue with the *FHE-400* evaluation and then to proceed with a follow-on class at a necessarily slower pace. Rather than precluding the hydrofoil warship, acquisition of the long-range aircraft would only have slowed the hydrofoil warship.[7]

Maritime Command's ships are still ASW-oriented; it is impossible to radically change the main thrust or role of warships within twenty years, let alone within twelve and without new ship construction. However, with the announced 'new' roles in the 1971 White Paper on Defence, the 'Multi-Purpose Frigate' has become the 'buzz' word of the 1980s.

If hydrofoil craft had been considered, it would have been possible to build a 'standard' hull/foil configuration, adapted to role by tailoring the weapons/sensor packages to meet specific requirements. Even at the time of writing, hydrofoil craft would be more cost-efficient than multi-purpose frigates in quite a few roles. However, this does not suggest that hydrofoil craft would supplant conventional surface combattants; far from it! Rather, the hydrofoil craft would compliment surface units and allow these extremely expensive units to be used in their prime roles of defence and anti-submarine warfare because, like it or not, the submarine threat is greater than ever and the Canadian Navy is still configured to this role and is considered to be very good at it by NATO partners.[8]

2. The idea that there wasn't any offshore purchasers for the hydrofoil craft has been debunked time and time again. Indeed, the then Minister of Defence, Donald MacDonald stated some months before *Bras d'Or's* demise;

> "There is still a high level of NATO interest in this hydrofoil development concept."[9]

The USN has developed a class of hydrofoil warships based on the PHM developmental craft. The Italians have adapted the Boeing Tucumcari design to their particular needs and have built the *Swordfish* class. Various European countries as well as Israel have adopted naval hydrofoil craft and a healthy commercial hydrofoil industry has grown up in Switzerland, Italy, the USA, USSR, China, France and Germany . . . but not in Canada. DeHavilland have beaten their heads against a brick wall of indifference on the part of the government (a major stock-holder) in proposing civil, coast guard, fisheries patrol versions of the *FHE-400* configuration.[10] Lots of offshore interest has been generated, but governmental backing necessary to seriously negotiate these deals with foreign governments has been noticeably absent and all tentative inquiries have fallen through.[11]

3. Next is the old chestnut about the programme being too costly. This is a complex subject and should be examined from all angles. If the original yardstick of $12 million projected in 1963 is applied to the equation, then a superficial 'yes' is true. However, examining the whole story from those forgotten days reveals the following factors;

(a) — It was not known just how complex the theories, simulation, construction and systems would become in 1963. Over 60% of the design changes were made in 1964-65 and were brought about through the identification of problem areas *as they occurred in the design and simulation stages*. It must be kept in mind that *Bras d'Or's* design pushed engineering knowledge into new and unexplored areas. Problems that arose were largely unforeseen and therefore required rectifying; it's an expensive procedure, whether designing a new automobile or a hydrofoil craft . . . except most of the problems with an auto fall within known engineering parameters. It would be more accurate to liken the process to designing a car that used anti-gravity to suspend the car and using a turbine for motive power.

(b) — The Defence Research Board and the RCN changed various components of the craft, with the latter demanding that the craft must be able to achieve 60 knots as mentioned as a *theoretical* top speed in the N.R.E. 1959 Report. The addition late in the design of controlled-incidence anhedral foil tips added six months to the planning and building of the craft, plus adding nearly $1 million to that year's budget. Whether the tips were needed or not has been discussed; the extra cost and engineering effort were expended. As far as speed, it wasn't known what the costs of the 60-knot top speed would be when the specifications went out. The first was that narrow, low-profile section hydrofoil elements would be necessary to control cavitation; both expensive to manufacture and difficult to make structurally sound, yet as light as possible. These factors, coupled with the excessive projected stresses from all sources of approximately 180,000 psi which necessitated the use of the relatively new NiCoMo 18% maraging steel, was bound to lead to difficulties. The narrow foil section spelt problems for the hydraulics people who had to devise the anhedral tip actuators to not only function properly, but to fit within very limited space.[12]

As a yardstick, after-the-fact, DREA estimated that for a requirement beyond 50 knots, the cost would be *$1 million per knot per ship*. This requirement in the design immensely inflated the costs of engineering and construction and wasn't really necessary, but this wasn't apparent until after the fact.

(c) — The November, 1966 fire at Sorel added $3.25 million to the actual cost of the vessel, but added $6.5 million to the costs of the programme overall, through re-engineering effort and loss of nearly eighteen months of precious time, the latter being a crucial blow to the assessment period of the hydrofoil programme. The fault and consequences of the fire have been covered in Chapter Five.

(d) — The continued problems with the CGE transmission systems cost a further six months of the pre-acceptance trial time. Due to the unique nature of the dual propulsion system, coupled with the low-weight/high-output specifications, the engineering effort was far in excess of comparable systems and pushed known engineering and metals to their very limits.

(e) — The excessive demands upon engineering the metals in the foil system was responsible in part for the two high-speed centre foil defects. Worse than the replacement costs in 1969-70, it robbed the programme of over eight months opportunity for foilborne testing. However, it should be stressed that under no circumstance was the craft ever in any danger from foil failure. Indeed, several runs, plus the Halifax-Bermuda-Norfolk-Halifax trip was made with the cracked foil section.

(f) — The lightweight, but high-power requirements with light feed-back requirements for steering, taxed the hydraulics industry to the maximum and beyond. Hydraulics capabilities and demands in pumps necessitated re-engineering of existing units available, with resultant failures of highly-stressed components. Indeed, it compelled the manufacturer to develop a new, high-output pump, the AP-12 V31B in 1970 to finally correct the situation of frequent pump failures.
(g) — The design, assembly and proving of the Action Information Centre and the weapons systems under a separate contract had been lumped into the research and development estimates for the *FHE-400* Programme and to this day they are included in the $52.7 million allocated by Treasury Board. These contracts exceeded $10 million and were never fitted. These are discussed later, but should *not* be attributed to the *FHE-400* actual cost.

If an actual follow-on hydrofoil ship class had been considered, the cost per unit without combat systems would have been in the order of $18-28 million (1972), depending upon specifications, per ship in a class of ten or more. Allowing for inflation over the intervening years, this cost would be about $53 million today, per unit, without weapons, for a 200-ton, open-ocean hydrofoil ship.

It can be seen by comparing hydrofoil ships to conventional ships that costs, per ton in design and construction, are 2-3 times greater. However, the manpower requirements of a nominal 40-45 for the hydrofoil ship compares very favourably versus the 230 projected for the new Patrol Frigate. This soon brings the cost within reasonable limits, since manning requirements account for 42.6% of the actual operating costs of each vessel in Maritime Command.[13] Additionally, with lower manning needs, it is possible to train, retain and pay crews to higher levels than is currently possible, largely because of greater selection of CAF recruits.

Was *Bras d'Or* a failure and a waste of the taxpayers money? The answers are a complex 'yes-no' exercise too.

Yes, *Bras d'Or* was a failure in that it was not allowed to complete its trials nor remain within budget. However these were conditions beyond the control of the vessel. Thus the answer to the first part must be a qualified 'no' as well. The ship did everything it was designed to do and more. It proved a 200-ton hydrofoil ship could survive and operate in open-ocean conditions in the North Atlantic, with reasonable range and endurance. That was all it was asked to prove.

For the second part of the question, it is 'yes'; the *FHE-400* project was chopped off in mid-stride, with only $6.5 million needed to install the Phase II fighting equipment and complete trials. All of the Phase II equipment was developed and built under a separate contract, hence bought and paid for before 1970.[14] Judging the spin-offs that occurred from the programme, the answer is a resounding 'no'. Sure, the tax-payer lost, but Canadian industry gained, making us that much more competitive on the world market. Additionally, the Navy gained in several important areas.
(a) — Up until the time of *Bras d'Or*, the computer was something utilized by the aerospace industry only. Canadian shipyards hadn't the need nor the inclination to install an analogue or the new digital computer. However, *Bras d'Or* served as a not-too-gentle reminder that the computer age was dawning. Today, no shipyard would consider doing business without a computer to calculate ship specifications in conjunction with their Lloyd's Specifications, to project material acquisitions and the timing of deliveries, to control running costs and to tabulate inventories.
(b) — The experience of building *Bras d'Or* left both DeHavilland and Marine Industries Limited with extensive knowledge and facilities to work and weld exotic steels and extensive aluminium structures. This knowledge has been applied in commercial applications over the past fifteen years.
(c) — The need for lightweight sensors and computer components brought the Canadian electronics industry the necessary surge of knowledge to bring it on par with American and Japanese manufacturers. Indeed, Canadian electronics are considered as good as any in the world today, with components being selected for the CF-18 and the U.S. Army's *Abrams* main battle tank. A healthy research and development programme has brought world-wide recognition and kept us in the forefront of electronic developments.

Development of the Action Information Centre, although never fitted aboard, was installed in the Maritime Warfare School, Dartmouth, N.S., and was utilized to train many personnel in using a computerized command centre, once the many teething problems were solved. It also served as basis for the CCS-280 system that was installed in the DDH-280 class of destroyers.

The AN/SQS-507 '*Helen*' lightweight sonar system research benefitted both the Navy and Canadian Westinghouse. The development of segmented fairing for tow cables to prevent 'off-kiting' of the submerged towed sonar body was applied to both the SQS-504 and 505 Variable Depth Sonar arrays on most of the Canadian frigates and destroyers. For Westinghouse Canada, it allowed them to develop a lightweight series of sonar sets in the HS-1000 series. One of the hull-mount variants has been sold to

the Netherlands for their new frigates and all remain among the lightest, most reliable sets in the Western World.
(d) — The development of the baffled, pressure-differential filters and housing led to the development of the system that found its way onto the *DDH-280* class. This class of warship enjoys the longest lifetime between overhauls for marinized gas turbines worldwide, outlasting similar applications of the FT-4 family by 800-1200 hours. Indeed, *Bras d'Or* was the first Canadian ship to utilize a gas turbine as a propulsive force and pointed out many areas of weakness that were successfully avoided in the 280 class.

What was the real reason *Bras d'Or* was laid up and abandoned in 1971? After throwing out all the stock reasons given as a smoke screen over the years, only one inescapable reason is left. Political policy of the government of the day. Frank B. Caldwell, Director of Programmes for the Navy League of Canada, put the reason in a nut-shell in the '1970 Maritime Command' article for *Canadian Shipping*;

> "Simply because they wanted to spend the money on other projects."

This somewhat elemental comment was in reference to the government's lavish increases in social programmes at that time. Since 1968, the Canadian military had faced a financial freeze when it needed increased spending for equipment in the worst of ways. Faced with ships that were only able to spend 82 percent of normal minimum requirements at sea because of reduced fuel allotment funds, it was easy to see how the Department of National Defence could be induced to chop the *FHE-400* Project!

However, the real underlying reason behind the cancellation of the *FHE-400* lies deeper in the Canadian mentality since World War Two. Although accomplishing great deeds in the industrial sector during the 1939-46 period, Canada has maintained an inferiority complex that contends it is unable to compete with the U.K. and to a greater extent, the USA in industrial/military research and development. This was aptly put by Rear-Admiral R. H. Leir, former Commander, Maritime Forces Pacific in a 1976 article in Canadian Shipping:

> "Unfortunately, we lost courage and gave up this very promising research with *Bras d'Or*. . . . we have lost courage so many times in the past just when pure research was about to blossom into new equipment."

Who is to blame then? The lack of confidence and courage in Canadians, in their ability to be innovative, original; echoed and amplified by our vote-seeking, faint-hearted, dithering political leadership, that's who.

Chapter Nine

Hydrofoils of the World, ...an overview

It is important to see *Bras d'Or* in the context of international developments in hydrofoil craft. During the period 1960 to 1972, the major hydrofoil developer was the United States, who faced the same challenges as Canada, but surmounted the obstacles and went on to a practical application in their PHM class.

1962-72;

By the early 1960s various manufacturers were involved in hydrofoil research for both the military and commercial interests. The real impetus was the 1961 Hydrofoil Accelerated Research Programme (HARPY), aimed at the accelerated development of bigger, better and faster hydrofoil craft. The initial craft was the Boeing of Seattle *Fresh-1*, awarded in June 1961, the '1' standing for the first version. It was powered by a Pratt and Whitney JT3D-3 turbine, which generated 18,000 lb of dry thrust and had two outboards for hullborne propulsion of four knots. This was a research vessel that achieved the enviable speed of 80 knots on May 3, 1963, a record that stands to this day for hydrofoil craft.[1]

However, a fundamental change to a 40-50 knot platform was made by the USN in 1963-64 and such craft as the revised *Fresh II* and *Denison* were laid up. It was considered worthwhile to continue with the Lockheed AG(EH)-1 *Plainview*, a 328-ton hydrofoil craft, delivered in June, 1965. *Plainview* was utilized as a platform to prove that large hydrofoil craft could operate in sea state five conditions at first, then as a hydrofoil test bed and weapon/sensor platform up until June 1978 when it was decommissioned.[2] The stripped hull was sold to commercial interests and information has it in northern Oregon being used as a mobile crab processing plant.

The first actual hydrofoil craft delivered to the USN was PCH-1 *High Point* from the Boeing, Seattle plant in August, 1963. It was used to prove the feasibility of inshore hydrofoil ASW systems until 1971 and then was overhauled in 1972. It was returned to the USN in March 1973, identified as PCH-1 Mod. 1 and configured to act as a test bed for PHM missile equipment and ASW devices. Harpoon surface-to-surface missiles were successfully launched in the US/Canadian Nanoose Range in December, 1973 and January, 1974.[3] It was further employed by the US Coast Guard in April 1975 in fisheries patrols, search and rescue and assessment trials before being handed back to the USN in 1979 to be used in assessing the USN's Extended Performance Hydrofoil Project. To this end, she was returned to Boeing and was being modified at the Puget Sound Naval Yard, starting in 1982, before beginning a two-year assessment.[4]

The next craft falling within this time frame was the 58-ton waterjet-propelled PGH-1, another Boeing product ordered in 1966 under a US Fixed Price Patrol Gunboat Hydrofoil Programme contract. The craft was constructed and tested in twenty-three months and delivered on March 7, 1968. The craft operated on both the East and West Coasts of the USA and took part in USN surveillance forces in Viet Nam. Indeed both PGH-2 and PGH-1 *Flagstaff* underwent intensive testing in Viet Nam in 1969. The PGH-2 *Tucumcari* was virtually destroyed when it ran aground seven miles east of Puerto Rico in November, 1972. She was towed off the reef and utilized as a fire containment test body at the US Naval Research and Development Centre before being scrapped.[5]

The last US hydrofoil to be examined is the Grumman PGH-1 *Flagstaff*, launched January 9, 1968 and delivered in September.[6] It underwent five and a half months of trials off South Vietnam between September 1, 1969 and February 19, 1970, undergoing operational testing in Operation Opeval and Operation Market Time, while based at Da Nang.[7,8] The ship, returned to the US, was modified between November and December, 1970 to accept a complete M-551 Sheridan light tank turret, containing a 152mm low-pressure gun. This gun is capable of firing conventional six-inch ammunition or the Shillelagh wire-guided missile, the latter being capable of hitting

USCG WPGH-4 Flagstaff, 1976

targets at four miles. The tests were successful, with little damage other than tripped electrical relays with full-charge loads.[9] *Flagstaff* underwent testing between 1974 and February, 1975 with the US Coast Guard and was permanently transferred in October, 1976 as Coast Guard vessel WPGH-4, operating off New England. However, the craft was far too expensive to operate, since one-off parts from Grumman were too costly and the ship was de-activated in 1977 before being scrapped.

It should be noted that the US opted for full-submerged, retractable foils from the very first. Indeed, this difference largely accounted for the exchange of information between Canada and the US. The US also opted for the standard main foils forward, support foil aft up, until the time of the Boeing PHM and PCH craft. These crafts had proven very good in inshore waters, but it is questionable if these vessels could have survived a stormy North Atlantic crossing without major damage or loss. *Bras d'Or* remained the only open-ocean capable hydrofoil for years after her demise.

The Soviets entered the military hydrofoil craft field with the 75-ton P-8 class wooden-hulled torpedo boat, equipped with oinly bow foils and gas turbine boost to become foilborne. These were largely obsolescent by the mid-1960s and have been retired. Most hydrofoil patrol boats that followed utilized only bow foils, the stern planing across the surface and negating the necessity of special propulsive pods or shafts. The next were the *Pchela* (bee) frontier patrol boats of which twenty-five were built between 1968 and 1972 and utilized by the KGB in patrolling coastal frontier waters. Several other improved classes have followed, but these lie outside the time frame and are mentioned later.[10]

Although late in this period, it should be noted that the Italian firm of Cantieri Navali Riuniti, SPA had acquired a licensing agreement to build an improved version of the Boeing PGH-2 *Tucumcari* in the late 1960s. They were awarded a contract in October 1970 to build these P-420 Sparviero class craft. The improved design, the first being called *Swordfish* was delivered in July 1974.[11]

PRESENT TRENDS:

Since 1970, a smaller, slower paced programme of developing hydrofoil combatant craft has been instituted by most countries. The US has pursued and built a class of PHM's that grew out of the 1970 NATO requirement. In 1971 the USN proceeded with the design studies, but one by one the interested NATO countries dropped out of the agreement as costs per unit escalated. By 1977 the US, fed up with the reluctance of NATO partners to participate, froze out the only country still actively interested, West Germany. In 1971, a $5.6 million contract had been awarded to Boeing to design a 230-ton craft and acquire parts for at least two more. Seventeen months later Boeing was awarded a $42,607,384 contract to develop the NATO PHM for the USN. Delivered in 1975, the *Pegasus* has been joined by five more sister ships by 1983, all allocated to Key West, Florida and are classified as open-ocean hydrofoil combatants.[12] However, the delay and cancellation of a hydrofoil flotilla repair and replenishment ship has seriously affected overseas deployment plans and the craft will likely remain in North American waters.

Grumman, singularly unlucky with their *Flagstaff* craft, succeeded in interesting Israel in a new improved variant first called *Flagstaff II* and later modified to M-161 or *Shimrit* (guardian). This was a much modified variant of the M-114 *Flagstaff*, with very sophisticated fire-control and attack capability. The first was built at the Lantana Boatyard, Palm Beach, Florida and launched in May 1981. After some frustrating teething problems, the craft managed to acquire some fifty trips in North American waters and had proven reliable. It was then shipped to Israel in early 1982 for further testing in operational settings. Meanwhile, the second of the class, *Livnik* (heron) was being built in Israel Shipyard, Haifa, lagging some eight to ten weeks behind the *Shimrit* so that unforeseen weaknesses could be rectified while in construction stages. *Livnik* slipped some three months behind *Shimrit* when defects were discovered in the latter and rectified, but she is now completed. It is planned to build ten of these hydrofoil craft but it is uncertain whether the Israelis will stick to this number. Nevertheless, Israel is blessed with two of the most advanced hydrofoil warships in the world, with advanced digital hybrid fly-by-wire automatic control systems. Craft state is sensed by appropriate sensors, the information is processed by a digital computer which generates foil commands through an analogue interface, which in turn commands the servo-actuators of the incidence-controlled flaps. This automatic system, coupled with the extensive missile mix (Harpoon and Gabriel III surface-to-surface missiles), Elta X and S-bands fire control and twin 30-mm Emerlec remote-controlled cannon make the Mk.II/M-161 a potent adversary.[13]

On the European front, Supramar of Switzerland, builders of hydrofoil ferry craft have proposed naval hydrofoil craft from the 100-foot *NAT.85* through the 250 tonne *MT 250*. However, the largest of these differs from former offerings by utilizing fully-submerged, canard-configuration foil systems rather than the fixed surface-piercing Schertel-Supramar air-stablized

USS *Tauris*, PHM-3, seen from above. Note the foil elements below the surface of the water and the two Harpoon S/S missile canisters.
Credit: Boeing Aircraft Co. Ltd. Seattle.

foil system. These are retractable, but since the ship mentioned has not come off the drawing board, little concrete information can be presented.[14]

The USSR has made the greatest effort to catch up with the western world in the hydrofoil field. Progressing from the *Pchela* craft, the Soviets have introduced progressively more sophisticated hydrofoils over the past fifteen years. The latest to enter service in numbers has been the *Turya* class, first seen in 1972. This 250-ton torpedo boat has a single main foil of trapeze configuration, set one-third of the hull length back from the bow. This allows the craft to obtain sprint speeds of 40-45 knots in calm water. Installation of a dipping sonar body suggests that a primary duty of the *Turya* class may be ASW in shallow waters, ASW weapons consisting of four 54cm ASW torpedoes in single fixed tubes. Six have been supplied to Cuba. Latest version has semi-retracting foils permitting the overall width to be reduced, thus enabling the *Turyas* to be berthed alongside in conventional facilities.

The latest Soviet hydrofoil to enter series production is the *Matka* missile-equipped fast attack craft. These will replace the twenty-year old *Osa* class and are based on the 39.3 metre steel *Osa* hull. A fixed surface-piercing trapeze foil is fitted forward to increase speed and lower wave impacts in rougher weather. The bow foil generates enough lift to raise the bows at about 24-28 knots and allows sprint speeds of 40-45 knots in calm waters. Series production began in 1978. Missiles consist of two SS-N-2C surface-to-surface missiles, plus one mount for a SA-7 *Grail* light AA missile launcher.

However, it is only with the advent of the *Babochka* class that the Soviets have entered the realm of the pure hydrofoil warship. This 400-ton hydrofoil craft, the largest in service in the world, first appeared in 1978 and is thought to use conventional configuration of surface-piercing bow foil and fully-submerged rear foil with automatic trailing edge flaps, utilizing sonic/electronic controls. It is thought that the *Babochka* class when they enter service will replace the 19-year old *Poti* class coastal anti-submarine vessel.

The forerunner of a new class of formidable fast strike missile craft, the 330-tonne *Sarancha* is one of the biggest naval hydrofoil craft in the world. Like *Babochka*, this hydrofoil is truly foilborne, utilizing gas turbines, 'Z'-drives and combined surface-piercing and submerged foil systems. The craft, first seen in 1977, is armed with four SS-N-9 anti-ship missiles, an SA-N-4 surface-to-air missile system and a 30mm Gatling type cannon. The foil system is fully retractable and the craft is auto-stabilized in the best Western manner. Top speed is 50 knots plus and if ever actively deployed in a 'bush war' in the Third World, should account very well against Western equipment.[15]

France has one developmental craft on the boards: a 185-ton fast patrol hydrofoil ship utilizing fully-submerged, sub-cavitating canard configuration foils, named *Saphyr*. 80% of all-up weight is carried by the aft, retracting foils and 20% by the bow foil. Camber of the foils is flap-controlled for low-speed stability.[16]

Britain has had little to do with developing hydrofoil craft since the 1950s, but have kept an active interest in the subject through NATO membership. In 1976 it extended its fisheries control zone from twelve to two hundred nautical miles and the onus was placed on the Royal Navy to provide inspection and interception craft within this zone. Obviously there wasn't a way that a craft could be in any specific area for long and the numerous boardings and inspections necessary were at odds with each other.

In the spring of 1977 the Boeing hydrofoil craft, *Flying Princess* made a tour of Northern European countries, plus a brief evaluation period with an RN team while in Britain. Based upon the versatility of the jetfoil, the RN commissioned Boeing to investigate a modified version of the hull for performing fisheries patrols. The resultant design was accepted by the RN and one was ordered in June, 1978. Christened HMS *Speedy* on July 9, 1979 and shipped to Britain after trials, to finally commission in April, 1980.

Although *Speedy* has yielded splendid results in this field, it was decided to decommission and sell her as part of the reduction of Fleet strength in mid-1982.[17]

Lastly, there is the People's Republic of China. Starting in 1966, the HuTang Shipyard in Shanghai began turning out a 40-ton hydrofoil torpedo boat for the Chinese Navy, generally known as the *Hu Chwan* (White Swan) class. Since that date, some 150 of these hydrofoil craft have been built, with another 32 lent or leased to the Albanian Navy, four to Pakistan, four to Tanzania and three to Romania, the latter building sixteen or more of a modified design within their own borders.

The hull is a high speed, 'V'-bottom design of corrosion-resistant light alloy. There is a sub-foil ahead of the main foil to assist take-off, where the main trapeze or shallow 'V' configuration foil raises the better half of the hull clear of the water's surface during calm weather. The same foil assembly retracts upwards when the ship is cruising hullborne or docking.

The engines are three 1,100 HP M-50 water-cooled, supercharged twelve-

A Soviet Turya class hydrofoil craft in the service of the Somalia Republic, 1976.
Credit: USN

Military Hydrofoil Craft of the World (Only Operational or Once-Operational Listing) Table 9-1

Class	Country Operating	Length × Width × Draft Overall	When Commissioned	Purpose	When Decommissioned	Remarks
P-8	USSR			MTB	Retired 1970s	75-ton wood-hulled, bow foil, gas turbine assist.
Turya	USSR	39.3m × 12.3m × 3.8m	First in 1972	MTB	operational (30 of)	250 tons, bow foil only.
Pchela (Bee)	USSR	27m × 8m × 2.6m	First in 1968	KGB frontier patrol	operational (25 of)	Strela-derivative, 60 ton.
Matka	USSR		First in 1977	missile FPB	operational (8 of)	Osa replacement.
Sarancha	USSR	51m × 23m × 3.5m	First in 1977	FSPB	forerunner of class	330 m. tonnes.
Babochka	USSR	50m ×?	First seen in 1978	ASW	in production	400 tons. ASW hydrofoil, replacing Poti.
PCH-1	USN	35.28m × 6.04m × 6.04m	August, 1963	Navy research	still operational in EPH testing	131 tons. Boeing built.
PGH-2	USN		March 7, 1968	Navy research	lost Nov./72, Puerto Rico	58 ton wt-jet propelled
NATO PHM	USN (to date)	40.5m × 14.5 × 7.1m	First in 1975	FMPB	six in class	241 tonnes. Boeing.
PGH-1 Flagstaff	USN/USCG	26.36m × 11.28 × 4.26m	Sept. 1968	weapons test platform.	deactivated 1978	67.5 tons, Grumman.
M-161/ Flagstaff II	Israel/USA	29.81m × 12.45m × 4.83m	May/81	FMPB	evaluation by Israel	built by Grumman, Shimrit by name. Livnik to be built in Israel.
AG (EH)-1 Plainview	USN	66.75m × 25.19m × 1.9m (retracted)	March 1969	experimental	deactivated 1978, disposed	328 ton. Lockheed.
HMS SPEEDY	USA/G.B.	27.2m × 9.2m × 5.2m	June, 1980	fisheries patrol	declared surplus 1982	based on boeing Jetfoil 929-115. Surplus as cutbacks in budget.
Swordfish	USA/Italy	24.6m × 10.8m × 1.6m (foilborne)	July, 1974	FMPB	seven in class	Sparviero class. Based on PGH-2. Italian. 64 M.T.

Military Hydrofoil Craft of the World (Only Operational or Once-Operational Listing) Table 9-1 cont'd

Class	Country Operating	Length × Width × Draft Overall	When Commissioned	Purpose	When Decommissioned	Remarks
Hu Chwan (White Swan)	People's Republic of China	22m × 6.5m (hull) × 1m (foilborne)	First in 1966	MTB	150 in class; 32 to other countries	foils forward, none aft. 40 tons f.1.
Houma	People's Republic of China	29m × 6.5m × 1.5m (foilborne)	prototype in 1970	FAC	in service	95 tonnes, based on Komar hull. Foils forward.
FHE-400	Canada	45.9m × 20m × 7.16m (static)	July, 1968	developmental	May 1, 1972	open-ocean intent. DeHavilland Canada.
Hu Chwan	P.R.C./Romania	21.8m × 5.02m × 1m (foilborne)	first in 1972	MTB	operational, 20 in class	modified Chinese foilborne MTB.
ST 3A	Switzerland/USN	10.32m × 3.6m × 1.55 (static)	1966	research	N/K	Schertel-Supramar air stabilization system. 5-ton.
PAT 20	Switzerland	21.75m × 8.6m × 1.4m (static)	1976	coastal patrol	current with several navies	69 tons, coastal waters only. Based on commercial PT 20B Mk.II
Shantung	P.R. of C.	25.1m × 6m × 1.8m (static)	1966	FPB	N/K	80 tons, few of, poor design.

NOTE: All measurements are overall, lengths including retracted foils, beams include widest foil measurement and draft is hullborne, with foils down unless otherwise stated.

FPB — Fast Patrol Boat
MTB — Motor Torpedo Boat
x FSPB — Fast Strike Patrol Boat
FMPB — Fast Missile Patrol Boat
FAC — Fast Attack Craft

cylinder V-type diesels, each driving an inclined shaft. Two 53cm (21″) torpedo tubes, plus four 15mm machine guns in twin mounts make up the weapons suite. Maximum speed in calm waters is 50-55 knots, with a range of 100-150 nautical miles.

The latest hydrofoil craft to enter service with the Chinese is a derivative of the *Hoku* class fast attack craft (missile) which is based on the Soviet *Komar*, but with a steel hull. The difference being that the *Houma* is fitted with a bow foil, is slightly longer and has another twin 25mm AA mount aft. The first was launched in 1970. The hydrofoil is situated approximately one-third of the hull length from the bow. It is approximately 95 tonnes and maximum foilborne speed is about 40-45 knots in calm waters.[18]

FUTURE TRENDS

Future trends have been based upon larger hydrofoil craft with greater and greater emphasis on hullborne seakeeping abilities. This has been made more apparent by the greater length-to-width ratios in projected designs and fine lines of the hull for greater sea-worthiness.

Most hydrofoil advocates point to development of higher-tonnage hydrofoils of 400 through 3200 tons. Investigating these craft, country by country, it is quickly seen that these hydrofoil ships are limited by their costs to large western countries and the USSR. Known Soviet developments have been discussed in the last section of this chapter already, so this leaves only the USA, France and to a lesser degree, Canada.

In 1979, Direction Techniques des Constructions Navales studied a proposal for a high-tonnage hydrofoil which would meet requirements outlined by the Chiefs of Staff of the French Navy for a vessel to be used in the 1990s.

The proposal was for an ASW vessel with a displacement of 2,000 metric tons, a calm water foilborne speed in excess of 50 knots and an ability to operate in sea state six, plus have a range of 2,000 nautical miles foilborne. The design study suggested a catamaran-type hull structure consisting of two welded light alloy lateral keels linked by a buoyancy tank, supported by fully submerged, canard configuration foils with one-third of the dynamic lift generated by the bow foil and two-thirds by the aft foils. Both foils would be hydraulically-retractable. Foil incidence angles would be controlled by sonic autopilot on both foils, with auxiliary foil surfaces on the rear strut, above the main foil, to operate differentially to provide roll control.

Engines would be two FT9 turbines of 30,000 kW maximum power each. Drives would be via mechanical 'Z'-drive, with two fixed-pitch base-ventilated propellers. Hullborne power would be via two diesels, each driving a fixed-pitch propeller. All power-plants would be installed in the lateral keels. Crew would be ninety-two officers and men, armament two *Lynx* ASW helicopters, six MM40 surface-to-surface missile tubes and a 100mm DP gun, with final armament suite to be defined by the purchaser.[19]

Since the cancellation of the *FHE-400* Project, Canada's studies have become low-key and closely related to US efforts. Lack of funding has assured that this will continue into the foreseeable future. Hence, to try to separate these efforts other than on important points would be confusing.

Coverage of the small displacement efforts to date fall in the NATO PHM and Flagstaff II/M-161 sections, so we will proceed to the intermediate, medium and large tonnage hydrofoil craft projections.

Studies done to project naval warfare into the last decade of this century and the first of the twenty-first century have shown that roles necessary will be best suited to intermediate and medium hydrofoil ships. Technology and the knowledge gained by the small hydrofoil craft of the 1960s through 1980s have shown these ships are feasible. To take full advantage of these two facts, advanced studies were initiated by Grumman, David Taylor Naval Ship Research and Development Centre, Advanced Marine Enterprises and Defence Research Establishment Atlantic, Canada. It should be clarified that all have been involved with intermediate sizes where Grumman has projected into the larger tonnage category.

First, let us examine Grumman, Bethpage, New York State;

Starting in September, 1974, Grumman began exploring the potential of hydrofoil craft as open-ocean combatants for the USN. Preliminary designs of ships ranging in displacement from 1,330 to 1,625 tonnes had been proposed, with both retractable and fixed hydrofoil alternatives. Ranges in the order of 3,000 nautical miles and speeds in excess of fifty knots, plus continuous operations in sea state six were parameters of these designs. Proposed powerplants are the twin General Electric LM 2500 gas turbine package, with optional gas turbines for hullborne operation. Power would be transferred by 'Z' drive to supercavitating constant-pitch propellers while foilborne and controlled-pitch propellers in hullborne mode.[20]

However, under the USN's Advanced Naval Vehicles Concepts Evaluation Study, Grumman delivered the conceptual design of a 2,400-tonne hydrofoil warship in March 1977 (see Table 9-2). The programme was restricted in that the design had to embody known parameters of design and materials so that a projected design could be evaluated and possibly initiated in the 1990s. The most noticeable design feature of the ship proposal is the accommodation for two LAMPS III helicopters, the canard, fully-submerged hydrofoil system with 40% of the ship weight carried by the bow foil and 60% by the aft foil, both foils being retractable in the hullborne mode.

Engines in this proposal were Turbo Power and Marine Systems FT9 gas turbines for foilborne operation and a single GE LM 500 gas turbine for hullborne operation. All would be amidships and drive four propellers, two foilborne and two hullborne through a combined transmission.[21]

During the late 1970s, the Canadian Exchange Officer (CED) at David Taylor Naval Ship Research and Development Centre documented a study entitled, "Fast, Light Frigate" as an example of a hydrofoil ship which would fulfill Canadian needs. The FLF took full advantage of a fixed, fully-submerged foil system. This was followed by a later CEO study entitled, "Canadian-US Hydrofoil" or *CUSH* for short, (see Table 9-3 for specifications.), a lower-cost alternative to the FLF.

The FLF study led the US to consider a hydrofoil ship which could be built with either fixed or fully-retractable foils. Combined-drive variants have been proposed, utilizing a common transmission for both foilborne and hullborne propulsion.

Starting in 1980, the Surface Ship Continuing Concept Formulation (CONFORM) Programme supported the 1981 Corvette Escort Study as well as the previous proposals. This study investigated many of the options and new developments for intermediate-sized hydrofoil ships, oriented toward a specific application. This and the 1982 CONFORM Light Battle Group Escort (KE(X)) Study were the most mission-specific designs performed in this weight class.

The major aims of new design studies will be to simplify the engineering, layout and reduce the costs of propulsion machinery and transmission systems. Reliability has greatly increased over the years, but 'Z'-drives by their very complexity, resist cost-cutting or simplification. Hence, most designers are looking at ways to eliminate these in future prospects. Additionally, combined power sources and transmissions are being actively researched for both hull and foilborne operations.[22]

The subject of projecting future classes of warships has been vastly complicated in the past fifteen years by outside forces, largely unpredictable. However, examining the future trends of the Canadian Armed Forces and Maritime Command in particular, a clear-cut projection is possible with a fair degree of accuracy. However to put these choices in perspective, the dilemma Canada finds herself facing in the 1980s must be detailed.

With the continued delay and final cancellation of the Fast Patrol Frigate in the 1960s, Canada was forced to consider a larger, more cost-inefficent ship, the *DDH-280*.[23] However, this class was a compromise in design and more importantly are manpower intensive. It was therefore a foregone conclusion that a follow-on class of this sort would not be possible with MARCOM's dwindling manpower base. Since 1974 not one new warship has been seen in Canadian shipyards.

The slip-shod method of ship acquisition forced on Maritime Command by over-zealous budget cutting and the dissolving of the Naval Design Team at the end of the *DDH-280* class programme, a process that had started in 1966 with the finishing of the *Annapolis* class of helicopter-carrying frigates, forced naval design and acquisition into the hands of commercial Canadian shipbuilders. Prior to this, a specific ship design and specification was devised by Department of National Defence Production and supplied to prospective competitors. Now the shipyards were thrown back on their own resources to design and define a warship configuration to meet a set of general demands and principles made by Maritime Command through Supply and Services. Canadian shipyards were ill-equipped to do this and it has led to a great deal of difficulty with the Canadian Patrol Frigate design time frame.

Starting in the mid-1970s, a vague process of acquiring a Canadian Patrol Frigate class was initiated. Despite the desperate need for haste, the programme has drifted along, with various delays, the least of which was not having a clearly defined role for the ship class from government. Conglomerate corporations such as SCAN Marine have resulted, bent on building ships with maximum Canadian manpower, utilizing off-shore hull designs modified to meet CPF requirements. To make matters worse, an impossible

Characteristics of the Grumman M-161 (HYD-2) Proposal — Table 9-2 .

Dimensions:	Length-(pp)	97.54m	320 feet
	Foils retracted (OA)	111.17m	364 feet 9 inches
	Foils Extended (OA)	106.85m	350 feet 7 inches
	Beam (OA) foils ret.	24.69m	81 feet
	foils ext.	35.62m	116 feet 10½ inches
	(hull)	15.87m	52 feet 1 inch
	Operational draft, foils ret.	5.72m	18 feet 9 inches
	Operational draft, foil ext.	13.41m	44 feet
	Nominal draft, foilborne-	5.43m	17 feet 10 inches
	Radar scanner height, nominal:		
	foilborne-	24.99m	82 feet
	hullborne-	17.07m	56 feet
Weight	2400 tonnes displacment		

Powerplants and Drives:
Foilborne- 2X FT9 gas turbines, 43,000 max. intermittant @4,000 RPM, 2 variable pitch prop.
hullborne- 1X GE LM 500 gas turbine, 5,100 SHP intermittant, @7,000 RPM, 2 variable pitch, reversible propellers with combined gearbox.

Electrics: 3X Lycoming T35 gas turbines, 2,800 SHP continuous at 15,000 RPM
Two for normal generators, one emergency or anchor operation.

Personnel: 155 officers and men.

Fast Light Frigate Option Comparison Table 9-3

Item	FLF(F) Fixed foils 2*	Retraction opt.	FLF(C1) Fixed Option 3**	Retraction Option 3**	FLF(C2) Retraction Option 4**	Fixed Option 5**
LBP	200 feet	NIL	196 feet	196 feet	196 feet	196 feet
Full Load Weight	4985 tonnes	NIL	536.7 tonnes	536.8 tonnes	519.7 tonnes	519.7 tonnes
Instrument HP, F.B.	21,000	NIL	24,000	24,000	24,000	24,000
Instrument HP, HB	2700	NIL	2,698	2,698	2,608	2,608
Usable Fuel Wt.	112.7 tonnes	NIL	112.6 tonnes	125.8 tonnes	109.3 tonnes	119.8 tonnes
Relative H.B. Range (13 kt., sea state 4)	1.0	NIL	1.05	1.18	1.01	1.13
Relative Acquisition Cost	1.0	NIL	1.04	1.03	1.04	1.02
Relative total Life Cycle Cost	1.00	NIL	1.00	1.03	1.01	1.00

NOTES: * — Three Detroit Allison 570 KB gas turbines with three propellers via three 'Z' drives for baseline.
** — Single G.E. LM 2500 Gas Turbines with split 'Z' drive to two propellers.
2 — MTU 12V493 diesels for H.B. operation X2.
3 — 2X MTU 12V331TC81 Diesels through three separate propellers.
4 — 1X 16V538TB81 MTU diesel with combiner gearbox.
5 — Additional Pratt and Whitney ST6J-70 gas turbine, reduction gear hull-mount propeller for retracted foil, hullborne movement.

set of demands was specified and a definite financial 'lid' placed on total cost, effectively saying; "We want this, but only have this much money", like shopping for champagne with a beer budget! The assembly of the programme has cost years in lead time and the first ships will not appear before 1987 ... if then. Meanwhile, the last ship will cost an estimated $300 million, a prohibitive cost now and an impossibility after 1990 with present projections of defence budgets and attitudes. Clearly, Canada must examine an alternative to the conventional surface warship.[24]

There are only three alternatives:

(a) The Small Waterplane Area, Twin Hull (SWATH) Ship. The first practical example of this type of ship was the 190-ton displacement *Kaimalino*, launched in 1973 for the USN. Progress in the US has been slow, largely because of a lack of funding, but the SWATH ship shows great promise in greater seakeeping ability and fuel economy through vastly decreased waterline areas. The ship is basically a catamaran in configuration, with two, narrow vertical hulls arising from two cigar-shaped underwater hulls that will contain the entire propulsion machinery in larger examples and the lower gears and propeller shafts in smaller models. Indeed, this is one of the problems in progress on this type craft; the larger ships are very easy to build, but down-scaling for smaller scale models testing involves having the propulsion machinery on the main deck and a complex series of 'Z' drives to the lower hulls.

Atop the narrow hulls would be the main deck platform and superstructure (see illustration.).

Other disadvantages to date have been increased resistances due to the immersed areas, something that keeps fuel economy low. However, this lies within research efforts currently underway and could be solved readily. Funding for research remains a barrier in both Canada and the U.S., however.[25]

(b) — A complete submarine fleet: this was advocated by one member of

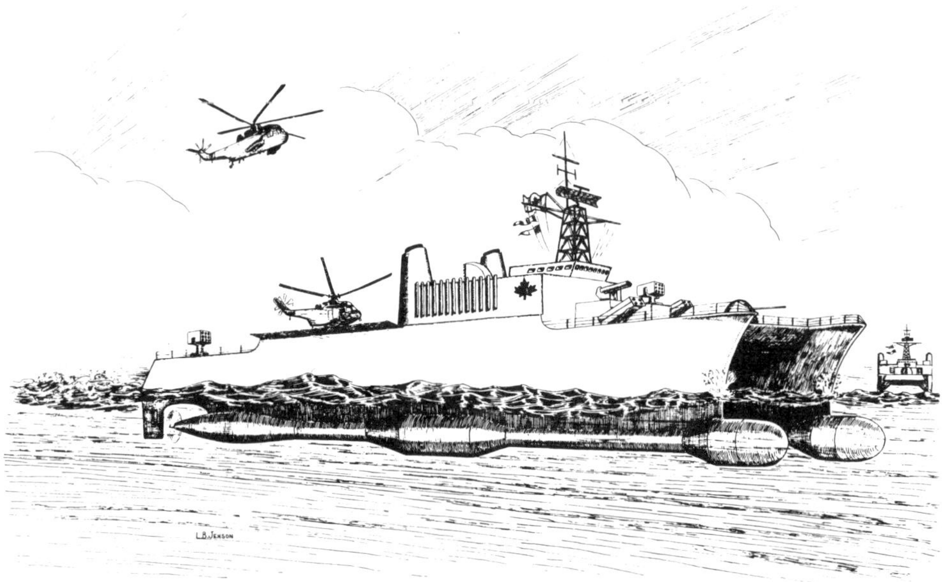

Drawing by L. B. Jensen of a possible follow-up to the CPF: the Small Waterline Area, Twin Hull — SWATH — ship.
Credit: DREA

the USN in early 1983 after obviously becoming disgusted with the mixed bag of ships that make up Maritime Command. However, with the multi-tasking of roles that Ottawa demands, submarines would not fill the bill to exclude surface units, but will play an important supportive role in a mixed fleet.[26]

(c) — Hydrofoil ships: although Canada has apparently dropped any idea of surface-piercing hydrofoil ships, the consideration of lower-intermediate (400-500 ton) hydrofoil craft with canard configuration, fixed, fully-submerged foil systems with flap-incidence controls is on-going with DND ship planners and DREA staff.[27] There are many advantages:

1 — Hydrofoil ships of this size are a viable option to conventional escorts using currently available or near-term technology.

2 — Hydrofoil ships, for their relatively small size, can be immensely effective and because of reduced cost-per-unit in series production, more of them can be purchased. Their superior performance and numbers afford the naval commander far greater flexibility and capability.

3 — With increased emphasis on seakeeping in the hullborne mode, endurance has increased markedly. This allows these fuel-critical vessels to remain in patrol areas for greater periods of time without refuelling.

4 — With increased diving depths and speed capabilities of Soviet *Typhoon* and *Alpha* class nuclear submarines, a vessel with high-speed 'dash' capability is needed more and more. This 'dash' ability of over fifty knots, combined with the ability to patrol at relatively slow speeds while conducting active or passive sonar searches makes the hydrofoil ship hard to resist by overworked, under-equipped naval services.

5 — The previously-mentioned ratio of manpower required per vessel still holds valid. Even with the 400-500 ton range, crew member numbers remain around 40-50 men per ship versus the 220-230 required by the CPF. This saving in turn converts into viable funds for increased salaries and/or equipment acquisitions for the near future.

Given the facts, it is possible to envision by the year 2000 a Canadian Navy of twelve Canadian Patrol Frigates, four *DDH-280s* (up-graded and nearing life's end), four new conventional submarines and twenty multi-tasked hydrofoil warships off Canada's coasts. Given the economic times and political/public indifference prevelant in Canada for the past fifteen years, Canada will have no financial alternative by 1990 if she wishes to remain a sovereign state. If this attitude and financial scenario holds true, the resultant warship might resemble the CUSH figure below;

One inescapable fact remains; Canada, by her termination of the *FHE-400* Programme, lost any advantages she had enjoyed in technology, skilled designers and engineers. Chances are that although these prospective hydrofoil ships may be built in Canadian yards, the basic design and know-how will be of US origin, tailored to meet Canadian needs.

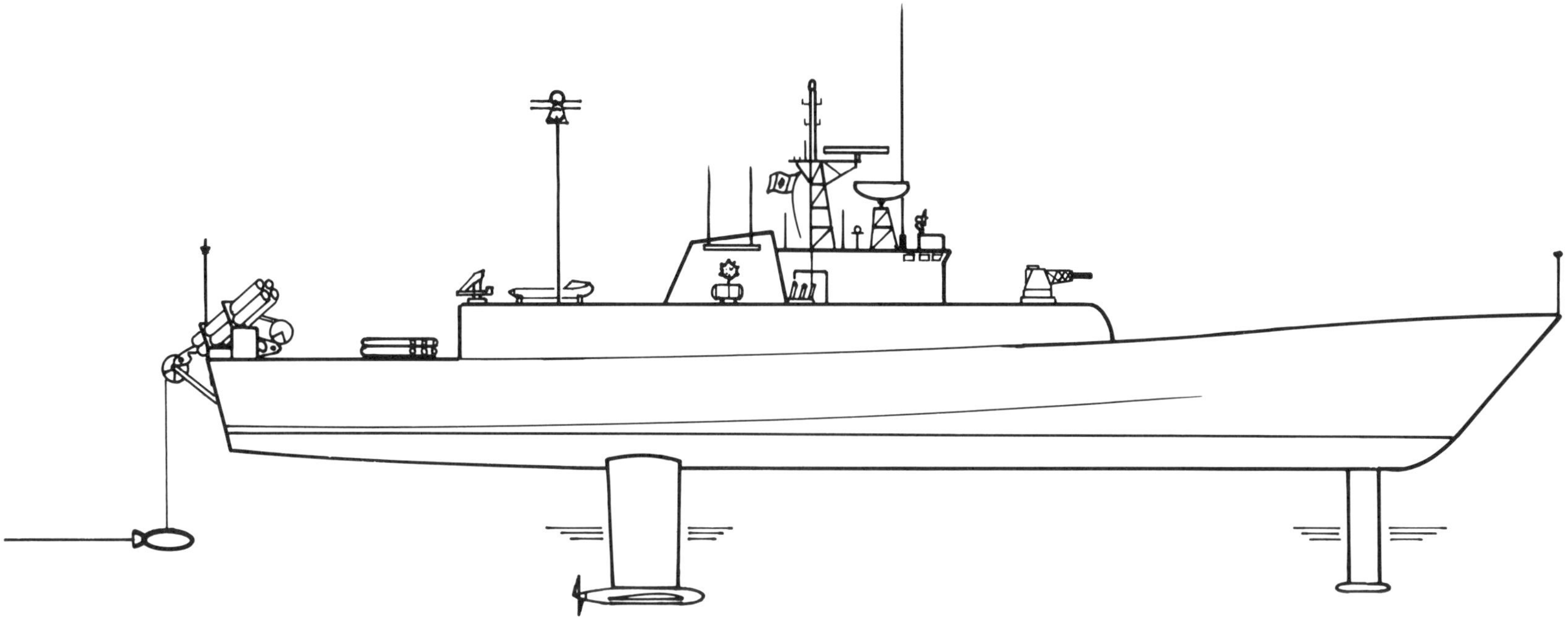

Diagram of the design proposed of the Canadian/US Hydrofoil — CUSH — ship.
Credit: DREA

Appendix A
References

References — Chapter One

1 Further information on this period is available from: J. H. Parkin, "Bell and Baldwin", (Toronto, University of Toronto Press, 1964), pp. 332-486.

2 "The Canadian Hydrofoil Project: Progress and Preliminary Trials of the R-100", Report number PHx-88, Dartmouth, Naval Research Establishment (N.R.E.), June 1, 1953, pp. 1-3.

3 J. W. Milman and Cdr. R. E. Fisher, "The Canadian Hydrofoil Programme", Ottawa, Department of National Defence, 1965, pp. 2-3.

4 Committee of Massawippi Boat Project, Minutes of, Defence Research Board, Ottawa, July 11, 1949, (DRBS-2-1087-101), Directorate of History (DHist).

5 Letter from Naval Secretary of Flag Officer, Atlantic Coast, Halifax. January 13, 1950. NSS 1660-36, DHist.

6 Letter from Cdr. (S.B.) Duncan Hodgson to Vice-Director General E. Ll. Davies, February 19, 1950, DHist. Ottawa.

7 "The Canadian Hydrofoil Project . . .", (N.R.E.).

8 Ibid.

9 Allotment Notification, DND Vote 400, Primary 70, A.N. No. 459, Ottawa, NSS 1660-36, DHist.

10 "The Canadian Hydrofoil Project . . ."

11 Report from Hull Inspector and Surveyor, HMC Dockyard, Halifax, to Manager Constructive Department, Dockyard on Survey of hull damage, October 9, 1953, NSS 1660-36, DHist, Ottawa.

12 M. C. Eames, "The Canadian Hydrofoil Project, Intermediate Hydrofoil System for the *R-100*", Report PHx-106, N.R.E., May, 1957, Defence Research Establishment Atlantic Library, Dartmouth, N.S.

13 A. J. Tachmindji, W. B. Morgan, M. L. Miller and R. Hecker, "The Design and Performance of Super-cavitating Propellers", Report C- 807, (Washington, D.C., David Taylor Model Basin, February, 1957).

14 Milman and Fisher, "The Canadian Hydrofoil Programme", 1966, pp. 2-3.

15 M. C. Eames, "A Review of Hydrofoil Development in Canada", IHSC, 1982, pp. 3-4.

16 Memorandum from Chief Superintendant, N.R.E. to Dr. F. H. Sanders, NDHQ, June 13, 1956.

17 P. R. Crewe, "The Hydrofoil Boat: its History and Future Prospects", Vol. 100, #4, Royal Institute of Naval Architects, London, October, 1958, pp. 357-359.

18 Report Nos. H/O/161 and H/O/171, Westland Aircraft Ltd., Saunders-Roe Div., 1958 and June 1963, DRE(A) Library.

19 Janes All the World's Aircraft, 1945-46, Janes, London, pp. 26d-27d.

20 *Crowsnest*, Ottawa, Queen's Printer, May, 1957, pp. 13.

21 M. C. Eames, "Hydrofoil Development in Canada", (IHSC), 1982, pp. 3-4.

22 Letter from Directorate of History, Ottawa to author, March 11, 1983.

23 Trial Data Sheets, 1957-58, N.R.E., 1958, DRE(A), Dartmouth, N.S.

24 P. R. Crewe, "The Hydrofoil Boat . . .", R.I.N.A., London.

25 Eames, "Hydrofoil Development . . . Canada", (IHSC), 1982.

26 Ibid.

27 Report H/O/171, Saunders-Roe Division, June, 1963, DRE(A).

28 M. C. Eames, "Experimental Bodies For High Speed Underwater Towing Research", *Canadian Aeronautics and Space Journal*, Vol. 13, no. 5, May, 1967.

29 Eames, "Hydrofoil Development . . . Canada", 1982.

30 J. H. Harris, "An Experimental Facility for High Speed Underwater Research", Canadian Aerospace Journal, December, 1969, pp. 417-421.

31 E. A. Jones, "*Rx*, A Manned Model of the RCN Hydrofoil Ship Bras d'Or", Journal of Hydronautics, Vol. 1, no. 1, July, 1967.

32 Halifax-Herald, November 13, 1962.

33 N. E. Jefferey, "Proteus — A Versatile Vehicle for Open-Ocean Hydrodynamics Research", (DRE(A), Dartmouth, 1969).

34 Canadian Shipping and Marine Engineering, Toronto, October, 1970, pp. 18-21.

35 Vancouver Sun, August 3, 1970.

36 Letter to author from Mr. D. C. Cameron, President, Canadian Aircraft Products, Ltd., Richmond, B.C., May 10, 1983.

37 Jefferey and Ellis, "Proteus . . .", DREA, Dartmouth.

References — Chapter Two

1 Bernard Fitzsimons, editor, "The Illustrated Encyclopedia of 20th Century Weapons and Warfare", Vol. 18, New York, Columbia House, 1969, pg. 1972.

2 Director of Naval Intelligence, "Understanding Soviet Naval Developments", Fourth Edition, Washington, Office of the Chief of Naval Operations, Dept. of the Navy, 1981.

3 Eames, "Hydrofoil Developments in Canada", IHSC, 1982.

4 Milman and Fisher, "Canadian Hydrofoil Programme", pp. 4-5.

5 Eames, "Hydrofoil Developments . . .", IHSC, 1982.

6 Milman and Fisher, ". . . Hydrofoil Programme . . .", pp. 4-5.

7 Capt. F. Harley to Mr. Philpott, BAI, correspondance, Ottawa/Montreal, August-October, 1960, DHist, Ottawa.

8 Letter to DRB Director-General from Captain F. Harley, September 23, 1960, DHist, Ottawa.

9 Stevens Report #LR-877, "Report on 1/25 scale model Trials", *FHE-400* files, November 28, 1961, DHist, Ottawa.

10 Hydrofoil Project Review Group, First Meeting, Minutes of, DeHavilland Aircraft of Canada Ltd., Toronto, April 12-13, 1961.

11 EDO Corporation, "Proposal For Dipped Sonar for Hydrofoil craft", Report 5165, Washington, September 15, 1960, DHist, Ottawa.

12 G. J. Biefer, "Stress-Corrosion Cracking of Neoprene Coated 18% Nickel Maraging Steel", Ottawa, Department of Energy, Mines and Resources, Aug. 30, 1967, DHist.

13 Cmdre R. P. Welland, RCN,A/CNO, "Operational Uses of Hydrofoil Craft", Royal Canadian Navy, Ottawa, NS-8000-36, vol. 6, Dec. 11, 1961. DHist. Ottawa.

References — Chapter Three

1 Andre Rochon, "Shipyard Approach to the Hull Construction of the *FHE-400* Hydrofoil Ship" Canadian Shipbuilding and Ship Repairing Association, Technical Section, Quebec City, February 14, 1967. Maritime Museum of the Atlantic, Halifax.

2 Hydrofoil Project Review Board, "*FHE-400* Hydrofoil Development Review of Progress, No. 3/05", DeHavilland Aircraft of Canada Ltd., Downsview, Ont., Oct. 12, 1965 HPO NS 8000-FHE-400 file, DHist, Ottawa.

3 Ninth Hydrofoil Progress Meeting, Minutes of, Ottawa, November 2, 1965, item 2.6, p. 4.

References — Chapter Four

1 DeHavilland Aircraft of Canada Ltd., "Engineering Procurement Specification: Transmission System for RCN Prototype ASW Hydrofoil Ship", Amendment B, Toronto, November 28, 1963 pp. 1-15.

2 Milman and Fisher, "Canadian Hydrofoil Programme", pp. 11-12.

3 M. C. Eames and E. A. Jones, "HMCS Bras d'Or, An Open Ocean Hydrofoil Ship", Report 69/9, R.I.N.A., London, DREA, April 22, 1970 p. 122.

4 Commander J. H. W. Knox, "Trials and Tribulations of a Hydrofoil", *Canadian Shipping & Marine Engineering News*, April, 1970, pp. 33-36.

5 DeHavilland Aircraft of Canada Ltd., Phase I Experimental ASW Hy-

drofoil Instructor's Handbook, Toronto, 1966. MARCOM Museum, Halifax.

6 Eames and Jones, "HMCS Bras d'Or. . . .", 1970.

7 Lt.-Cdr. Burman, C. Crate, "Report of a Visit to Jarry Hydraulics, Annex 'A' ", (unpublished), September 17, 1966, Ottawa, Memo NS 8000-FHE-400-10 (DGES), DHist.

8 Treasury Board Submission, RCN, April 21, 1966, HPO-8000-FHE-400 TD 6105, DHist, Ottawa.

9 FHE-400 Hydrofoil Development Review of Progress no. 3/65, Toronto, Oct. 12, 1965, DHist, Ottawa.

10 Eames and Jones, ". . . Bras d'Or . . .", 1970.

11 Biefer, "Stress-Corrosion Cracking . . ." Ottawa, August 30, 1967.

12 FHE-400 Hydrofoil Development Review of Progress no. 1/65, Toronto, June 18, 1965, points 3.4.1 to 3.4.2, DHist, Ottawa.

13 131st Meeting of the Defence Research Control Board, Ottawa, Dec. 20, 1963, NSS-1279-33 (DSS 10-2A), DHist, Ottawa.

14 Eames and Jones, "HMCS Bras d'Or . . .", 1970, London.

15 DeHavilland, "Phase I . . . Handbook", 1966, Toronto.

16 DeHavilland Aircraft of Canada Ltd., Eighth Quarterly Technical Report Design Progress of the *FHE-400* Hydrofoil Ship, March 1 to May 31, 1965, Toronto, DHist, Ottawa, p. 6.

17 DeHavilland Aircraft of Canada Ltd., "Final Engineering Report", Toronto, 1971, DHist, Ottawa.

18 DeHavilland Aircraft, "Phase I . . . Handbook", Toronto, 1966, MARCOM Museum.

19 Cdr. G. L. Edwards, "HMCS *Bras d'Or* Extended Cruise Report", July 20, 1971, Item 20B, NDHQ, Ottawa.

20 DeHavilland, Halifax Hydrofoil Trial Group, "HMCS Bras d'Or Hullborne Trials Report", NDHQ, Ottawa, Nov. 2, 1970, Item 5B, DHist, Ottawa.

21 Col. G. L. Edwards, "HMCS Bras d'Or Trials Habitability, Reliability, Seakeeping", Appendix B 10081-1, FHE-400 files, Feb. 23, 1971, DHist, Ottawa.

22 DG Ships, "Review of Progress, no. 1/65", Ottawa, 1965 p. 4.

23 Ninth Hydrofoil Progress Meeting, Minutes of, Ottawa, Dec. 31, 1965, p. 7.

24 Project Management Report, March 1, 1970, NDHQ, Ottawa p. 1, DHist.

25 FHE-400 Hydrofoil Project Status Report, Hydrofoil Project Office, Ottawa, March 31, 1970, p. 1.

26 Ninth Hydrofoil Progress Meeting, Minutes of, Ottawa, Dec. 31, 1965, pp. 9-10.

27 Hydrofoil Project Office, "Hydrofoil Project Status Report", Ottawa, DND, March 31, 1970, p. 1, DHist.

28 Minutes . . . Ninth . . . Meeting, Ottawa, Dec. 31, 1965, p. 10.

29 Ibid, item 32.

References — Chapter Five

1 Letter to author from Col. J. G. Boulet, Director Information Services, Ottawa, May 4, 1979.

2 Standing Committee on Public Accounts, First Session, 128th Parliament, Ottawa, March 11, 1969 and March 13, 1969, pp. 375-389 and pp. 391-407 respectively.

3 Message from Canadian Forces Headquarters, DGMS to Naval Overseer's Office, Sorel, P.Q., November 23, 1966. DHist, Ottawa.

4 Standing Committee, March 18, 1969, pp. 409-420.

References — Chapter Six

1 Office of the Superintendant, Halifax, "Canadian Forces Auxiliary Vessel Monthly Proceedings Report," July, 1968, HMC Dockyard.

2 Press Release, DND Office of Information, Halifax, September, 1968.

3 SRIO Press Release, Halifax, N.S., July 23, 1968.

4 Flight Test Number HI-H-003, DHist, Ottawa.

5 Letter and report from DeHavilland Project Manager to DG Maritime Systems, Ottawa, Nov. 1, 1968.

6 Cdr. J. H. W. Knox, "Trials and Tribulations . . .", April, 1970, p. 34.

7 Ibid.

8 Flight Test HI-H-881, March 15, 1969: resumed March 24-29 as Flights 2-6.
9 SRIO Press Release, April 10, 1969, Halifax, N.S.
10 Flight Test Number HI-H-783, DHist.
11 Flight Test Number HI-H-883, remark 3, June 14-19, 1969, DHist.
12 First mention in Flight Test Number HI-H-883, June 19, 1969.
13 Knox, "Trials and Tribulations . . ." April, 1970, p. 36.
14 Author's Letter from S. Morita, Project Engineer, DHC, May 28, 1979.
15 Project Management Office, "FHE-400 Hydrofoil Project Report", Ottawa, March 31, 1970. DHist, Ottawa.
16 Ibid — Milestone 3.9.3(b), pre-acceptance trials.
17 Flight Test Numbers HI-H-791, Feb. 24-27; March 9-12, 1970. DHist, Ottawa.
18 DeHavilland Aircraft of Canada, "Final Trials Report", Item 7.6.3 Hydraulic System Components, Toronto/Halifax, 1970. DHist, Ottawa.

References — Chapter Seven

1 See: Frank Fillmore, "World's Fastest Warship", *Canadian Shipping and Engineering News*, Toronto, March, 1970, p. 49.
(Staff), "Another Setback for *Bras d'Or*" *Cdn. Shipping & Engineering News*, Jan., 1970, p. 37.
Dan Slovett, "Bras d'Or Skipper Sees Many Roles for Hydrofoil", Ottawa Journal, Nov. 17, 1970.
2 SRIO Press Release on G. L. Edwards, June, 1978. DHist, Ottawa.
3 Flight Test Number HI-H-888, Flight 4 (35th take-off.)
4 G. L. Edwards, "HMCS *Bras d'Or* Hullborne Rough Water Trials Report", DND #10081-1, Halifax, Nov. 2, 1970, DHist.
5 Flight Test Number HI-H-889, Flight 6, DeHavilland Trials team, Halifax.
6 Flight Test Number HI-H-889, Flight 8, and Final Trials Report Item 6.1.6.
7 HI-H-889, Flight 9-10, note 2 and Flt. 11-12 Note.
8 HI-H-890, Flight 1-3.
9 HI-H-890, Flight 9 and G. L. Edwards, "HMCS *Bras d'Or* Trials . . . Feb. 23, 1971.
10 Final Trials Report, 1971, Item 6.1.3.
11 Flight Test Number HI-H-896, Flight 5, May 20, 1971.
12 G. L. Edwards, "Extended Trip Report, HMCS *Bras d'Or*", SITREP, Halifax July 23, 1971, DHist, Ottawa.
13 DeHavilland Aircraft, "Final Trials Report", Toronto, 1971, Hullborne propulsion, items 6.4.1 to 6.4.8, DHist, Ottawa.
14 Edwards, "Extended Trip . . .", July 23, 1971.
15 Ibid, auxiliary engines and systems, point 12d.
16 Aide Memoire — Capt. J. H. W. Knox, "Crack", DND, Halifax, July 13, 1971. DHist.
17 Staff, "Bras d'Or Battles On", *Canadian Shipping and Marine Engineering News,* Toronto, March, 1971, p. 28.
18 The Mail-Star, Halifax, June 28, 1971, p. 11.
19 G. L. Edwards, Aide Memoire, "Status of HMCS *Bras d'Or*", SITREPS, Halifax, July 23, 1971. DHist.
20 Statement Minister of National Defence, Commons, Ottawa, Nov. 2, 1971, Hansard, p. 9239.

References — Chapter Eight

1 Press Release IA-72-54P, Base Information, Halifax, May 2, 1972.
2 Technical Bulletin TIP.3.16.4, "Shell VPI-260; An Effective Volatile Corrosion Inhibitor for Internal Surfaces", Montreal.
3 See: Jim Essex, "Canada's Hydrofoil: A Multi-Million-Dollar Nightmare", *Atlantic Advocate*, June, 1980.
"One *Bras d'Or* For Sale", *Canada Weekly*, Ottawa, Dept. of External Affairs, Dec. 6, 1978.
Hattie Densmore, "Hydrofoil Future Still Undecided", *Mail-Star*, Halifax, May 22, 1975.
Robert Gordon, "*Bras d'Or* Not Wanted in N.S., Quebec-Bound", *Mail-Star*, Dec. 31, 1982.
4 Author's conversation with Mr. Neils Jannasch, Maritime Museum of the Atlantic, September, 1982.

5 Statement by Director Maritimes, Parks Canada to author, June 6, 1983, Halifax.

6 See: "Info and Ship Swallowed in Fog", *Daily News*, Halifax, June 7/82.
J. P. Mason, "Few Watch as Navy Hydrofoil Towed Away", *Daily News*, June 7/82.
Gerry Arnold, "Hydrofoil's Final Journey", *Chronicle-Herald*, June 7/82
Gerry Arnold, "Vessel Goes to Quebec Museum", *Mail-Star*, June 7/83.

7 Minister of National Defence, Donald MacDonald, White Paper on Defence, "Defence in the '70s", Ottawa, Government of Canada, August, 1971, pp. 21-22.

8 Lyndon Watkins, "The Shape of Things To Come", *Canadian Shipping and Marine Engineering News*, March, 1974, pp. 21-23.

9 Gerald Porter, "In Retreat: The Canadian Forces in the Trudeau Years", Toronto, Deneau & Greenberg, 1978, p. 47.

10 Letter from S. Morita to author, Dec. 6, 1982, detailing scuttling of the DCMP-100 proposal.

11 Ibid.

12 Ibid.

13 Dept. of National Defence, "Defence '82", Ottawa, Dept. of Supply and Services, 1983.

14 Minister of National Defence, Statement of, Ottawa, House of Commons, Nov. 2, 1971.

References — Chapter Nine

1 Capt. R. J. Johnson, USN, Ret'd., "History of U.S. Involvement in Developing the Hydrofoil", First International Hydrofoil Society Conference, Ingonish Beach, N.S., July 27-30, 1982, pp. 42-45.

2 "Jane's Surface Skimmers", London, Janes, 1981, p. 294.

3 Ibid, p. 278.

4 R. T. Crowley, "Jetfoil As An Offshore Patrol Vessel (OPV)", Seattle, Boeing Aircraft Co. Ltd., 1979.

5 "Janes Surface Skimmers", London, Janes, 1981, pp. 279-280.

6 Ibid.

7 Ibid.

8 USNI, "Proceedings Naval Review", Annapolis, United States Naval Institute Press, 1973, p. 256.

9 Grumman Aircraft, "PG(H)-1 Comparison Study, 152mm Gun Mount Feasibility Study Report no. M114.30", Bethusda, N.Y., Jan. 31, 1972.

10 "Jane's Surface Skimmers", London, 1981, p. 270.

11 James King, "The Evolution of the Nibbio Class Hydrofoil From Tucumcari", I.H.S. Conference, Ingonish Beach, N.S., July 27-30, 1982, paper no. 9.

12 D. S. Olling, R. G. Merritt, "Patrol Combatant Missile Hydrofoil Design Development and Production: A Brief History", Seattle, Boeing Aircraft Co., D312-80948-1, December, 1980.

13 H. C. Frauenberger, "Shimrit: Mk.II Hydrofoil For the Israeli Navy", I.H.S. Conference, Ingonish Beach, N.S., July 27-30, 1982.

14 "Jane's Surface . . .", London, 1981, pp. 241-255.

15 Ibid, pp. 257-271.
Director of Naval Intelligence, "Understanding Soviet Naval Developments", Fourth Edition, Washington, Office of the Chief of Naval Operations, Dept. of the Navy, 1981.
Norman Polmar, "Soviet Naval Developments", Washington, Nautical & Aviation Publishing Co. of America, 1979, pp. 32-33.

16 "Jane's Surface . . .", London, 1981, pp. 214-215.

17 Crowley, "Jetfoil As An Offshore . . ." Boeing Marine Systems, 1979, pp. 3-4.

18 "Jane's Surface . . .", 1981, p. 214.

19 Ibid, p. 215.

20 Ibid, p. 296.

21 G. Pieroth, "Grumman Design M-163, A 2400 Metric Ton, Air Capable Hydrofoil Ship", AIAA/SNAME Advanced Marine Vehicles Conference, San Diego, CA, April 17-19, 1978, Grumman Paper 78-749.

22 J. H. King, et al, "AIAA's '83 Intermediate Size Hydrofoil Investigations", New Orleans, AIAA/SNAME/ASNE 7th Marine Systems Conference, Feb. 23-25, 1983.

23 A. A. Purvis, "The General Purpose Frigate", London, Naval Technical Review, Vol. 1, no. 3, 1962, pg. 20-30.

24 CPF Project Office, "The Canadian Patrol Frigate: Program Specifications," Ottawa, 1978.

25 T. Lang, "The SWATH Ship Concept and It's Potential", AIAA/SNAME Advanced Vehicles Conference, San Diego, CA., April 17-19, 1978.

26 United States Naval Institute, "Proceedings", Annapolis, USNI Press, March, 1983, p. 124.

27 Pieroth, "Grumman Design M-163 . . .", Feb., 1983.

Appendix B
Powerplant Specifications

Powerplant, *R-100 Massawippi*

Type: Packard Merlin 31, 12-cylinder, 60°-V, supercharged, gasoline engine.

History: Manufactured in the USA, the Merlin 31 differed from the Rolls-Royce Merlin XX only in that Packard utilized the British design of separate cylinder heads, something that could not be done at the Rolls-Royce facility in Britain in 1942 since it would have seriously disrupted vital production. In US production circles, this engine was identified as V-1650-1.

Specifications:
Length: 75.078 inches, OA
Height: 41.175 inches, OA
Width: 29.825 inches, OA.
Bore: 5.4 inch (137.16mm)
Stroke: 6 inch (152.4mm)
Swept Volume: 1,647 cubic inches (27 litres)
Maximum HP: 1,280 at 3,000 RPM (sea level)
Compression Ratio: 6:1
Dry Weight: 1,450 pounds.

Description: Two piece block of cast RR.50 aluminium-alloy, with separate heads and integral coolant jackets. Two banks of six high-carbon steel liners were directly in touch with the coolant circulation. Pistons were RR.59 aluminium alloy forgings, carrying three compression and two scraper rings, with one of the latter above the connecting pin and the other below. Both rings and grooves were drilled to return scraped oil from the walls. Full-floating connecting rod wrist pins are of hardened nickel-chrome steel, retained in position by circlips. Connecting rods were of 'H'-section nickel-steel forgings. Each pair consisted of plain rod and forked rod, the latter carrying nickel-steel bearing blocks, lined inside and out with lead-bronze.

Crankshaft: One-piece, six-throw, chrome-molybdenum steel.

Crankcase: Two halves, aluminium-alloy castings.

Wheelcase: Aluminium casting.

Valves: Two inlet, two exhaust valves per cylinder, of K.E.965 steel. Exhaust valves were hollow-stem, sodium-cooled, with hardened stem surfaces and facings. Two concentric coil springs per valve. Separate steel rockers per valve. Camshaft was atop each cylinder bank head, supported by seven bearings and was driven by inclined shaft and bevelled gears in the wheel case.

Induction: Twin-choke updraught carburettors of Rolls-Royce/SU design, supplying the air/gas mixture to the supercharger. Twin fuel pumps.

Supercharger: Two-speed, single-stage supercharger.

Ignition: Two twelve-cylinder magnetos, metal-braid wires to plugs, heat-resistant on the exhaust side.

Lubrication: Dry sump system; one pressure and two scavenge pumps of gear-driven type. Two centrifugal filters, external cooler, oil reservoir tank.

Coolant: One centrifugal pump, thermostat-control, seawater medium.

Starting: Electrical, with hand-turning geat at 14:1 ratio

Status: Still in *Massawippi*, Halifax, N.S.

Powerplant, *R-103 (Bras d'Or) Baddeck*

Type: Rolls-Royce Griffon III 12-cylinder, 60° upright 'V', supercharged, gasoline.

History: Planned in 1939 to supplement the Merlin series, the Griffon had a larger swept area. The Griffon was introduced in 1941 and was virtually interchangeable with the former engine in most airframes. It incorporated such new innovations as a remote gearbox, shaft-driven from the engine. Although the Griffon III was rated at 1720 HP at 3000 RPM as an aircraft engine, it was detuned to 1500 HP at 3000 RPM in its marinized application.

Description: Two blocks of six cylinders were mounted at 60° to each other on an inclined upper surface of a two-piece crankcase. Each block comprised of a light alloy skirt with a separate light alloy cylinder head. Separate cylinder liners were fitted and supported, top and bottom of the block. Soft aluminium jointing rings assured gas-tightness. Silchrome valve seatings were renewable.

Pistons: Machined from close forgings of RR.59 aluminium alloy, carried two compression and two scraper rings, one of the latter above the connecting rod wrist pin, the other below. The scraper rings were drilled to allow excessive oil from the cylinder walls to drain.

Connecting rods: Nickel-steel forgings, machined to 'H' section shanks and finished as in the Merlin 31 entry.

Crankcase: Two halves, cast aluminium alloy, the upper containing the cylinder heads and the lower the crankcase and running gear.

Crankshaft: Clockwise rotating, viewed from the rear. One-piece, balanced, six-throw, machined forging of nitrogen-hardened, chrome-molybdenum steel.

Wheelcase: Bolted to the rear. Cast aluminium case.

Valve Train: Two exhaust, two inlet valves per cylinder. KE.965 steel used in both valves, 'Brightray' plating covering the combustion face and seat of the exhaust valve and the seat on the intake valves. Sodium-cooled, hollow-stemmed exhaust valves in the Griffon III. Two springs per valve. Single camshaft per bank atop each head, supported by seven pedestal bearings. Individual rocker arms per valve. Camshaft driven by spur, bevel gears and inclined shafts from the reduction gear wheel.

Induction: Single Rolls-Royce-Bendix updraught, three choke/-throat type.

Supercharger: Two-speed, single-stage, centrifugal type.

Ignition: Two 12-cylinder magnetos in combined unit, tube guide/braid wire connectors to plugs.

Lubrication: Dry sump system; one pressure, two scavenge gear-type pumps.

Coolant System: Centrifugal pump, thermostat-controlled, seawater pick-up and return.

Starting: Electric 24-VDC.
Compression Ratio; 6:1
Dimensions the same as Merlin 31.

Unit History: Two delivered in *R-103*, 1957. Camshafts were rounded off in 1962, from use and two replacement engines were acquired in Ontario. These units remain aboard *R-103* at Shearwater. Original engines were sold as surplus in mid-1970s.

Powerplant, *Rx* Research Craft.

Type: Chrysler Imperial Type M-45-S V-8 gasoline engine.

History: This heavy marine engine was developed in the early 1950s and was preferred over a comparable auto engine because of the severe duties anticipated in service. Further history is included in the Notes at then end of this entry.

Bore: $3^{13}/_{16}$ inch.

Stroke: $3^{5}/_{8}$ inch.

Swept Volume: 331.1 cubic inches (2136.12 cm^3).

Description: V-8, 90° inclined angle between cylinder banks, cast-iron construction block, separate heads.

Main Bearings: 5 of, bronze-phosphor, split-shell, self-draining. Grant racing connecting rods in latter engine.

Crankshaft: Stock, balanced.

Crankcase: Stock pillar-block crank support, split-shell bearing surfaces.

Valve train: Poppet valves, hydraulic lifters acting on pushrods to rocker arms. All driven from the camshaft. One intake and one exhaust valve per cylinder, with the exhaust valves having sodium-filled stems.

Induction: 4 Carter Model YH dual-throat carburetors.*

Superchargers: Single-speed, single-stage Latham axial supercharger, Type 21-L, belt-driven by external pulleys from crankshaft pulley.**

Ignition: Dual-point Mallory distributor.***

Lubrication: Standard gear sump, filter, five quart capacity pan.

Cooling: Centrifugal pump, inlet pipe via scoop at bottom of propeller strut, saltwater cooling, temperature thermostatically controlled.

Starting: 12vDC electric motor, engaging flywheel teeth.

Maximum HP: 365 HP at 4500 RPM.****

Notes: The investigation of this engine proved more complex than any other, largely because very few notes had been kept. However, through several employees and former employees of DRE(A), the following was assembled.

* **** The original engine supplied N.R.E. in 1954 was a M-45-S. When it arrived, it was equipped with twin four-barrel Carter carburetors by N.R.E. employees. However, on the test bench, the engine would only yield 150+ horsepower. A fuel change to high-test aviation gas brought no improvement, so a switch to Esso Premium was tried with a small improvement. Despite constant tinkering the engine refused to yield anything near the advertised 235 horsepower and an inquiry was made to Chrysler of Canada for an explanation. After some delay, a technician arrived from Detroit with boxes of parts and an explanation. The M-45-S supplied to N.R.E. was one of 50 developmental engines that should have been destroyed rather than sold. The technician then set to work bringing the engine up to specifications with the new parts and local machine ship facilities.

*** During the test bench runs in 1954, a Swedish magneto was tried to improve reliability, but this failed under testing and the standard ignition distributor was fitted.

** Two McCulloch superchargers were fitted before installation in the craft, and these proved a dismal failure. These units would allow boost pressure to escape through one unit or the other, if one was not engaged. Indeed, if not perfectly balanced, one blower would suck air, while the other blew and the sequence could be reversed by covering the inlet of the sucking unit with one's hand! Additionally, when the units worked, fuel was forced out through the gaskets and the arrangement never worked satisfactorily. As an interim measure, eight Stromberg single-throat carburetors were fitted, but required constant tinkering.

In the fall of 1960, *Rx* was being refurbished for the testing of the R-200/ASW hydrofoil ¼ scale foil system. The engine was tested with one of the first transistorized ignition units, but this was found sadly wanting. While doing a run-up of the engine at high revs, a connecting rod let go, twisting the rod, taking a piece out of the lower flange of the block and breaking the crank. The block was non-repairable and a new one was ordered.

Mr. George Bennom attempted to obtain a new block from Chrysler, but all block manufacture was tied up in current engine production. N.R.E. was forced to purchase an entire new engine, very akin to the 1961 Series 300 automobile engine. The engineering staff installed an Iskederian ¼ racing cam, somewhat modified locally. Grant connecting rods with beefed-up bronze-phosphor bearing shells were installed. Four

Carter Model YH dual-throat carburetors were installed on a custom manifold and a Latham axial supercharger, supplying .5 atmosphere boost obtained. Total horsepower on the bench was 365 at 4500 RPM and water-cooled manifolds helped dissapate heat.

As can be seen, the Jones figures would appear to be a composite of the two engines that actually saw service in "Rx".

Powerplant, *FHE-400*, Foilborne:

Type: Pratt-Whitney FT4—A2 gas turbine.

History: In the spring of 1961 the Bureau of Ships initiated the competitive procurement to develop a 30,000 HP gas-turbine for marine use. Pratt and Whitney was selected to develop their proposed FT4-A2, utilizing the J75 jet engine as the base generator, with the addition of a power turbine. The resultant engines were the FT4, FT12 and the smaller ST6 series.

General: The FT4 A2 gas turbine comprises the gas generator and the power (free) turbine. The independant power turbine accepts the kinetic energy of the gas generator and converts it to mechanical energy through a shaft which extends through the exhaust duct elbow.

Description:

Type: Simple-cycle two-spool turbine. A low pressure compressor is driven by a two-stage turbine and a high pressure compressor is driven by a single turbine. The burner section has eight burner cans which are equipped with a duplex fuel nozzle system.

Air Intake: Cast steel casing with 18 radial struts supporting the front compressor bearing and equipped with a bleed air anti-icing system.

Low Pressure Compressor: Nine-stage axial flow on inner of two concentric shafts driven by two-stage turbine and supported on ball and roller bearings.

High Pressure Compressor: Seven-stage axial flow on outer hollow shaft driven by single-stage turbine and running on ball and roller bearings.

Combustion Chamber: Eight burner cans located in an annular arrangement and enclosed in a one-piece steel casing. Each burner has six duplex fuel nozzles.

Turbines: Steel casing with hollow guide vanes. Turbine wheels are bolted to the compressor shafts and are supported on ball and roller bearings. A single-stage turbine drives the high compressor and a two-stage turbine drives the low compressor.

Power Turbine: Clockwise rotation of the gas turbine was chosen for *FHE-400*. The power turbine housing is bolted to the gas generator turbine housing. The three-stage turbine shaft assembly is straddle mounted and supported on ball and roller bearings. The output shaft is bolted to the hub of the power turbine rotor and extends through the exhaust duct.

Bearings: Anti-friction ball and roller bearings.

Accessory Drive: Starter, fluid power pump, tachometer drives for low compressor, high compressor and free turbine.

Lubrication System: Return system and scavenge pumps with internal pressure, 45 PSI (3.09 kg/cm²)

Lubrication System, Oil Specs: Type 2 synthetic lube oil PWA-521.

Marine Applications: Meets installation, high shock and ships seaway motion requirements.

Starting: Pneumatic or hydraulic.

Dimensions, FT2A-2:
Length: 312″ (26′) 7,925mm
Width: 76″ (6.34′) 1,930mm
Height: 85″ (7.08′) 2,159mm
SHP: 22,000 (max.) 30,000

Fuel Specs: Light distillate (Naphtha), Aviation Grade Kerosene, Marine Diesel, heavy distillate.

FT4A-2 only: 30,000 SHP intermittent, 25,500 SHP max., continuous, 21,500 SHP normal at 3000 RPM and ambient temperature of 80° F at sea level.

Powerplant, *FHE-400*, Foilborne:

Fuel Consumption:	.49 pound (222gr.) SHP/hr. max. intermittent, .50 pound (226 gr.) SHP/hr. max. continuous, .52 pound (235 gr.) SHP/hr. normal.
Oil Consumption:	.4 gal. (1.82 litre) hr. maximum continuous, service operation average .1 gal. (.45 litre) hr.
Jet Pipe:	Exhaust pipe dimensions 31.5 sq. ft.
Dry Weight:	14,200 pounds.
Turbine Operating Temperature:	1450° F°

Powerplant, ***FHE-400***, Hullborne:

Paxman Ventura 16YJCM Diesel:	Manufactured by Paxman Diesels Ltd., Hythe Hill, Colchester, Essex, C01 2HW, England. These were advanced diesels of V-configuration, suitable for propulsion of high-speed craft.
Type:	Direct injection, 60°, V-form 16 cylinder, turbocharged four-stroke diesel engine.
Output:	2,000 BHP, 1600 RPM.
Bore and Stroke:	197 by 216mm (7.75 by 8.5 inches).
Swept Volume:	(per cylinder) 401 cubic inch (6.67 litres).
Housing:	Fabricated high quality steel plate.
Crankshaft and Main Bearings:	Fully nitrided shaft carried in aluminium tin prefinished steel-backed main bearings. Engine fully balanced against primary and secondary forces.
Connecting Rods:	Fork and blade type with steel-backed, aluminium tin lined large end (forked rod) and steel-backed, lead bronze lined, lead tin flashed bearings (blade rod).
Pistons:	Conventional aluminium alloy, oil cooled with Alfin bonded insert for top ring. Three compression rings and one oil control ring are fitted.
Cylinder Head:	High grade casting carrying four valve direct injection system.
Liners:	Wet type seamless steel tube, chrome plated bore and water side surface honeycombed for surface oil retention.
Fuel Injection:	External Monobloc pumps located below air manifolds. Pump plungers and camshaft lubricated from main engine pressure system. Feed and injection pump driven from engine drive and gear train; a fuel reservoir and air bleed system are fitted. Injectors of the multi-hole type spray fuel into the toroidal cavity in the top of the piston. Injectors are retained by clamp and are external to the head cover.
Governor:	Standard hydraulic 'Regulateurs Europa' unit with self-contained lubricating oil system; mechanical, electrical or pneumatic controls.
Pressure Charging and Intercooling:	Napier water-cooled exhaust-gas-driven turbo-blower mounted over the engine. Air to water intercooler of Serck manufacture for after-cooling version.
Exhaust:	Single outlet from turbochargers.
Starting:	Air starting, starter engaging toothed flywheel.

Auxiliary Powerplant: *FHE-400*

ST6A-53 — Type:	A simple cycle, free turbine engine incorporating a multi-stage compressor, single-stage compressor turbine and single-stage counter-rotating free turbine with planetary reduction gearing.
Air Intake:	Screened annular intake.
Compressor:	3 stage axial compressor followed by one centrifugal stage, 6.1 pressure ratio.
Fuel Grade:	JP1-JP5, light distillate marine diesel conforming to UACL Sec. 92
Turbine Gas Generator:	Single stage axial flow-turbine directly drives the compressor and the accessory gear-box. 38,000 RPM.
Combustion Chamber:	Annular reverse flow combustion chamber with 14 simplex fuel nozzles.
Bearings:	Anti-friction ball and roller bearings are used throughout except on the planet gears in the reduction gear.

Jet Pipe:	Single oval outlet atop turbine for exhaust effluent.
Accessory Drives:	Gearbox driving fuel pump, controls, oil pump, starter FWD of intake.
Lubrication System:	Return system with integral oil tank and filter. Internal pressure and scavange pumps circulate oil intercooler.
Mounting:	Horizontal to 28° nose up or 23° nose down, 20° either side of vertical. Mounting inclination may exceed above values.
Starting:	Electric-starter generator drive: two stage planetary gearbox with 15:1 reduction ratio.
Dimensions:	Length: 62″ (1,575mm) Diameter: 19″ (483mm) Weight: 335 lb. (152 kg.)
Ratings:	(at 59°F sea level) Max. 550 HP @2200 RPM Int. 445 HP @2100 RPM Cont. 390 HP @2100 RPM
Fuel Consumption:	Max. .670 lb. (304 gr.) hp/hr. Int. .720 lb. (327 gr.) hp/hr. Cont. .750 lb. (486 gr.) hp/hr.
Oil Consumption:	Less than .5 (227 gr.) per hour.
Remarks:	This was the only ST6 A53 ever delivered according to Pratt & Whitney Canada records. It was delivered in 1965 and approximate cost was $30,000.

Powerplant, Proteus ST6A-64 gas turbine

Specifications were as for the ST6 A53, other than the following:

Ratings:	Max. SHP: 550 @2,200 RPM Int. SHP: 445 @2,100 RPM Cont. SHP: 390 @2,100 RPM
Notes:	Two ST6A-64 units were delivered to N.R.E. in March, 1967. Cost: $31,700 per unit. Both in storage with Proteus, Dockyard, Halifax, N.S.

FHE-400 **Emergency Powerplant — AiResearch GTCP85-291 Gas Turbine.**

History:	This small gas turbine evolved from earlier efforts during the late 1940s into small, dependable gas turbine compressors. The original 85 Series turbines were used by the USAF and the USN from 1955 onward to provide both air, electrical and pneumatic services to start aircraft. In 1963, the improved 85 Series with two bearings went into production. The FHE-400 was the first hydrofoil application for the GTCP85-291.
Type:	Auxiliary gas turbine, simple, two-stage compressor, providing bleed air for diesel start and system pressurization, plus emergency services.
Air Intake:	Radial inlet plenum.
Compressor:	Two-stage centrifugal, two radial outward flow impellers.
Fuel:	JP-1 to JP-4 and kerosene.
Turbine Gas Generator:	Single stage, axial flow turbine.
Combustion Chamber:	Annular, with fixed-area nozzle ring against turbine wheel.
Bearings:	Anti-friction, two ball-bearing type of turbine wheel, one roller type per compresser stage.
Jet Pipe:	Single circular outlet to rear, insulated exhaust pipe.
Assessory Drive:	400 Hz. AC generator, AP6 hydraulic pump, air bleed at 120 lb/min @ 59°F., Tach-generator, overspeed switch, and 44 hp water pump.
Lubrication:	One pressure, two scavenge pumps, oil filter, by-pass, oil supply self-contained.
Starting:	28v DC electrical.
Dimensions:	Length: 88 inches, overall. Width: 28.5 inches, overall. Weight, (dry, without options): 260 lb.
Ratings, at Sea Level:	Cont. HP-190 HP at 6,000 RPM

Appendix C
Glossary

A.I.C. Action Information Centre. That position within the *FHE-400* superstructure allocated to the computerized tactical and weapons control centre (not fitted.)

ASW Anti-Submarine Warfare.

Abeam position of another craft alongside or 90° from ship's head.

Actuator Unit designed to translate sensor information and/or computer instructions into mechanical action. Energy is transferred to control surfaces hydraulically, pneumatically or electrically.

Aeroplane Foil System Arrangement in which main foils are forward of the centre of gravity to support 75% to 85% of load and the auxiliary foil, supporting the remainder, is aft as the tail assembly.

Air Entry Entry of air from atmosphere that raises low pressures created by flow due to foil's cambered surface, effectively impairing or destroying lift. Commonly referred to as ventilation.

Amidships Midway between stem and stern of the hull. Generally refers to rudder position, with rudder in mid-position or zero rudder angle.

Angle of attack Angle made by mean chord line of hydrofoil with flow.

Angle of incidence Angle made by mean chord line of hydrofoil in relation to fixed struts or hull.

Anhedral Sloping upwards from the horizontal.

Aspect Ratio Measure of ratio of foil's span to it's chord, defined as

$$\frac{\text{span}^2}{\text{total foil area}}$$

Athwartship Transversely across the hull from one side to the other.

Base-ventilated foil System of forced ventilation designed to overcome reduction in lift/drag ratio of foil at supercavitating speeds. Air is fed continuously to the upper surface of the foil, unwetting the surface and preventing formation of critical areas of decreased pressure. Alternatively, air may be fed into the cavity formed behind the square trailing edge.

Beam-on Sideways movement of craft, i.e. at 90° angle of yaw.

Blades Early name for individual hydrofoil elements.

Bow-up Trim position or attitude when craft is high at the bow.

Brest To take waves at 90° to their crests.

Broach Sudden breaking of the surface by foils or part of the foils, resulting in loss of lift due to air flowing over the foil's upper surface. To broach to — to swing sideways in following seas under wave action.

Bulkhead Vertical partitions, either transverse or longitudinal, which divide or sub-divide the hull. May be used to separate accommodation areas, strengthen structure, form tanks, act as a fire barrier and to compartmentize flooding.

Buoyancy Reduction in weight of floating object. If object floats, its weight is equal or less than the weight of the water it displaces. Reserve; buoyancy in excess of that required to keep undamaged craft afloat.

Camber Convex form on upper surface of foil; high-speed flow over top surface decreases pressure and about two-thirds of lift is provided by this surface.

Canard Foil System Foil arrangement with foil of wide span near the stern, aft of the centre of gravity, bearing between 65-90% of A.U.W. and a smaller centre-mounted foil at the bow.

Cavitation Formation of vapour bubbles due to pressure decrease on upper surfaces of a foil or back of a propeller's blades at high speeds. Non-stable cavities or cavitation bubbles of aqueous vapour form near the foil's leading edge and extend down the stream, expanding and collapsing. At points of collapse, positive pressure peaks can rise to 20,000 psi, causing erosion and pitting of the metal. Cavitation causes unstable water flow over the foils, resulting in abrupt changes in lift and therefore discomfort to crew members. Foil sections being developed either delay onset of cavitation by reduced camber, thinner sections or sweepback, or if the craft is required to operate at supercavitating speeds, stabilize cavitation to provide smooth transition between sub- and super-cavitating speeds.

Chord — Distance between leading and trailing edges of foil section measured along chord line.

Chord-line — Straight line joining leading and trailing edges of foil or propeller blade section.

Clearance — Distance between hard structure and water's surface.

Coastal vessel — Able to operate in up to sea state 5, seeking shelter in greater sea states.

Contour — Motion of hydrofoil when it more or less follows the wave profile.

DWL — Displacement water line.

Deadrise — Angle with horizontal made at keel by outboard rise of vessel's hull form at each frame.

Dihedral — Sloping downward from the horizontal.

Displacement — Weight in tons of water displaced by floating vessel. Light displacement; craft weight exclusive of ballast, fuel, etc.

Draught or draft — Distance between water surface and bottom of craft.

Drag — Hydrodynamic resistances resulting from wave-making, which is dependant on craft shape and displacement, frictional drag due to viscosity of water, total wetted surface and induced drag from foils and transmission shafts and their supporting struts and structure, due to their motion through the water.

DRB — Defence Research Board; set up in late 1940s to guide defence research work.

DRE(A) — Defence Research Establishment, Atlantic; portion of DRB concerned with naval acoustical and related hydrodynamic studies, based at Dartmouth, N.S.

Delayed Cavitation Section — Foil section with decreased camber at leading edge to delay onset of cavitation, thus allowing greater speed.

Drift Angle — Difference between course and actual track of the craft.

ECCM — Electronic counter-counter measures; ability of search radar stations to overcome enemy jamming, chaff launchers and other countermeasures.

ECM — Electronic counter-measures — devices to either jam, mask or deceive the enemy's electronic detection devices.

ESM — Electronic support measures; active, passive and analysing electronic equipment, including chaff launchers and flare dispensing systems.

Efficiency — Ratio of useful work performed (thrust times relative velocity through water) to total input power.

Extended-range vessel — Small warships capable of up to 14 days continuous unsupported operations away from base at 14-18 knot speeds for 2,500-4,000 nautical mile ranges or a vessel capable of over 1,000 nm at maximum speed.

FWL — Foilborne waterline.

Fences — Small partitions at short intervals down upper and lower surfaces of hydrofoils tending to prevent air ventilation passing down to destroy lift, attached in direction of flow.

Flare — Upward and outward curvature of freeboard at bow, presenting additional rising surface to oncoming waves.

Foilborne — With hull raised completely out of the water and wholly supported by lift from the foil system.

Foil flaps — (1) Trailing edge flaps for lift augmentation during take-off and to provide control forces. (2) Upper and lower flaps to raise cavitation boundary.

Foil Systems:

1-Surface-piercing — More often than not V-shaped, the upper parts forming the tips of the 'V' and piercing the surface on either side of the craft. The 'V' foil, with its marked dihedral is area stabilized and craft employing this configuration can be designed to be inherently stable and for stability, geometry dependant. The forces restoring normal trim are provided by the area of the foil that is submerged. A roll to one side means the immersion of increased foil area on the other, which results in the generation of extra lift to counter the roll and restore the craft to an even keel. Equally, a downward pitching movement at the bow means an increase in submerged area of the forward foil, the generation of added lift, raising the bows once more. If the bow rises above even keel, a corresponding decrease in lift will restore normal trim. This type of foil is known as a emerging foil system in some circles.

2-Ladder Foils Also come under the heading of surface-piercing foils, but are not used that much any more. This system was pioneered by Forlanini in his hydro-areoplane, which was the first successful hydrofoil. Bell purchased the patents to this foil specification in 1911 and developed several versions that were used in various experimental craft. Early ladder foils, with single sets of foils beneath the hull, fore and aft, lacked lateral stability, but this was rectified by the use of outriggers and eventually offset foils, port and starboard and toward the bows. Early configurations were straight and at right angles to their support legs, but later these were 'v' shaped, the resultant dihedral preventing a sudden change of lift as the foils broke surface. The V-foil had the added advantage of being more rigid, lighter and cheaper to construct. The disadvantage over the conventional submerged foil system was the inability of the v-foil craft to control, without specialised controls, downward orbital velocities at wave crests when overtaking waves in a following sea, a condition that generally decreased the foils' angle of attack, reducing lift and causing wave contact or stall. On large craft, the weight and size of the system was considerably greater than that of a submerged foil system. Restoring forces to correct a roll had to pass above the centre of gravity of the craft, necessitating the placing of the foils only a short distance beneath the hull. This meant that a relatively low wave clearance resulted and therefore the V-foil was not suitable to routes where really rough weather was encountered in most cases. The modified canard system of the *FHE-400* was the outstanding exception.

Grunberg Foil System First patented in 1936, the Grunberg principle of inherent angle of attack variations comprises a 'stabilizer' attached to the bow or forward projection from the latter and behind this a 'foil'. Both foil and stabilizer can be 'split' into several units. The lift curve of the stabilizer, plotted against it draught, is considerably steeper that its corresponding foil lift curve. Hence as the operational conditions (speed, weight, CG travel) change, the foil sinks or rises relative to the stabilizer, automatically adjusting its angle of attack. The 'foil' is set at an appropriate angle of incidence in order to prevent it from approaching the interface. The system is fully compatable with Forlanini's concept of area variation and both can be incorporated in the same structure.

Shallow-draught submerged This system which incorporates the Grunberg angle of attack variation approach, is employed almost exclusively on hydrofoils designed and built by the Soviet Union and is intended primarily for passenger-carrying craft used in long calm water rivers, canals and inland seas and lakes. The system, also known as the immersion depth effect system, was evolved by Dr. Rostislav Alexeyev. It generally comprises two main horizontal foils, one forward, one aft, each carrying approximately half the weight of the vessel. A submerged foil loses lift gradually as it approaches the surface from a depth of about one chord, which prevents it from rising completely to the surface. Means therefore have to be provided to assist take-off and prevent the vessel sinking back to the displacement mode. Planing subfoils, port and starboard are therefore provided in the vicinity of the forward struts and are so located that they are touching the water surface; the main foils are submerged at a depth of approximately one chord.

Submerged Foils These have a greater potential for seakeeping than any other, but are not inherently stable to any degree. The foils are totally immersed and a sonic, mechanical or air stabilization system has to be installed to maintain the foils at the required depth. The system has to stabilize the craft from take-off to touchdown in heave and all three axes-pitch, roll and yaw. It must also see that the craft makes coordinated banked turns in heavy seas to reduce side loads on the foil struts; insure that vertical and lateral accelerations are kept within limits in order to prevent excessive loads on the structure and finally, ensure a smooth ride for passengers and/or crew. The control forces are generated either by deflecting flaps at the trailing edge of the foil or varying the incidence angle of the entire foil surface. Incidence control provides better performance in a high sea state. The key element of a typical automatic control system is an acoustic height sensor located at the bow. The time lag of the return signal is a measure of the distance of the sensor from the water. Craft motion input is received from dual sonic ranging devices which sense the height above the water in relation to a fixed reference; from three rate gyros which measure yaw, pitch and roll; from forward and aft accelerometers which sense vertical acceleration fore and aft and from a vertical gyro which senses the angular position of the craft in both pitch and roll. This information is processed by an electronic computer and fed continuously to hydraulic actuators of the foil control surfaces, which develop the necessary hydrodynamic forces for stability, producing forces imposed by wave action manoeuvring and correct flight. There are two methods of incidence control; mechanical incidence control and air stabilization system.

Mechanical — The most successful purely mechanically operated incidence control system is the Hydrofin autopilot principle, designed by Christopher Hook, who pioneered the development of the submerged foil. A fixed, highriding crash preventer plane is mounted ahead of and beneath the bow. The fixed plane, which is only immersed when the craft is in a displacement mode, is also used as a platform for mounting a lightweight pitch control sensor which is hinged to the rear. The sensor rides on the waves and continuously transmits their shape through a connecting linkage to vary the incidence angle of the main foils as necessary to maintain them at the required depth. A filter system ensures that the craft ignores small waves and that the hull is flown over the crests of waves exceeding the height of the keel over the water. Two additional sensors, trailing from port and starboard immediately aft of the main struts, provide roll control. The pilot has overriding control through a control column, operated in the same manner as that in an aircraft.

Air Stabilization — Designed and developed by Baron Hanns von Schertel of Supramar AG, Lucerne, Switzerland. Air from the free atmosphere is fed through air exits to the foil upper surfaces and under certain circumstances the lower surface as well (into low pressure regions). The airflow decreases the lift and the flow is deflected away from the foil section with an effect similar to that of a deflected flap, the air cavities extending out behind producing a virtual lengthening of the foil profile. Lift is reduced and varied by the quantity of air admitted, this being controlled by a valve actuated by signals from a dampened pendulum and a rate gyro. The pendulum causes righting moments at static heeling angles. If exposed to a centrifugal force in turning, it causes a movement which is directed towards the centre of the turning circle, thereby avoiding outside banking (co-ordinated banking). The rate gyro responds to angular velocity and acts dynamically to dampen rolling motions.
(end of Foil Systems)

Forepeak — Space forward of the fore collision bulkhead, frequently used as storage space.

Frames — Structure of vertical ribs or girders to which a vessel's outside plates are attached. For identification, frames are numbered consecutively, starting aft.

Freeboard — Depth of exposed or free side of hull between water level and freeboard deck. Degree of freeboard permitted is marked by Plimsoll or load lines.

Freeboard deck — Deck used to measure or determine loadlines.

Free power turbine — Gas turbine on which the power turbine is on a separate shaft from the compressor and its turbine.

Furrowing — Condition of foilborne operation of hydrofoil caused by contact of lower part of hull and/or keel with crests of larger waves. Contact is brief and does not prevent craft from remaining foilborne.

Gross tonnage — Total tonnage of vessel, including all enclosed spaces, estimated on the basis of 100 square feet equalling 1 ton.

Hard chine — Hull design with topsides and bottom meeting at an angle, rather than curving to a round bilge.

Hard structure — Any structure (hard or flexible) which may cause capsizing or right moment when in contact with water.

Head Sea — Sea approaching from the direction steered or directly ahead of the ship.

Heave — Vertical motion of craft in response to waves.

Heave Stiffness — Rate of change of restoring force in heave direction with displacement in that direction.

Heel — (1) Incline or list in transverse direction while underway. (2) Lower end of mast or derrick. (3) Point where keel and stern post meet.

High-speed vessel — Vessel with a speed of 36 knots or greater.

Hull cresting — Contact of hydrofoil's hull with waves in high seas.

Hull slamming — Contact of hydrofoil's hull with water following foil broach.

Hydrofoils — Small wings, almost identical in section to those of aircraft and designed to generate lift. Since water is 81.5 times denser than air, the same lift as an airplane wing is obtained for only 1/81.5 of the area (at equal speeds).

Hydrocurves — Early simple curved hydrofoil surfaces.

Hydrodrome — Patented name for a hydrofoil craft designed by Bell-Baldwin.

Inclined shaft — Marine driveshaft used in small V-foil and shallow-draught

	submerged foil craft with keels only a limited height above mean water level. Shaft is generally short and inclined at about 12-14 degrees to the horizontal. On larger craft, designed for operation in higher waves, the need to 'fly' higher necessitates alternative drive arrangements such as "V" and 'Z'-drives or a water jet system.
JP-4	Liquid fuel, based on kerosene, used widely in gas turbines.
Keel	(1) Backbone of hull. (2) Extension of unitized hull rigidizing the entire unit.
Land	At the end of a run, hydrofoils are said to land or settle down into the water.
Leading frequency of sea waves	Sea wave of greatest energy content. See Significant wave height.
Load factor	Relationship between pay load capacity available and capacity filled.
Long-range vessel	Small warship capable of up to seven days continuous unsupported operations away from base at 14-18 knots for 1500-2500 nautical miles.
Medium range vessel	Warship capable of up to 3 days' operation from base, patrolling 1500 nautical miles or 500 nm at maximum speed.
Medium speed vessel	Vessel capable of 18-24 knots or more.
Multi-role craft	Small warship with facilities for fitting a range of interchangable weapons at short notice (6 hours).
MIG welding	Semi-automatic, consuming a continuous wire electrode (wire) under a protective atmosphere of argon and argon inert gas mixture. The arc is exposed, allowing the operator to guide and watch the welding process, with transfer of material nearly 100%.
Net tonnage	Total tonnage of craft based on cubic capacity of all spaces available for carrying revenue-producing cargo less an allowance for areas needed to operate the craft.
N.R.E.	Naval Research Establishment. Founded during W.W. II, this was based in HMC Dockyard until the new facilities were built in Dartmouth, N.S. This became DRE(A) in the early 1960s. It's purpose from the beginning was solving marine problems for the Navy.
Open-ocean vessel	One that is capable of operating in open-ocean conditions at all times in all but the worst of weather conditions.
Patrol craft	Small warship fitted with light armament.
Payload weight	Weight of revenue-earning load, excluding crew and fuel.
Pitch	Rotation or oscillation of hull about transverse axis in a seaway. Also angle of air or water propeller blades in relation to the hub axis.
Pitch angle	Pitch a craft adopts relative to horizontal datum.
Pitch attitude	Instanteous angle between surface (roll attitude) traversed and longitudinal (lateral) datum of the craft.
Platform	Approximately level flight of hydrofoil craft over waves lower than calm water hull clearance.
Porpoising	(1) Oscillatory motion in pitch and heave of high-speed planing craft caused by incorrect trim rather than wave action. (2) Oscillatory motion in pitch and heave of early surface-piercing hydrofoil craft caused by partial or complete loss of lift by ventilation of these foil surfaces. Ventilation usually occurred by air travelling down the vertical struts. Fences were found to cure this problem in large part.
RCN	Royal Canadian Navy; founded in 1910 under the Naval Services Act, it was the predecessor of Maritime Command. It ceased as a separate force in 1968.
Roll	Oscillation or rotation of hull about longitudinal axis.
Roll attitude	Angle of roll a craft adopts relative to longitudinal axis.
Roll stiffness	Rate of change of restoring roll moment with roll angle. Slope of applied roll moment versus roll angle.
SSM	Surface-to-surface missile system; anti-shipping missile; often referred to simply as S/S in tables.
Sea State	Scale of sea conditions classified from Sea State 1 to 8, precipitous, according to wind duration, fetch and velocity, wave length, period and velocity.
Service Speed	Cruising speed obtained by average crew in average craft on a given route.
Short-range vessel	Small warship capable of 36 hours continuous operation and which can cover up to 600 nautical miles at cruise speed or 250 nm at top speed.
Significant	Arithmetic means of highest third set of measurement, i.e., wave heights or lengths.
Significant wave height	Sea waves are composed of different frequencies and have different wave heights (energy spectrum). A wave with the lead-

ing frequency of this spectrum and energy content is called the significant wave. It is from this wave that this measurement is obtained.

Split foil — Main foil system with foil area divided into two, either to facilitate retraction or to permit location of foil/control surfaces well outboard, where foil control and large roll correcting moments can be applied for small changes in lift.

Standard speed vessel — Patrol vessel capable of speeds up to 18 knots.

Stringers — Longitudinal support structures generally linking the ship's vertical ribs.

Submerged foil system — Foil system employing totally submerged lifting surfaces. Depth of submergence is controlled by mechanical, electronic or pneumatic systems which alter angle of incidence of the foils or flaps attached to them to provide stability and control. see Foil Systems.

Supercavitating foil — General classification given to foils designed to operate efficiently at high speeds while fully cavitated. Since at very high speeds foils cannot avoid cavitation, sections are designed which induce onset of cavitation from the leading edge and cause cavities to proceed dowstream and beyond the trailing edge before collapsing. Lift and drag of these foils is determined by shape of the leading edge and undersurface.

Take-off speed — Speed at which a hydrofoil vessel's hull is raised clear of the water, dynamic foil lift taking over from static displacement or planing of the hull proper.

Tandem foils — Foil system in which area of the forward foils is approximately equal to that of the aft foils, balancing loading between them.

Tetrahedron — A solid having a base and three sides of equilateral triangles.

Thickness-chord ratio — Maximum thickness of foil section in relation to its chord.

Tietjens-type foil — Forward swept (surface-piercing) main foil almost amidships and slightly ahead of the centre of gravity. It was intended that pronounced sweep of the V-foils would result in increasing the area of the foil further forward coming into use to increase bow-up trim of the craft when lift was lost. The considerable length of unsupported hull ahead of the centre of gravity meant the craft was constantly in danger of 'digging-in' in bad seas and was highly sensitive to load arrangements.

Transcavitating foil — Thin section foil designed for smooth transition from fully wetted to supercavitating flow. By loading the tip more highly than the root, cavitation was first introduced at the tip, then extending spanwise over the foil to the roots as speed increased.

TIG welding — (Tungsten Inert Gas); tungsten electrodes are non-consumable. Wire is pre-heated by arc under inert gas shield and deposited in the weld joint. AC high-frequency, stabilized current is normally used, but DC reverse polarity can be used successfully to $^3/_{32}$ inch. Ceramic or glass cups are used to 250 ampheres and water-cooled cups above this ampherage. Cold wire feed was utilized in the M.I.L. construction the *FHE-400* hull.

Torsion — Lateral twisting forces acting upon a structure.

Transom — Last transverse frame of a ship's structure, forming the stern board.

Transverse framing — Steel frames running athwartships, from side to side, instead of fore and aft.

Trim — Difference between draughts forward and aft in displacement vessels and hydrofoil hull attitude relative to line of flight.

Trim angle — Pitch or roll angle which results under steady running conditions.

Variable-pitch propeller — Propeller with blades which can be rotated about their longitudinal axes to provide variable forward and reverse thrust.

VCG — Vertical height measurement from appropriate datum to centre of gravity.

Ventilation — See Air Entry.

Wave height — Vertical distance from wave trough to crest or twice wave amplitude.

Wave length — Horizontal distance between adjacent wave crests.

Wave velocity — Speed at which a wave form travels along the sea surface, the latter without forward motion.

Walchner 'C' — A particular design of hydrofoil section for delayed cavitation.

Yaw Angle — Rotation or oscillation of craft about its vertical axis.

'Z'-drive — Drive system that normally is employed on hydrofoil craft to transmit power from the engine in the hull to a screw through horizontal shafting leading to bevel gears over the stern, then via a vertical shaft and second bevel gear to the horizontal propeller shaft, thus forming a 'Z'-shaped power train.

Appendix D
Acknowledgements

There seem to be hundreds of people that I am indebted to for assistance in assembling this book, but I will only mention a few dozen who figured in a large manner. To those not mentioned, my apologies and thanks for your assistance.

Mr. M. C. Eames, for his patience in interviews early in the research when I didn't know a ladder-foil system from a broomstick. Also, for suggesting pertinent papers to fill in the gaps in my knowledge which were huge.

Mr. W. (Bill) Carty, DREA, who shared so many thoughts and rememberances, not to mention his personal photo collection! Sorry we couldn't use the personal stories; they would have been a riot.

Rear-Admiral G. L. Edwards, CMM, CD., for his personal rememberances, photos and thoughts during the research, plus his thoughts in the Foreword of this book. Hope this helps bring back some pleasant remembrances in the future. Bravo Zulu.

Mr. T. Drummond, DREA for sifting through many records to find obscure data on the N.R.E./DREA craft and odd bits and pieces. Also Walter Ellis, who went out of his way to find long-stored blueprints, photos and records that were invaluable in the *R-100* and *R-103* sections of Chapter Two.

A big thanks to the following for their experience with the *Rx* engines; Gordon Pizantson, Charlie McManus and George McLeod, all former N.R.E. employees.

Mr. Barry Davis, who supplied so many of the Flight Test Reports on *FHE-400* and was instrumental in straightening out the sequence of events through other records. Also for the many colour slides and pictures, some of which appear in this book, albeit in black and white. Hope the low-head turbine project is a smashing success.

Commodore C. 'Tino' Cotaras, CAF, Ret'd, for sharing his experiences in the two first years of *Bras d'Or's* trials and tribulations. Another Bravo Zulu.

To S. Morita, project engineer, DeHavilland for all the patient letters which required so much digging in musty files and memories, a big note of thanks. Also with the DHC gang, Ron Nunney, Chief of Photography, who supplied so many of the building shots. Lastly, a big thank you to DeHavilland for taking the time to assist me through their busy schedules with DASH-Eight.

To J. D. F. Kealy, Senior Researcher, Directorate of History, Ottawa. So many thanks for the opportunity to go through the hydrofoil material last February . . . thought we'd never see the end of it, didn't we? Also for the many letters that filled in the smaller gaps after I returned from Ottawa.

Captain Ian Sturgess, who now pilots B.C. Ferries, a great round of thanks for his memories of the X.O. of *Bras d'Or* and the agony that was his as the last C.O. of *Bras d'Or* during the lay-up period. The latter were instrumental in understanding the lay-up procedure, since few written records remain . . . if they ever existed.

The following people and corporations for their assistance in particular fields;

Mr. R. M. Sachs, Marketing Director, Pratt and Whitney of Canada Ltd.

Mr. Conrad W. Sanders, General Council, Garrett Engine Company.

Mr. D. C. Cameron, President, Canadian Aircraft Products Ltd., Richmond, B.C.

Mr. Bill Harper, CBC Halifax for viewing file footage.

Mr. Paul Pleau, Crown Assets, Ship Disposal, Halifax, for tracing bits and pieces.

Mr. Graham McBride, Maritime Museum of the Atlantic, Halifax for literature on the turn-over of *Massawippi* to the Museum.

Mrs. Marilyn Smith, Curator of the Maritime Command Museum, whose many pictures of *Bras d'Or* grace these pages and make the book come alive. A big Bravo Zulu.

Captain Paul Brick, Superintendant of CFAV, Atlantic for sharing his observations on the *Bras d'Or* tow to Quebec in June, 1983 and the opportunity to photograph her leaving. Many thanks.

To Lt. (N) Mike Considine, BINFO for the many trips into Dockyard to cover events.

To Lt. Ron Moore, long-departed from the SRIO's Office, Halifax, who learned *Bras d'Or* with me on our 1979 crawl-through. Hope you get your tank back, Ron.

And finally to all those who supplied snippits of information, told me where to go for further information (and otherwise when questioning became too hectic!) and generally assisted, a great vote of thanks.

Appendix E
Index